For the Family's Sake

Crossway Books
by Susan Schaeffer Macaulay

For the Children's Sake
For the Family's Sake

FOR THE
FAMILY'S
SAKE

∾

The Value of Home
In Everyone's Life

Susan Schaeffer Macaulay

CROSSWAY BOOKS

A DIVISION OF
GOOD NEWS PUBLISHERS
WHEATON, ILLINOIS

Cover design: David LaPlaca

Cover illustration: Debra Chabrian

First printing 1999

Printed in the United States of America

Scripture taken from the *Holy Bible: New International Version®*. Copyright © 1973, 1978, 1984 by International Bible Society. Used by permission of Zondervan Publishing House. All rights reserved.

The "NIV" and "New International Version" trademarks are registered in the United States Patent and Trademark Office by International Bible Society. Use of either trademark requires the permission of International Bible Society.

Scripture verses marked PHILLIPS are from *The New Testament in Modern English*, translated by J. B. Phillips © 1972 by J. B. Phillips. Published by Macmillan.

Scripture references marked KJV are taken from the King James Version.

Scripture verses marked AMP are from the *Amplified Bible. Old Testament* copyright © 1965, 1987 by the Zondervan Corporation. The *Amplified New Testament* copyright © 1958, 1987 by the Lockman Foundation. Used by permission.

Every effort has been made to contact owners of copyrighted material quoted in this book and to secure permission.

Library of Congress Cataloging-in-Publication Data

Macaulay, Susan Schaeffer
    For the family's sake : the value of home in everyone's life /
Susan Schaeffer Macaulay.
        p.   cm.
    Includes bibliographical references.
    ISBN 1-58134-111-3 (alk. paper)
    1. Home—Religious aspects—Christianity. I. Title.
BR115.H56M33   1999
248.4—dc21   99-33107

VP		13	12	11	10	09	08	07	06	05	04
17	16	15	14	13	12	11	10	9	8	7	6	5	4	3

*This book is
dedicated, with thanks
to the Lord
and with love,
to Philip and Abigail.*

CONTENTS

CONTENTS

ACKNOWLEDGMENTS

Without the work of Elaine Cooper, my friend and the administrator of Child Light, this book would not have been possible. We all thank you.

Thank you also to my husband, Ranald, to my children, and to my grandchildren for their support and encouragement at a personal cost to themselves.

Thanks to L'Abri Fellowship, which has allowed me to devote so much time to writing.

Thanks to the members of the Charlotte Mason College Association, who welcomed Elaine and me to their reunion in Ambleside. We appreciate their generous friendship and the many conversations with us that helped us to understand their student experience at Scale How and the Parents' National Education Union (PNEU) schools they taught in during their professional careers.

Thanks to Miss Eve Anderson for the generous gift of her time and energies in helping us all as we seek to apply the PNEU ideas in homes and schools today.

Thanks to Phil Matthews for the hours spent telling me about Amy Carmichael and Dohnavur and also to Margaret Wilkinson for the long telephone conversations and the loan of letters. Thanks to the Dohnavur Fellowship office and Jean van der Flier for her help.

I thank my mother and my father for my early childhood and for so much more than could ever go into a book. Thank you, Nancy Barker, for my beloved Sunday school class when I was four and five years old. Her teaching forged for me a lifelong link with the Bible.

PREFACE

This is a book about life at home. Just as the use of the word *home-maker* has fallen into an uneasy past, the concept of having time for rich home life is also being relegated to history. I'm referring to a time when friends would congregate in threes or fours on front porches to laugh and chat while children played outside in the twilight, when neighbors knew each other and would pause to exchange words and events over the back fence.

HOME. Do we have to give it all up? We, whoever we are—the unmarried professional, the single person devoted to a vocation teaching inner-city children, the parent left alone to bring up children, the widow wondering how to go on and make a life that still has shape and meaning, the elderly person making decisions about everyday life patterns, the postgraduate student facing several stressed-out years, the Christian worker with never a spare moment, parents of all sorts and in different circumstances—we all need a fresh look at what we are aiming for at home.

Women ask whether it is worthwhile to give generous time and energy to the home. Is it necessary? And what should the home look like? Is it possible to find a map that shows? Can we see a stabilizing infrastructure that will clarify our priorities as we wade through details?

What do the most vulnerable of persons, little children, need?

In our real-life circumstances, how can we give them a satisfying childhood? What does that look like?

This book will address these questions and more. Of course, because human life is anything but obvious, getting to the answers takes some telling! The questions are like icebergs floating in a deep sea. To give worthwhile answers, you have to look deeper than the obvious. Is there a big picture beyond the details, a reality below life's surface? Christian believers think so. If the Judeo-Christian Scriptures are reliable, they offer a view of our lives that explains matters and directs us. Hopefully, we can discover a balance in our practical lives that is life-giving and works well. For hundreds of years people have found life-giving ideas this way.

In a short book like this, the big view can only be sketched briefly. Many questions can't be answered. There is an appendix at the end of the book with suggestions for further reading and a list of addresses that may be useful to you. There you'll also find a short description of people and organizations mentioned in the book—Charlotte Mason, Amy Carmichael, Francis and Edith Schaeffer, and L'Abri Fellowship.

1

~

Who Needs a Home?

If you were to stop and ask a miserable refugee, "Who needs a home?" he or she would not think it a question worth answering. The cold winds of winter and gusting rain make the covering of canvas provided by a relief agency a poor shelter, and it is too noisy for conversation anyway.

Turn to a sophisticated young business person in any city, and you might be rewarded for using such an old-fashioned word with a supercilious gaze. That person might also be speechless. "*Home!*" the gaze seems to exclaim. "That word isn't in my vocabulary or life. Nor is marriage. My parents used those words, and they are retired in a backwater."

The dictionary tells us that home is the place where we live, whether we are single, married, young, or old. The definition also includes the idea of a family or another group living in a house. Further, it says that home is the place we are at ease.

What is a tree without its roots held deeply in the soil? What is a cup without its saucer? What are letters if they aren't put into words and sentences? What is a child's life like if there is no home and no family to belong to?

Most people agree that children need stable, loving homes. Are homes then a temporary arrangement for their care and development? Or, as many people seem to think, do homes only go with marriage? Novelist Jane Austen didn't think so. She lived in a little Hampshire village and made her home with her sister.[1] This gifted writer stayed unmarried, but it never prevented her from having a balanced life within the ease of home and community. She wrote:

> *Our Chawton home, how much we find*
> *Already in it to our mind;*
> *And how convinced that when complete*
> *It will all other houses beat*
> *That ever have been made or mended*
> *With rooms concise or rooms distended.*[2]

We all need to think hard, or we may find ourselves rootless and drifting whatever our age. For many the very words *family, home, commitment,* and *neighborhood* convey agonies, fears, and questions. Others dream romantically about a warm, settled, creative, and satisfying life. But they find that nothing in the cold light of the everyday, the ordinary, can even begin to resemble the dream. They can become hopeless, bitter.

On top of this, for children there are special considerations. As fewer of the routines and less of the atmosphere of everyday life can be taken for granted, the resulting confusion has caused uncertainty about how children thrive. They are like little seedlings, and they do need a particular environment to do well. The more we've learned about children's development, the more we realize that the hours and days from birth onward are the most formative in the whole of life. We now know that whether the child's brain will be fully utilized or not depends on early care. We know that children's emotional balance for life grows out of early relationships.

The main reason I am writing this book is that *we all need homes.* And, as we are made in a particular way, this life and home must suit human beings. There is a basic pattern that fits us, holds us, serves us.

It is too easy to make excuses about why we cannot follow these patterns. It is easy to excuse ourselves from working at our everyday lives with the words, "if only . . ."

"If only I were married."

"If only I were married to another person."
"If only we could leave this miserable home and have a nice place."
"If only my spouse had not died/left me."
"If only I had more money or a better job."
"If only I had more time/energy/ideas."
"If only I'd had a good childhood model."

Homes are for everybody—single persons or families with children, young or old, people with good jobs or bad ones. Homes are not a romantic idea to dream about wistfully; homemaking needs to be put into practice as a priority. A good home life is too basic a human need to whine and fuss about with the plaintive words, "if only."

It is essential that older adults have the rootedness of a home. Probably those who are single have an even greater need to consider what goes into making home life for themselves and "neighbors" or friends than do families for whom homemaking might seem more obvious. For instance, widows often have to be reminded to cook nutritious meals again for themselves after being left alone. It can seem hardly worth it "just for me." We more naturally follow good patterns when we are caring for others.

Sometimes life *is* too hard, and we go down. And that experience should find its place in this book too, for that is real life. It is also real life to find a way to go on. Today we expect so much that many of us are dissatisfied with simple basics in every area. We can also be confused about what matters and what does not. Commercial and media pressures mislead us there and breed discontent.

It is helpful to remember that we don't have to do everything or have everything. What are the basics exactly? What is most important when we can't have it all or do it all? What ingredients make up a good home? I believe that a mixture of common sense, realism, traditions that have worked, and a look at how different kinds of people have made a success of life will provide an excellent map to help us in our individual circumstances. Today we have so overcomplicated and stressed our lives, minds, and bodies with the "too much" that we've lost a "pearl of great price": the basics of wholesome everyday life at home. A balanced life.

As we rush along this way and that, we may find an echo of our own dreams when we read the following Irish poem:

AN OLD WOMAN OF THE ROADS

O, to have a little house!
To own the hearth and stool and all!
The heaped-up sods[3] upon the fire,
The pile of turf against the wall!

To have a clock with weights and chains
And pendulum swinging up and down!
A dresser filled with shining delph,
Speckled and white and blue and brown!

I could be busy all the day
Clearing and sweeping hearth and floor,
And fixing on their shelf again
My white and blue and speckled store!

I could be quiet there at night
Beside the fire and by myself,
Sure of a bed, and loath to leave
The ticking clock and the shining delft!

Och! but I'm weary of mist and dark,
And roads where there's never a house or bush
And tired I am of bog and road
Amid the crying wind and the lonesome hush!

And I am praying to God on high.
And I am praying Him night and day,
For a little house—a house of my own—
Out of the wind's and the rain's way.[4]

PADRAIC COLUM

Pity the tiny child who never has the peaceful comfort of the "humdrum" everyday home life described here. Watching such a child is like seeing a plant designed by the Creator for a sunny patch in the garden put instead into a chemical dish under a glaring light. The plant may sprout and put out leaves, but the roots wander miserably looking for . . . home.

This book is intended to be a practical help in creating homes that work well in a variety of circumstances. The special thrust is to encourage us all gladly to take the time and effort making a home requires. There are few shortcuts on the essentials—homemaking has to be a chosen priority in life for men and women. To create welcoming homes requires thought and then action.

Many kinds of "winds" blow on all of us in our generation. There are multitudes of lonely, tired, weary souls tramping through various sorts of mires or bogs. Although Prozac-type medications help in medical depressive states, no quick pill can substitute for *the satisfaction of a contented life based at home.* Why not look back and harvest the wisdom of past days? Our human makeup, needs, and nature have not changed. And so here is a book about the foundational place *our homes* have in our lives.

The primary example and references included will be to young children's needs in home life. Home is the first part of our educational path; it is the place where our characters and personalities develop.

Writing about such a subject, I knew I'd draw on my own life, thoughts, and ideas. My husband, Ranald, and I have been making a home together since our marriage in 1961—thirty-seven years at the time of writing. And of those years, thirty-six have included children. We still aren't finished with parenting! We had four children born into our family. During the years while they were fairly young, we also included other children occasionally who needed the shelter and the care of an established home. The three who shared our family life like this stayed for times ranging from three months to one and a half years.

Then twelve years ago two children for whom we were

guardians were suddenly bereaved and needed "stand-by" parents to swing into action. Thus we found ourselves once again being mother and father to young children when our previous youngest one was a teenager. So it is that while some of our friends have empty nests, we have steadily continued the routines that go into making a family home. Of course this has been of benefit to us all. We were not tempted to give up on homemaking! Such a personal lifetime story could not help but become part of this book.

However, I've wanted to refer to other wise guides also. It was nineteenth-century educator Charlotte Mason's writings that first gave Ranald and me a theory that explains how a child's life "works" in practice and a clear educational philosophy. Charlotte Mason valued home as the primary setting for a child's life and relationships. Just as she said that "education is an atmosphere, a discipline, and a life," so we can say that the *home is an atmosphere, a discipline, and a life.*

As I write, I feel that I am saying, "Miss Mason, let us together sit down in the drawing room of your home in the Lake District." The evening light comes in through the window; the peace of the lake and mountains is refreshing. "This is a good place to talk together about our primary concerns and insights."

"First things first," I can almost hear both of us saying, a century apart. "One of the most important aspects of life is the home. And then communities of homes."[5]

My imaginary conversation between Charlotte Mason in, say, 1898 and Susan in 1998 will be in these chapters. Other people whose writings, choices, or examples are applicable will also "join in."[6]

I hope that a clearer map for our homes and lives will emerge. May we be rooted and live generous lives. That is good.

2

୧୬

Home—the Best Growing
Ground for Children[1]

Before plunging into this book about home and the lives of people
who make them, I would like you to have a picture of the home and
community I lived in as a little girl. An author's thinking comes out
of a life, and my life will especially be part of this book.

The 1940s neighborhood where I rode my tricycle along sidewalks and played with friends in the vacant lot is now part of inner-
city St. Louis, Missouri. In that era my friends and I were not
warned not to trust grownups we didn't know. In fact we were told
the opposite. We were instructed to obey grownups along the way
and turn to them for help if we were hurt or in need.

Our mothers hung out their washing in the yards while we
played. We had a lot of freedom—going in and out of each other's
houses wherever our play led us, occupying long free hours in our
own ways. We were, however, always under the caring eye of some
grownup in the neighborhood.

Our homes were different. On one side was a Catholic family
with one adopted child; on the other, a Jewish home full of children.
We believed different things as families, but we as children had
more in common than we had differences.

Neighborhood children were called in to supper at about the
same time. We'd sit down with family arranged around the table.
Most of us were read to before bedtime. There was no television. If

we did wrong, we had to go and apologize to the neighbor. Sometimes this was very hard. I'll never forget my despair at having to face my neighbor and apologize for picking her tulips!

When we were old enough, we walked to school. There the teachers expected the same sort of obedient behavior as our parents and neighbors. I, like so many others, loved school. There I could learn how to read; this I wanted to do very much. I also enjoyed art and games.

Our lives had form and freedom—routines and moral framework on one hand and yet a rich and generous childhood of safe freedom with many hours of play, fun, friendship.

Church was important, for my dad was a pastor. But I didn't like sitting still at all. In fact, although graying Grandma Susan now enjoys certain church services immensely, there are still times when I can find myself more like the four-year-old Susan and can struggle to follow what seems a dreary grind!

Yes, I do understand myself as I look back. When I was really small, I sometimes deeply and urgently longed to stand up in that quiet place and make a huge, exciting noise, shouting and surprising everybody into good cheerfulness. One of our playmates, the young son of an elder, did call out in a clear, shouting voice in the middle of the hush of Communion. He then made a rapid escape, crawling out under all the pews. From then on, starting in my fourth year until much later, he was my hero.

Although the church service was a weekly test and trial for me (and more for my poor young mother as she coped with an unruly child), I was blessed with the immensely interesting and foundational Sunday school teaching of Nancy Barker. She told stories vividly, and when we acted them out, I felt as if I too had been called and was following the Lord Jehovah Himself.

Indeed, her teaching is still something I mull over with thanks. It was life-changing for one naughty little child. How can you not be affected for life when you had actually marched out of Egypt, had walked through the towering Red Sea pushed back for a path to escape from the terrible might of Pharaoh, and a few weeks later had found yourself camping under Mt. Sinai? Any child who has experienced that before the age of five or six obviously still shivers when remembering the holy cloud fearfully blotting out the higher levels of the mountain.

Why, I'd even had to watch out so that the family animals did not stray too near, or they'd have been zapped dead! And I was old enough to know what death meant in reality, unlike children today who encounter death only on TV screens. In my St. Louis life, I'd known people who had become ill. I had visited them with my dad in the hospital and later had gone to a few funerals. In that place and culture, I had sometimes seen the dead body.

Yes, of course in the Israelite camp I'd kept well away from that mountain so powerful that mere mortals died if they strayed too near. But Moses was especially called by God into the cloud, and so he was protected as we watched him disappear from sight. We still trembled though as we watched him trudge up to the mountaintop.

Upstairs in church there were recompenses. One of the elders always shook our hands after church, and he'd leave a yummy wrapped caramel in our palms. Also, my dad would sometimes let me choose one of the hymns for the whole church to sing. I loved the organ and singing. Usually I'd choose "Holy, Holy, Holy." I liked to be "in" the brightness of the early morning rays approaching the tremendous might of the Lord God, just as Nancy Barker and the hymn described. God is powerful and yet all-shining and beautiful with light and total goodness and love.

Of course, when I started singing, I knew my full-hearted voice was praising God in *another* place as well as in the city church with its pews. I'd have a sort of "Narnia excursion" as I sang, joining in with the wonderful throng about the heavenly throne. I didn't see them very well, but I "saw" their light, and I loved sharing in the wonder of doing something along with those who were in heaven right now. For I knew that reality was not only in everything I could see. The unseen was all around, just behind the edge of what is visible here. And I knew that my final destination would be through the seen barrier, right into this singing, enjoyable, great place. In fact when I was small, I'd pray I could get there before the next dreaded visit to the dentist!

Anyway, while I remembered Moses and the great throne in the heavenlies at church, I came to know the everyday Lord Jesus within the intimacy of a truly homelike home. My mother often sang songs of gladness about the goodness of Jesus as she worked around the kitchen. I could see He made her glad. Or on Sunday evenings when Dad went back to church, we'd be alone in the kitchen listening to a program on the radio that had lots of Christian singing. I think that because it was a special once-a-week program, it never disappeared into background noise for me. We'd sing along, happy together and cozy.

One warm spring St. Louis evening, Mother started whirling and dancing gaily as we both sang about the greatest love in all of life—our sweet Lord Jesus. This love sparkled and was enjoyable and gave gladness. I laughed as I joined in the dancing with a joy that can still bubble up. I'll always remember this lovely young mother, the atmosphere and home I grew up in, and that special scene.

Other times I had nightmares or was sick in the night with croup or measles. But this meant all-night comfort when my mother sat near me. Sometimes my dad would stumble into my bedroom and rock me in his arms in the rocking chair as he sang his favorite song, "Jesus loves me, this I know."

There is so much more that I could tell, for I was taught Bible stories clearly, even in those years when I was six years old or under. So I knew this Lord Jesus by word, by song, by hugs and comfort, by forgiveness and faithfulness and meals all together, blessed with prayer.

A childhood home like this is a very great and godly gift. Such a legacy does not come from perfect parents, thank God. In fact perfect parents could not prepare us for a life that is to be full of our own and other people's failings. My parents were always open about the fact that they weren't all that good. Anyway, all children see parents as they are!

How could anyone dare to suggest or say that working at the huge task of making a home and carrying on through years and years of ups and downs is not one of the very few truly worthwhile ways to spend our energies and gifts in human life?

We cannot start with homes. We have to begin with the *people* who make and live in them. We are part of a generation and culture that has forgotten the very framework and the truth of who persons are and why being human is special and wonderful. With this loss, personal self-understanding also disappears, along with a sense of purpose.

Having forgotten or turned aside from these roots, we've gone on to throw out the fruits that grew on the tree of this understanding. Our culture has changed rapidly. Fundamental knowledge of right and wrong is disappearing, and in the subsequent confusion, people sell their souls for a "mess of pottage." Our schools, workplaces, houses, and apartments are filled more and more with lonely people seeking someone who will love *them* and not just use their bodies. Counselors are kept fully busy as persons seek "self-worth" and try to decide who and what they are.

Good relationships grow out of the lives of persons who have roots and who are living in a balanced way. Relationships have always needed perseverance, compromise, consideration, priority, enjoyment, forgiveness, and unself-centeredness. So of course, with so many persons unsure of who they are, relationships dwindle and start evaporating like the morning mist on a hot day.

Without a clear sense of purpose or firm self-confidence, myriads of young people have given in to peer pressure and to pressure from the money-making media to give up their fresh virginity and try to win the crowd's acceptance. Too often adults have stopped protecting these immature young persons, and many youths have suffered the long-term abuse of having been pushed into trading their souls and bodies for someone else's temporary satisfaction. I think girls have suffered the most abuse, as resulting pregnancies have frequently been terminated by powerful adults who override the teenagers' maternal feelings.

We have also witnessed the disappearance of trust and neighborly goodness in epidemic proportions. Often because of the parents' fear, children today are not allowed to walk to school alone, not allowed to play Cops and Robbers around the neighborhood in the dusk and finish with catching fireflies. Many of the elderly people endure terror as they live alone, and they walk as quickly as they can with sideways glances when they go anywhere.

Children no longer have the security of knowing that the houses on the streets where they live are mostly "all-day homes"— homes peopled by known neighbors and friends. Children may, in fact, only know the inside of their own home, and for too many that is a lonely place as well.

In Rochester, Minnesota, a few years ago I saw a leaflet for parents telling them what a child should be told to do when they go home to the empty house after school. "Don't touch the stove." (So no hot drink on a bitterly cold Minnesota winter day.) "A young child should have several telephone numbers to call." There is a daily surge on the nation's telephone system as schools close for the day. That surge is the nation's children calling a parent, usually Mom. A phone call is different indeed from Mom's lap, her welcoming comfort and preparation of food, her meeting children's needs! These children experience fear too.

I am writing this because there is a primary need in human life. *We all need a home.* Home is the place we return to when we are old enough to go out. For a baby and toddler, home *is* the world. Home, the place where a person *belongs*. The place where we each live the rhythm of life with its joys and duties. A shelter, a growing place; a place to be alone and private, to share friendship, fun, and conversation; the place for quiet rest and sleep; the place we love.

We need input on what is essential for making a home for ourselves, other adults, our young, and our elderly. Amid the welter of advertisements and fragmented points of view confronting us, we need to sit down to think while we let confusion clear. Often someone is trying to make us spend money. Or people have a political agenda. Or they are destroyers of reasoned, balanced, whole thinking. We are left with ideas that are not usable or clear. In contrast, it is possible to make and enjoy a home that is "good enough" in spite of flaws. Good enough for what? Good enough to provide a home that, as Charlotte Mason said, "would be the best growing ground for children." A good-enough home too for contented life for *any* person of whatever age. We all need a place for the creativity of life to take root and flourish. We need a home ground that is secure.

Yes, just as a house needs its infrastructure, so homes need certain basic patterns. Yet as long as the necessary basic routines and patterns are in place, all *sorts* of variations and adaptations will grow. In such a diverse world, to be good growing places or living places homes must adapt to actual persons, places, and situations. There is no one model. But certain qualities will be found in all these good-enough homes. What are these elements? How *do* we make good homes for ourselves and/or our children?

Charlotte Mason was a single woman. In contrast I have been married since I was young and have had a family to care for as the top priority in all the many interesting responsibilities of my life.

Not much about Charlotte Mason's childhood is communicated in her writings or in books about her. But we find enough to know that her early life was in what today would be termed "disadvantaged" circumstances. Her great advantage was a loving home where, among other things, books were read aloud to her. Thus, like many others, we find a great person coming from a situation where all needed courage just to survive. As for Charlotte, she enjoyed a great love of life always. The light and strength of that still shines on when we get to "know" her from her books.

I enjoyed a secure childhood with respected parents. But although so different from Charlotte Mason's early life, mine was not the scene of ease and plenty people expect today! Charlotte and I both loved and trusted the Lord God as the center of our lives. We both have understood that this is not an imaginary or mythical hope but the unifying truth that explains the mystery of all reality, all that exists. We accepted (and I still accept) the claims of Christ as revealing to all persons, including ourselves personally, the love and "rescue" of God. We believed that this was not "got up" as one mere human idea among many such ideas, but that God's Word, the texts of the Old and New Testament, are a true communication from the God who exists, a God who actually "is there." We both based our lives and work on this belief, as have the countless numbers of believing Christians in history before us.

Of this Jesus, Charlotte Mason wrote in the introduction to her book *The Saviour of the World* (Vol. 2): "That 'He is Lord of all,' the dominion, supremacy, the universal authority of our Lord appears to be the salient idea in this second volume." She wrote the book in poetry form because she thought that form would be more vibrantly influential than prose in her readers' lives. Later on in the book, she explains the only way this knowledge is learned:

> *Once more; The Scriptures search ye—*
>   *These are they*
> *Which, line on line, tell out the history*
> *Of Jesus, Virgin-Born, of men denied. . . .*[2]

She points us to the source of this knowledge—the Scriptures, God's Word. When Charlotte Mason, who so valued historical knowledge, uses the word *history*, she means just that—something that happened in space and time.

Her biographer Essex Cholmondeley writes, "The love and knowledge of God, of Jesus Christ the Saviour of the world, of the Holy Spirit as supreme educator of mankind, these themes are never absent from her thoughts."[3]

At the beginning of this chapter we read, "Any attempt to tell the story of Charlotte Mason must lay stress upon that 'life hid with Christ in God' upon which she based her teaching. . . ." And a bit further on: "There was only one word underlined in the prayer book which Miss Mason used: 'This I _know_' (Psalm 56:9)."

Hers was not just a belief in a distant intellectual truth; her beliefs were part of her life. She gave her practical, everyday life a lot of thought. This way her routine included the spaces needed to practice the presence of God—time to read His Word, ponder it, and pray. She set aside her very best hour of the day for "Bible reading and earnest prayer." She chose the time when she said, "I feel quite fresh," so that she could give the Gospel "that full gaze of the mind we call attention."[4]

Rain, snow, or shine would find Charlotte Mason walking down to the village parish church for morning and evening services every Sunday. The rest of the day was also a true "day of rest unto the Lord," which was a delight.

My own life has also been based on the central truth/belief in the historical Judeo-Christian teaching. Trying to put it into practice *is* a lifelong challenge! When I was eighteen, the reason I allowed myself to look toward marriage with Ranald was because I knew he meant it when he wrote, "I have set my face like a flint because the Sovereign Lord helps me."[5] That was to be our life's base, road, light, and help. For me, the thought of marriage could only be considered with such a person.

When our oldest daughters were doing their A-level exams,[6] I was able to write a book about Christian belief for their generation.[7] Their peers, like mine, asked then and still ask lots of questions. The majority of people do not believe that Christianity could have the authority of truth. When the Christian faith is respected at all, it usually is viewed as an experience of "personal faith" in some unclear myth-like belief that, people think, can vary. The content per se doesn't matter—"but it is nice to have faith." For many people this vague conception has now given way to the hopeless idea that there is no truth at all! In contrast to this, understanding Christians have throughout history believed that "in the first place, Christian faith turns on the reality of God's existence, His being there."[8]

"True Christian faith rests on content. It is not a vague thing which takes the place of real understanding, nor is it the strength of belief which is of value." "The true basis for faith is not the faith itself, but the work which Christ finished on the Cross."[9] This Jesus, Son of the living God, was born a flesh-and-blood person so as to win "mercy to me, the sinner" (as Christians have prayed for nearly 2,000 years now, and all have meant the same thing).

There is a wonderful unity of thought and understanding of life among these believers over two millennia. Often we are only struck by the diversity, or we have been scalded by corrosive arguments between groups of believers. Of course, it is in our collective history that the purity of truth again and again is clouded over through incorrect interpretations and practices.[10] We *do* tend to go down side lanes, forgetting essentials; we add rules and ideas. Sometimes even the basic core of belief was/is obscured.

However, the believer who honors God's Word as holy truth and His Son as an actual historical person has more in common with other believers than he or she has differences. The Judeo-Christian view of history means that there is a "before," "present," and "after" in space and time. We all learn from those who have walked ahead of us, even if only to disagree with some details in their ideas or practices. But we all regard God's Word as *His* speaking/telling us the truth; the Bible is (or should be) our shared, unchangeable foundation.

This viewpoint is now past history for the majority of people in the Western world. We live in a post-Christian culture. When C. S. Lewis gave his inaugural lecture at Cambridge University,[11] he called attention to this transformation. He first spoke of that earlier cultural shift from paganism to Christianity that took place as Antiquity gave way to the Dark Ages. This is where we find the fall of the Roman Empire, the invasions by barbarians, and the coming of Christian belief to Europe.

Lewis points out that our ancestors thought this "christening of Europe" was irreversible. Instead we are witnessing "the opposite process." He discerns three major periods in our history—the pre-Christian, the Christian, "and what may reasonably be called the post-Christian." The coming of this last stage has made a "momentous difference" in our culture. Values have changed; new values have in turn changed our lifestyles, and our whole society has been transformed.

According to Lewis, it is wrong to think that "Europe can come out of Christianity . . . and find herself back where she was. . . . A post-Christian man is not a Pagan; you might as well think that a married woman recovers her virginity by divorce." What we have in this post-Christian world, Lewis argues, is far worse than paganism.

You may wonder why I'm quoting from a university lecture while beginning a book dealing with the most everyday, ordinary concerns in life—home life and the children in our homes, especially in the early years. A good question!

The profound truth is that the way we as persons live every day is based on our belief about who we actually are and what life is about. For instance, if I am an accident of probability in a universe with no rhyme or reason and no right and wrong in an objective sense, then *how am I to live?* What will a culture be like when people believe that there is no truth, no purpose, no meaning—that there are no moral absolutes?

This kind of thinking devalues life to such an extent that many younger people (and older ones too) now lack motivation and *la joie de vivre* (the joy of living). Holding this life-denying post-Christian view, many are ignorant of the value and joy of having an everyday life rooted in a home and community. The ordinary for them becomes boring or like a prison. The media and advertising reflect and intensify this warped view. Is it any wonder such life-cheated persons (for so they are) cannot enjoy simple delights and satisfactions?

Charlotte Mason was finishing her work in the first part of the twentieth century. She died in 1923. She saw the agony of World War I and the growing confusion of thought. Because of her beliefs, she was not disillusioned. For if there is truth, people can always enjoy with integrity the goodness and glory of God and His creation. In this way, individuals can return to the original "marriage" with their Creator. They can experience the true gold of abundant life itself. Their lives can be redeemed.

So can cultures be redeemed. If enough people live according to the truth of who they are in relation to God and His goodness, then goodness spreads like a light. It can grow again like a spring after the harsh winter of disaster.

Like all other believers, Charlotte Mason, Susan, and indeed C. S. Lewis thought (and I am still here to put that into the present tense!) that everyday, ordinary life lived faithfully is where the glory of God is best reflected—in our homes, communities, jobs, our art, charitable enterprises, and so on. Of course, truth is *told* and believed first (truth has content), but after that comes the actual living, being, and doing.

Ordinary home life matters for everyone. How we arrange for children's lives matters *terribly*. Starve them physically, emotionally, or mentally; cheat or abuse them in the formative days, and we will throw away their opportunity to develop properly. We can and will destroy lives. And this is a most terrible thing. Not only will their personal lives be damaged, but if that damage involves enough young human beings, the culture will become distorted.[12]

Most of us now feel we live in distorted communities. Many people are already so scarred that they can no longer enjoy the simple things of life—such things as nature, a good conversation with friends with laughter punctuating thought-provoking discussion, a meal enjoyed in leisure, the company of a child, the peace and quiet of gazing at the afternoon sky as one rests after work, lingering over a cup of tea. For C. S. Lewis, it was a tramp along lanes with a friend and a welcome pint of beer at the village pub along the way. For Charlotte Mason, it was also a row on the lake or the joy of seeing the first flowers of spring. For all of us, it can be the company of great minds and interesting lives through books.

These sorts of joys are another reason I link Charlotte Mason, the pioneer in education, with myself in order to write on our combined viewpoints about home, childhood, and life itself. We both always found special refreshment in the beauty of nature. This love of nature was not only a personal feature of the educator's life, but she guided children and their teachers to appreciate the natural world too. One hundred years apart in time, she and I both have enjoyed the glory of the Hampshire countryside.[13] We have soaked up the song of the skylark over the Downs.[14] We have tramped through bluebells in woods near Alton.[15]

In my childhood I had enjoyed myriads of wild flowers in the Alpine meadows I loved.[16] In Charlotte Mason's time, English hedgerows were likewise jeweled with a rich variety of color. She wrote vividly descriptive books about this Hampshire countryside.[17] Ranald and I with our children were to crisscross the same paths a hundred years later. Only after that did we discover Charlotte Mason.

I, like Charlotte, enjoy children. We have appreciated children as valuable persons—different from each other, fascinating, often with amazing thoughts. We both believe that the care and education of children is one of the greatest tasks any human being can have.

Both Charlotte and I had a desire to work with children. At eighteen years of age, she went into teacher's training at a time when this was a new initiative in the United Kingdom. I went at eighteen to a college for occupational therapy near Oxford with the goal of specializing in the care of children with special learning needs.

Charlotte was unable to finish the training as a resident in the college, possibly due to financial restraints or her fragile health. She went to teach in a small school in a seaside town on the south coast of England.

My plans changed, and I withdrew from my college after my theory exams, as I was by then engaged to be married. I taught a class of English-speaking children in a Swiss school that year—children aged four and a half to twelve in one class. I also taught high school biology plus Bible classes for all ages. Then Ranald and I were married and blessed with the birth of children.

Charlotte Mason taught and loved the children in her first school. Many of her ideas were formed there. In her "free" time, she carried on with her studies to finish the courses sent to her by the

London college—we'd call it distance learning today. So she accomplished her work for the exams and certificate from the Home and Colonial Training College in London.

Much of Charlotte Mason's childhood education had been at home, as was usual at that time. Her mother and father taught her for most of her childhood, although she also attended a "board" school for a limited time and was probably a monitress[18] with some teaching experience before she went to college at eighteen. As we saw, this was also a fairly brief spell, for she finished the course "by correspondence" while teaching; most of her higher education was self-taught.

I went to school first until seven years of age in the United States of America. (And once again for a year when I was twelve.) Otherwise, I was in small classes in Switzerland taught entirely in French. However, at the age of thirteen, I developed rheumatic fever. From that time until I was seventeen and went to the University of Lausanne (to matriculate in the Ecole de Français Moderne), I taught myself from an excellent school course that came in the mail. First I studied this much-loved Calvert School course[19] and then later high school correspondence courses from the University of Nebraska.

In fact it was through the use of the lesson manuals on my own that I developed the discipline of study. My experience brought the satisfaction of self-taught accomplishment and a growing love of learning for its own sake rather than to make a teacher happy. Thus Charlotte and I both profited from self-motivated learning—an ongoing habit in life! Like her, I know its value, and I desire that children in my care should likewise love learning and books.

Charlotte Mason spent time living in the home of a friend who had children. Therefore she knew what it is to be a loved and intimate member of such a family. She wrote in her *Essay Towards a Philosophy of Education*:

> While still a young woman, I saw a great deal of a family of
> Anglo-Indian children who had come home to their grandfa-

ther's house and were being brought up by an aunt who was my intimate friend. The children were astonishing to me; they were persons of generous impulses and sound judgment, of great intellectual aptitude, of imagination and moral insight.[20]

Charlotte next described a particular incident and her own reaction to it:

> Such incidents are common enough in families, but they were new to me. . . . I had an elementary school and a pioneer Church High School at this time, so that I was enabled to study children in large groups; but at school children are not so self-revealing as at home. I began under the guidance of these children to take the measure of *a person* and soon to suspect that children are *more* than we, their elders, except that their ignorance is illimitable.[21]

Thus in her clear analysis of what is necessary for a strong educational framework, method, and life and of how children (and all of us) learn with understanding, she realized that it is in the family home that children can best be seen for what they are—*persons*. She knew that the home is fundamental for a child; it is the first priority in their life and development. She gave lectures and wrote books to encourage parents to give thought and time to creating good homes for their children.

Charlotte Mason also developed a clear educational philosophy. After much lecturing and writing, she had an ever-growing influence in England. Many parents[22] found guidance for their families through her teaching. It changed their lives; they saw their children benefit. They urged her to train teachers. Finally she moved to Ambleside, a village surrounded with hills in the Lake District. Here in a rented house the first students came to train as teachers.

Did she begin an institutional training college? No. Charlotte Mason spent her most productive years and gave much time and energy to *creating a home* and a balanced life for herself, some friends who worked closely with her, and the young adult students who came to study there. This was *their* "growing and learning place" for life, whatever they did later on.

Not long after beginning the work, she moved out of the rented house and purchased a distinguished home perched high on lawns that sloped down toward the lovely mountain-rimmed Lake Windermere. Charlotte Mason decided that this house, Scale How, was the God-given place for her training establishment. She did not have the capital, but she believed that God would provide. She quietly went forward in prayer and trust. The last payment on the house was made just before she died.

"God-given" is the correct designation. To begin with, she wanted to call it the House of the Holy Spirit. She, as a Christian, believed that the source of life is God and that all departments of life are governed and breathed into by the "Lord who is Lord of all of Life." She knew that life cannot be divided into compartments with one labeled "religious"—the Lord made the whole of life, and He has a place in each part.

A friend persuaded her to call it the House of Education, for although Charlotte Mason understood her first designation, not everyone else would. Charlotte Mason was gifted with the strength of everyday common sense. Part of her wisdom was the knowledge that this should be a home and that all who came to be part of it were sharing a life—a rich, generous life. This philosophy is different from that in an institution teaching courses that are passed or failed.

In fact, once as a young student arrived in the cold of January to begin the course, Charlotte Mason asked her, "What have you come for?"

"I have come to learn to teach," was the answer.

Charlotte Mason gave what may have been a startling response: "You have come to learn to live."

Learning to live! How enviable is the person who succeeds in mastering the gift of a life well lived. And what is that? we might all ask. Whatever it is, all persons need to know and practice life. The sooner a wee baby is welcomed into such a life-place, the better. For the lessons learned endure, once they have become entrenched within, for a lifetime.

Charlotte Mason comments here on our Lord's words in St. John's Gospel: "*Hath eternal life*"—not a joy merely reserved for the future, but fullness of living now—"hath the *full* life."[23]

Life. Our Lord appears to be speaking in this connection of that liberty of soul, that vitality and joyousness of spirit, of which He speaks again when He says: "I am come that ye might have life, and that ye might have it more abundantly."

> *It is more life and fuller that we want,*
> *that we crave sometimes with a sick craving . . .*
> *life of joyous, generous expansion,*
> *free . . . as a bird's life,*
> *dutiful and humble as the life of angels—*
> *this sort of glad living is the instant reward and*
> *   result of that recognition*
> *of the SON which we call faith. . . .*[24]

3

～

Free as a Bird, Dutiful and Humble as the Angels

Children brought up in a home or school that practiced Charlotte Mason's educational philosophy enjoyed a wonderfully varied and yet balanced life—on the one hand free and on the other carefully structured within the stable framework of Christian boundaries. There is sweet naturalness in this balance for persons of all ages.

We all need structure, a "shape," that contains also areas "free" for choice and creativity, including first our *own* personal responses to life. The personal response of the child to an aspect of life can be illustrated in many ways. For instance, I remember going to the Rijksmuseum in Amsterdam when I was seven. Rembrandt's *Night Watch* covered an entire wall. I still remember its power interacting with me. I stood and gazed, absorbed. Charlotte Mason would have been glad that no "educating adult" broke into my rapt response. For in such ways do artists actually speak to us—whether we are seven or seventy. No one tried to tell me all the facts about the painting. No one rushed me away. This painting alone met me that day, met me for life. How I remember! I can remember thinking to myself, "Ah, *this* is what kindergarten painting is to lead to!" Aloud I added, with a sigh my mother still remembers, "Aahhh. If only I had enough paint, this is what I'd do someday."

This is a perfect example of Charlotte Mason's theory and work—a child in direct contact with an original rich resource. In response a child's soul expands, and the idea of what he or she can achieve also expands. Such an experience truly brings a joyous, soaring freedom for mind and soul, fires the imagination, and gives ideas inwardly to fuel later motivation. This kind of experience is what has to come first.

The individual's joyous response is cut short by preaching/teaching explanations that get in the way. The direct two-way "conversation" between any person and the source is called by Charlotte Mason "Masterly Inactivity." In this instance, my parents had taken me to the museum, but stood back to let me actually "connect" with the painting myself (experience a living relationship).

We don't get excited by other people telling us how we should feel. (So if somebody had insisted at that point that I "notice how beautiful this is, etc.," it would have been yet one more weary lecture for Susan. The magic moment would have been shattered. No, my parents displayed the "inactivity" that was masterly. They let ME be the important person. What I felt and thought mattered. It was *my* moment with Rembrandt. And I was left to drink it all in for as long as I wanted to.

"Oh," I can almost hear readers sighing, "all well for a child taken to the great art galleries (actually only an occasional few in my childhood), but I live in (wherever). Nothing 'original' and 'special' is here."

Do you have puddles where you live? Is there mud anywhere? Is there grass or trees, flowers or ants? "Small children want to do a lot of things that get them dirty, and those things are good for children too. They love to dig in earth and sand, wade in mud puddles, splash in water in the sink. They want to roll in the grass, squeeze mud in their hands. When they have chances to do these delightful things, it enriches their spirit, makes them warmer people, just the way beautiful music or falling in love improves adults."[1]

NATURE! Unless our homes are located in the most naturally deprived places, basic elements are nearby to be explored and enjoyed. They have been designed and created by the greatest artist of all—God. Don't think you *need* a Rembrandt original for you or your child's spirit to soar, inner self to be satisfied, or creativity to be nurtured.

Yes indeed, I do remember many such satisfying contacts when I was still in my preschool years in plain, old St. Louis! One corner of the yard had been left without flowers or grass so we could dig— "mess about" the English would say. It turned into an often-quarried hole. Water would be poured in, and we'd mix it all around with a stick. Then claylike mud could be extracted for pies, etc. Inspired one day, I filled a bucket with the appealing chocolatey liquid and painted my parents' white front porch. Although their response to my creativity was really disappointing from the young artist's point of view, I survived these critics, which included chastisement. Before that cloud descended, my soul had expanded with joy as I'd wielded the real grown-up paintbrush with satisfying strokes. Nobody could now take that away!

The "mud, glorious mud" with its joys was a contrast to other aspects of that yard. There I watched full of wonderment as tall slender leaves surrounded stems pregnant with fattening buds. When the rich purple iris flowers emerged, I loved the velvety depths. My finger would touch them gently. I gazed as some petals reached up while others curved down.

In my overalls I used to squat down to enjoy smelling the lily-of-the-valley clumps. I think it was in this yard with its small square of lawn that my lifelong love of flowers was born. The irises were so rich. The lily-of-the-valley was so dainty and scented in delicate whiteness. I see them still, impressed forever by their loveliness. On the front strip of grass another joy—dandelions with sunny saucers of fringed light and glory. Naturally, they were picked. And I grieved when their beauty that was worthy of angels wilted. Later we would puff and blow away the light heads of seeds. Again a finger would touch the lightness. One's tongue would sample the milky juice from picked stems.

Keeping my examples here to an urban area, let me say that our environment provided me with plenty of generous life-expanding experiences in that early, vital part of my life. One day my dad, a young minister, had interrupted his busy schedule for a very important event. The Mississippi River was in flood. He found it exciting, and he wanted to share this with his two young daughters.

I remember the dreary cityscape, parking the car, walking. And then, wonder of wonders, the world from there on disappeared completely. Instead, there was an expanse of muddy water that stretched on—on—and more on. No shore in sight. Maybe that was when a sense of awed awareness at the concept of infinity stirred in me. The expanse of water seemed infinite. That sense was intensified when we were allowed to remove our shoes and socks and wade at "the edge of infinity." Then you knew how little you actually were—how big things could be. I remember clearly how glad I was my mom was not present! I knew that for some reason or other, she'd not allow this masterly inactivity. In fact, I still remember when we arrived back home, muddy and exuberant, for supper how her, "Ohhh, Fran!" spoke volumes!

"Life. Our Lord appears to be speaking in this connection of that liberty of soul, that vitality and joyousness of spirit. . . . It is more life and fuller that we want . . . life of joyous, generous expansion, free . . . as a bird's life. . . . "[2]

This is part of the quote I used at the end of the last chapter. All the permissive educators would be saying loud "amens" to this aspect of Charlotte Mason's idea on the abundant life needed for healthy personal growth. But they would shrink from the next words, stung to the core. For the path of life has two sides. We are led on a single path, yes. But to be balanced, we must navigate the narrow space between two sides. I always visualize this path as running along a mountain ridge.

So although on one side we allow for others and ourselves time and space for the bubbling up *joie de vivre*[3] with all the energy, well-being, and freedom that come when we spend some of our time according to personal choices, on the other side we need structure. To be beautiful, the river needs its boundaries, or the waters actually become like the muddy Mississippi flood. So with our lives.

The Road of Life

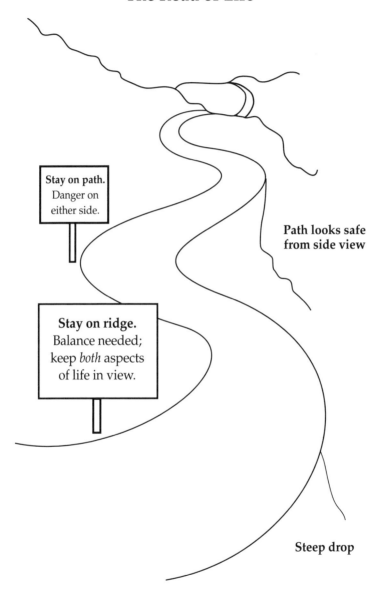

Stay on path.
Danger on
either side.

**Path looks safe
from side view**

Stay on ridge.
Balance needed;
keep *both* aspects
of life in view.

Steep drop

Path Along Top of Ridge, Cut-Away View

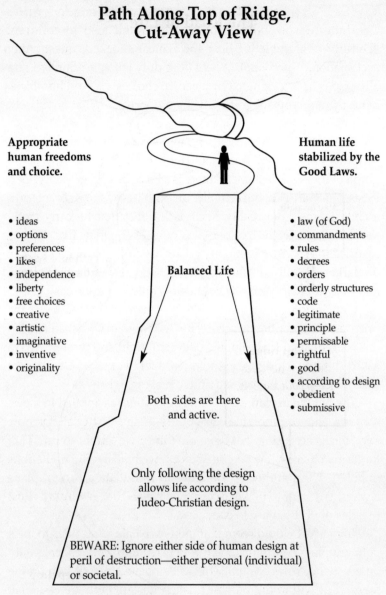

Appropriate human freedoms and choice.

Human life stabilized by the Good Laws.

- ideas
- options
- preferences
- likes
- independence
- liberty
- free choices
- creative
- artistic
- imaginative
- inventive
- originality

Balanced Life

- law (of God)
- commandments
- rules
- decrees
- orders
- orderly structures
- code
- legitimate
- principle
- permissable
- rightful
- good
- according to design
- obedient
- submissive

Both sides are there
and active.

Only following the design
allows life according to
Judeo-Christian design.

BEWARE: Ignore either side of human design at
peril of destruction—either personal (individual)
or societal.

God made persons nonprogrammed.
They have actual choice—free will.

God is there. His goodness and truth
are loving and holy.

"Life—dutiful and humble[4] as the lives of angels," writes Charlotte Mason, both to us as adults and also to children. "Dutiful?" "Humble!" I hear the typical shocked, questioning exclamation. "Surely not. Where does duty come in? Surely I and all persons have a right to our personal choices! . . . And humble—honestly! Are you suggesting being a doormat? What about self-esteem?"

The entire Bible presents a single view. From the Hebrew Scriptures of the Old Testament right through to the final paragraph of the New Testament, there is a basic design to reality: God exists, not as an idea, but actually, "in truth"—the same sort of truth a child learns from reality, such as the fact that he can't crawl *through* a table leg or that one plus one never equals five. God as revealed in His Word is entirely good: "God is light; in him there is no darkness at all" (1 John 1:5). Jesus said, "Listen to me, believe, and *do what I say.*" And "Be not hearers only, but doers also."

Duty is doing what is required. This instruction to follow is the price tag of the confident, secure, freely abundant Christian life. No one is ever called to design the pattern of right and wrong. We are asked to fit in. More, we are told to be followers, to obey. We are asked to choose what is good and to walk in light.

The word *duty* (from which we get *dutiful*, as applied to a person) is seen as a miserable concept in our age. "After all," people say, "this is accepting that there are things we 'ought to do'! That limits my choices." As people of today, we hate having limitations imposed by an authority. We want to formulate our own plans always. We want to make up our own rules. That is why we resist the idea of ever having to obey.

To many it would seem that these two balancing sides to life's path are plain contradictions (proper freedom, choices, creativity on one hand; rules and patterns to be obeyed and fit into on the other). But within the Judeo-Christian design, both are essential. Tip over too much on one side or the other in any area of thought or practice, and you get disasters, rather like the flooding of the "free" Mississippi on one hand or the asphyxiation of life by a hard, mindless legality on the other. John Bunyan illustrates this balance in a passage from *Pilgrim's Progress*:

> So Christian turned out of his way to go to Mr. Legality's house for help: but behold, when he was got hard by the Mill, it seemed so high, and also that side of it was the way side, did hang so much over, that Christian was afraid to venture further, lest the Hill should fall on his head: wherefore there he stood still, and wotted [knew] not what to do. Also his burden, now, seemed heavier to him, than while he was in his way. There came also flashes of fire out of the Mill, that made Christian afraid he should be burned: here therefore he did sweat and quake for fear.

Bunyan pictures the menace of being shadowed by the fear of legalism without mercy. Yes, legalism will kill human life—*if* all you have in a household or school is rules. The beauty of the Christian life, at home or otherwise, comes from clear structure and form on the one hand and yet a creative and maturing free choosing on the other. Both are essential.

Another influential writer, Benedict, in about A.D. 530, said:

> Listen, child of God, to the guidance of your teacher. Attend to the message you hear and make sure it pierces to your heart, so that you may accept with willing freedom and fulfill by the way you live, the directions that have come from your loving Father. It is not easy to accept and persevere in obedience, but it is the way of return to Christ, when you have strayed through the laxity and carelessness of disobedience. My words are addressed to you especially, whoever you may be, whatever your circumstances, who turn from the pursuit of your own self-will and ask to enlist under Christ, who is Lord of all, by following him through taking to yourself that strong and blessed armor of obedience which he made his own on coming into our world.[5]

In our day, many of us are startled by the paradox of these words: "accept with *willing freedom* ... the directions that have come from your loving Father ... strong and blessed armor of obedience." And yet this *is* the pattern of life to which Christians have committed themselves. We are all under authority—God's authority.

It is through the act of obeying God that adults and children follow a safe, definite path that leads to the liberty of green pastures and still waters for the soul and in actual life too. If we listen to the words of God, we never ignore His directions. We are to listen, understand, and take His offer of forgiveness to heart. We bow before the Creator, and a desire to follow and obey will increase as we stumble along. God's rules and ways *are* the way of life. His way followed is a gift, not a test.

The design portrays such a person as already liberated from the penalty of having broken the rules, but not excused from obeying. This person is freed from God's final judgment. There is law, order, and design without a threatening mountain of legality.

This is the historical Judeo-Christian teaching. Biblical words such as *grace, forgiveness, benevolence, goodness, kindness, love* and *mercy* confuse many people. They think of the rules as like a ton of bricks about to fall. They can't see the beauty of grace that is like fruit on a tree or the shade of a cool, green leafy beech woods on a hot summer's day. The strong structure of God's rules are like the trunk and roots of a tree. The rules are not designed to crush but to provide the structure that holds through the storms of life and that gives the gift of beauty, shade, fruit, and variety.

A good illustration of being under authority as the Bible describes it is that of the good father. He walks into the room as the three-year-old is just biting into a forbidden chocolate laid out for a birthday party. The child's disobedience is not excused, but neither does the father stop loving the child. (In this instance Dad may hide his smile at the chocolate-covered mouth!) He is stern for the child's own sake, but soon Dad is the very life of the party and swoops up the toddler in the joy of a game. They laugh with mutual love and enjoyment.

Some evangelical believers have made the mistake of feeling so totally safe—saved from guilt once for all—that they fall into the deathtrap St. Paul wrote about in Romans:

> Now we find that the law keeps slipping into the picture to point the vast extent of sin. Yet, though sin is shown to be wide and deep, thank God His grace is wider and deeper still! The whole outlook changes—sin used to be the master of men and in the end handed them over to death: now grace is the ruling factor, with righteousness as its purpose and its end the bringing of men to the eternal life of God through Jesus Christ our Lord. Now what is our response to be? Shall we sin to our heart's content and see how far we can exploit the grace of god? *What a ghastly thought!* (Rom. 5:20—6:2 PHILLIPS, emphasis mine. The King James Version exclaims, "God forbid!")

Believers who know that they are safe and forgiven can become casual about goodness and obedience. It becomes easy then to break rules without trying too hard to obey. When we start doing wrong, the practice escalates, becomes a habit. Wrongdoing hardens a person.

It is true that we *all* are still sinners. Yes, believing in Christ's death offers assurance of God's gift of forgiveness. The penalty was paid by His death like none other. But, no, we cannot ever feel free to disregard God's basic instructions on how to live. Just wanting to do something is not a reason for doing it—not at three, thirty, or sixty, for that matter. Trying one's hardest to obey is not just being "nice." Obedience has been commanded. It is central to being Christ's follower, a believer. The question is not, "What do I want?" or "What will make me (or my child) happy?" but "What is right?"

However, obedience is only the infrastructure of life. When we obey the ground rules, we find that suddenly we are like the sheep who have been behind their shepherd; they obediently and humbly follow and find themselves in an open pasture with much space to frolic or go right or left. The quiet sheep can chew the cud in the shade, while a mischievous young lamb enjoys skittering everywhere, all with safe boundaries.

The God of creation tells the creature what the rules of operation are. Just as airplanes cannot fly unless they follow the laws of aerodynamics, so we are eventually "grounded" when we ignore the basic rules of life to do whatever seems interesting. But there is more to flying than the rules! Flying is not a math lesson! The few among us who get to soar find immense joy and a sense of freedom as we pilot a craft obeying aerodynamic laws, and yet we plot our own course. Hang-gliding is a good example, because even though there *are* choices and those doing it seem as free as birds, they and the birds fly because they continue to observe the laws of nature. Listening, obeying, and following in this example allows the freedom of flight.

In the same way, we are liberated in all aspects of life by staying within the structures God has given. Human beings do this through choice. It must be said that in this fallen world staying within God's boundaries is not an easy matter at all, and no one is perfect. We all experience failures.

The humility that stops our self-centered chatter so that we can listen costs us something. How we love to prance into the limelight and live there! This is the opposite of biblical humility. The quote at the end of the last chapter mentioned people whose own desires are stilled so that they can hear God's voice. After listening, they plan to obey. And then, like some childhood party magic trick, it turns out that it is the humble, dutiful person who finds uncluttered joy in giving full attention to life's demands. Proper foundations enable a creative, satisfying, and interesting personal life.

Children growing up today on the streets I played on no longer ride tricycles around the block by themselves. They can't be free that way. The neighborhood elementary school's windows are still cheerful. Recently it delighted me to see a row of paper tulips all along a window there—a sight I'd enjoyed fifty-three years ago. The old kindergarten room with its high ceiling and small-paned windows is now a welcoming library. Children still feel safe in the halls; they are well looked after in the school. The education they are receiving is like a ray of light for many of them. Their safety, however, is secured by the police unit based in the school near the entrance door. The easy freedom I knew of coming and going without a care in the world is lost as more and more persons do whatever they feel like doing, rather than obeying life's basic rules. Following God's laws produces creative freedom, trust, and respect—all life-giving—both for individuals and for all of society.

4

∾

This Is Where I Put My Feet Up and Thank God

We've covered several basic areas of thought. Charlotte Mason and C. S. Lewis have suggested that the central beliefs of both individuals and cultures determine the way life is lived in practice. It is useless to talk about homes until really basic questions such as "Who are we?" or "What is life's aim?" have been resolved. For instance, if a human baby is regarded as an accident of probability, a cog in a meaningless machine, the "proper" environment for the child will be different than in a home where "God is there," and "all's well in His care."[1]

The writer Ellis Peters, who had a Christian worldview, will start us off on our quest to discover what home is and how to create it. She quoted from Rudyard Kipling:

> *God gave all men all earth to love*
> *But since our hearts are small,*
> *Ordained for each one spot should prove*
> *Beloved over all.*

Peters goes on:

Now it is perfectly true that this one spot does not necessarily have to be where we were born. I can think of places in other countries, where I can imagine being happy every moment of the day and night. But none of them displaces this vague circle of earth, three miles or so in diameter, in which I have lived, or at least made my base, all my life. I can travel joyfully to any of my favorite haunts abroad, but only to this place can I come home. . . . Other places can be where I exult and wonder. *This is where I put my feet up and thank God.* [Italics mine.][2]

Ellis Peters, who was single all her life, wrote this paragraph in a book describing the beautiful part of England that was her home. She was one of the persons whose personal home of four walls, garden, and kitchen with its ever-warm Aga[3] was nestled into a bit of the world that was also home to her. For such lucky ones, there is double meaning to being at home. First the house itself is home. It's the feeling of being "home again" as the returned person makes a cup of tea or the tired child nestles back into the cozy, familiar bed.

But for people like Peters, home also means the area all around the abode. She obviously loved travel and enjoyed places such as Venice, Prague, and Kashmir. She called them "Sunday treats to be visited, marveled at, enjoyed and remembered . . . graces to ornament and vary the basic stability of a weekday life, the spinal cord that binds everything together, the place where I live, work and coordinate all the experiences into a personal reconciliation, which is the point of living."[4] Notice that these experiences only had a richness for her *because* they were "graces to ornament" a stable everyday life.

She might have used the image of a tree trunk with its roots to convey the idea of unifying stability, but instead she refers to the spinal cord, which connects everything else together and provides a solid base.

In our age of rushing about hither and yon in fast-moving vehicles, we need to pause and consider whether it is worth making some major choices so that we too can be at home and belong in one familiar place.

As a young woman, Charlotte Mason visited a friend in the

Lake District. When she eventually chose to settle there and make Scale How her home, she not only bonded with the house but also with the area. She loved the hills and lakes. She took long walks every day—enjoying the rich fabric of her surroundings. The first snowdrops of the season or a bird returned for the summer brought her delight. Although she became a woman with great responsibilities, she did not allow the stress to rush her past her home countryside without time "to stand and stare."

LEISURE

What is this life, if full of care,
We have no time to stand and stare.
No time to stand beneath the boughs
And stare as long as sheep or cows.
No time to see, when woods we pass,
Where squirrels hide their nuts in grass.
No time to see, in broad daylight,
Streams full of stars, like stars at night.
No time to turn at Beauty; glance,
And watch her feet, how they can dance.
No time to wait till her mouth can
Enrich that smile her eyes began.
A poor life this if, full of care,
We have no time to stand and stare.[5]

W. H. DAVIES

Since I've already brought myself into this story, let me say how, as a college student in England in 1959, I'd longed for my home. It was "home" in both ways. I looked forward to telling the family all about my interesting experiences in Oxford, looked forward to having my own bedroom again instead of the dormitory with eight girls. But maybe even more I would anticipate returning home to *my* mountains. I leaned out the window as the train chugged up the last pass into Switzerland at Vallorbe. I welcomed the dark pines as friends and breathed in great draughts of cold, sweet air. HOME!

Homes are not only set in the geographical places we come to know and enjoy. Homes should also be part of a community. Norman Rockwell painted a wonderful picture that speaks more than many chapters. It portrays a redheaded GI in uniform and boots, bag in hand, appearing at the back door of a red-brick tenement house. The ground underfoot is scruffy, no softening grass in sight. But out of his own home comes an excited and happy family, welcoming him with relieved smiles shining with that greatest of all beautiful "things"—love. The kid brother jumps off the step; the plump, redheaded mother spreads arms wide; Pop's pipe is pulled out in frozen attention and surprise. The neighbors peep and smile over the back fence and from upstairs windows.[6]

Homecoming. The family. But not the family alone—all the neighbors too. No doubt on Sunday, all dressed up in best clothes, the family parades proudly to church with returned soldier, glorious in his uniform.

Down at the corner store, Mr. Cree leans over the counter. "Suzy, I hear yer brother's home on leave. I've slipped in a bit extra on the usual order."

Community. Belonging. Books are full of such descriptions. They are part of life, from an Italian village to New York or Chicago in the days of first-generation immigration.

Home. Family. Community. Surroundings. "This is where I put my feet up and thank God." Homes are part of the security of settled life, which is such a contrast to the terrible suffering of the refugee or homeless person.

Homes are not just for couples with children. All of us from babyhood to oldest age, single or married, benefit from the comfort, familiarity, and security of having a real home.

In all societies, to be invited into a home for a meal is the greatest sign of friendliness. "To be given to hospitality" means we have a welcoming home to share. Because we all suffer from being in the flawed (or fallen) world, homes also can be seedbeds of harm, pain, rejection, selfishness, sin, and damage. The Bible is stark in describing this: The pay packet of sin is death (Romans 6:23).

Contemporary playwrights, authors, and artists overwhelmingly join in the relentless chorus wailing out in a cynical cry. Their post-Christian doctrine is that permanent loving relationships are a romantic notion to be feared like imprisonment, that families and homes breed more trouble than good. Therefore, films that portray faithfulness, forgiveness, or enjoyment of permanent relationships are labeled sentimental. We are bombarded with the message that the only way to live is to seek personal gratification and fulfillment. "Trust nobody enough to be tied down together."

This is tragic. In fact, although we have all suffered from the imperfect nature of our parents and homes, this does not mean that it is better to dispense with homes. That would be like saying that because some food supplies are so toxin-laden that they cause more sickness than health, we should stop eating food. No, the answer is to clean up the water and food supply, find out which foods are most needed for health, and secure these.

In the same way the fact that homes contain people who are flawed individuals does not make all home life hopeless. Such pessimism rules out growth and change. There is plenty of evidence of substantially healed, satisfying, faithful relationships—people who've won through good and bad times. We see single people, married couples, and families maturing into generous persons. One of the most disastrous tendencies, that seems to be gaining strength year by year, is giving up too soon when life gets tough. What is happening to perseverance?

Well, homes can't be homes at all if they are dissolved when problems come. If they are to endure, it means sticking to homemaking when it all seems bleak. Everybody feels unhappy at times—and perhaps even caught in what feels like a trap.

One of the beautiful things about some elderly couples I've known is the sense that although there were many challenges to endure and no quick cure for the ills of life, they stuck it out and now have the peace and enjoyment of an "Indian Summer" in the relationship. They share memories, home, grandchildren, places, people, failures, victories, and, for Christians, the fruit of the Spirit (Gal. 5:22-23).

I find the same magnanimity displayed in the lives of many older single people. We all admire and enjoy those who have accepted life's boundaries, built within the framework, and become rich and wise, full of love.

It is hard to try to write about home without either sounding pessimistic or too rosily romantic. There are always elements of both! "Good-enough homes" can be and are built by perfectly ordinary, everyday people. It is not a project for the exceptional. Home is the base for all of us—with our actual strengths and weaknesses.

The stability and sense of community a home gives is necessary not only for the child's well-being but also for persons of any age. Home is the comfortable base where we all belong. Because of its healing and nurturing quality, we can be creative without getting confused by unconnected changes leading to fragmentation. In fact, a sense of belonging and a home that is real actually enables the constructive change of personal growth and creative projects.

Another important point is that there are many varieties of homes. In fact, there is no one model. For instance, some homes have beds; others have mats by the fire for sleeping on. Some homes use only food produced and cooked by family members; others rely on food brought in from supermarkets.

Some homes have a full-time mother in charge; in others this responsibility is shared. It was a time-honored tradition that while the mother was in the fields or working at the loom or elsewhere, the granny or a young aunt or uncle cared for the baby and tended the fire. Today the mother may be out regularly for a few hours while the father is home. All sorts of patterns have been and can be used. In fact, it is only in the relatively recent past that suburbs and long commutes isolated women in houses far from the buzzing community that included workplaces. This sterile home life existing "in little boxes" apart from community enterprise, places of learning, and shared fun/culture/leisure/worship is an aspect that needs our attention. In other words, we do not have to accept it as inevitable.

Many homes, rich in life and hospitality, that hold a strong place in the community are created by single persons or by combinations of people other than husband and wife, such as a mother and daughter.[7] Homes are too basic and vital to be talked about only in connection with married couples or fathers, mothers, and children. From ancient biblical days onwards, believers have models of single and married people creating homes. Neither situation is better than the other. There is a place for both.

However, the Bible gives rules for this area of life—not to condemn us but rather to enable us to live life at its best. After all, the Designer knows how the created person "works" properly! His way will be the happiest way to live too. If a man and a woman are so drawn to each other that they want to live together, they are to take the lifelong restrictive vow of commitment called marriage— "for better or worse, richer or poorer, in sickness and in health until death do us part."

Full stop. No ifs, ands, or buts. Only a man and woman are created to take such a life-binding vow (not persons of the same gender). God never forces marriage upon us. In this area, as in others, He allows us the dignity of a personal choice. The Christian view is that we, men and women, are equally responsible persons who should enter into such a tie by choice but not casually. In fact, the Bible actually says, "drawn by love." It has been the sad tale of sin that gave power to one gender (male) or matriarchal matchmakers (female) to "lord it over" or use others for his or her own ends only.

Side by side, man and woman are to agree to bind their lives into one unit—for life. As far as families go, it is impossible for the "plant" of the home to take root and grow unless both persons give up solely individualistic interests. Mind you, we're not really talking about a sacrifice here at all! It is a gift to be planted in the rich earth of marriage and home. "Two are better than one. . . . If one falls down, his friend can help him up. . . . Also, if two lie down together, they will keep warm. But how can one keep warm alone?" (Eccl. 4:9-11).[8]

"Shacking up together" has tragically become the norm today, whereby young men and women satisfy the inborn needs for marriage. Eventually this practice becomes a destructive experience for most, when one or the other is finally rejected, and the relationship breaks down. No lasting promises were made, nothing permanent given or received. It is truly terrible that so many couples are now following this transient and frequently wounding pattern. If couples living together choose to move on into marriage, then they have ended up well. But without the initial commitment, the outcome remains uncertain and offers no stability.

None of us wants or needs "fair-weather friends." In this phrase we acknowledge that sometimes we'll hit an unpleasant or difficult stretch in our lives, but that is exactly when our true friends are so valuable. And if that is so for friendship, how much more for marriage and families! A sure home base is a priceless strength in life because we need the shelter it gives us in the storms of life. How terrible when troubles make marriages and homes collapse!

Faithful commitment for a lifetime is like the foundation under the home. Yet Christians know that they, like everyone, are far from perfect. Also we sometimes make promises but then waver when it comes to keeping them. That is why we should understand that the security of our lives and homes is not built on our own goodness or on how good we think our marriage is or on the strengths of the other person. If we lean on each other too much, we'll flounder into sinking sand because of our weaknesses. *The only base for life, either as a single person or for marriage (and for any home or community), is the perfectly dependable Jesus Christ.*

Building our homes on Christ is not some pious idea that has nothing to do with real, everyday problems, fears, tears, and troubles. We do not have to do with an imaginary Jesus. He is actually there! Christians through the ages have found out that the Rock is *real*, a firm foothold. The Bible is bursting with promises and practical instruction. But we won't find out how it all works in real life unless:

1. We actually believe it is true.

2. We learn to live it every day and night of the week, rather than leaving it for the Sunday-in-church part of our lives.

3. We start actually living in relationship with God through His Son Jesus in a choice made once and then lived out on a day-by-day basis. He becomes the "always there" and best person in life.

4. We *listen* to God in His word—not inventing our own ideas about how to go about living life.

5. We obey His directions.

It seems harder and harder today for people to realize that in order to be rooted people who bear fruit, they must accept limitations. In deciding to make a stable home, we do relinquish many other choices. "*Here* I live, stay, relax, offer hospitality. *This* is my home."

In this book I'll be discussing family homes especially. Within a family both father and mother need to be fully committed to playing their parts in establishing and sustaining the home. Male and female, brought together in the marriage promise, complement each other. The subsequent life together grows out of the one unit they make as a team. Both are equally responsible and valuable in this all-important life task. They are like two strands in a rope. "Two are better than one." This is how the original design was planned.

Unfortunately, many of you reading this do not enjoy the basic blueprint. In many homes, a cord *has* broken; there is a lone human strand left. If you are in this situation, don't despair and lose hope! It is not easy to be a lone parent, but more and more of us today are in this situation for one reason or another. Often a lone parent who grows in love and wisdom is able to provide a fine home, especially with God's help. This is rather like a musician who is an accomplished pianist without eyesight. Not the perfect pattern/design, but it can work.

Look first at God's arrangement; in marriage there are two

cords. But, no, not only two cords. There is to be a third cord that gives the marriage (and home) its immense stability. That stabilizing cord also is there for lone-parent households and for friendships too.

I'll tell you a funny story. Dear Basil Atkinson from Cambridge chose to preach from this text at our wedding in 1961: "Two are better than one, because they have a good return for their work. If one falls down, his friend can help him up. But pity the man who falls and has no one to help him up! Also, if two lie down together, they will keep warm. But how can one keep warm alone? Though one may be overpowered, two can defend themselves. A cord of three strands is not quickly broken" (Eccl. 4:9-12).

I stood there listening to every word carefully. I was almost twenty years of age, in love, without any idea of the stresses and strains those two cords would face ahead. When Basil first quoted, "A cord of three strands is not quickly broken," I immediately said happily to myself, "That is the baby." I laugh now. No, little nearly twenty-year-old Susan, you and Ranald need a cord of unbreakable, perfect strength twined in with yours. You will fray, maybe even both at the same time (and often babies add to the stress).

My attention snapped back to Basil: "The securing cord is Jesus." *Of course*, I thought. But at that time it was like Sunday school words, teaching for the future. Now, thirty-seven years later, I know the very tactile reality of that third cord holding on through thick and thin. None of us is able always to be or do enough in relationship with each other. We have failures too. We are sinners, not yet perfected. Often the needs of a home and our lives become overwhelming. It is pretty horrible to become overwhelmed. That is why the two strands are reinforced with the third gold-like fiber. Knowing Jesus' promises and asking for His help are part of the securing strength. So is the obedience to God's instructions. Christians can enjoy God's comfort, strength, and guidelines if they ask and listen.

Furthermore, no individual or home should be absolutely alone in life. It is part of God's plan that we all have further help as we bear each other's burdens practically in community. This is all part of the biblical picture of how life works best in a fallen world.

Of course, many homes today don't have the three-stranded cord. For a start, many couples try to be strong enough using only their own resources. They ignore their need for God's help and the necessity of obeying His instructions. Together they are only two cords.

Then in numerous homes one parent struggles alone to provide what is hard work for two to supply. Those in that situation can especially cling to the gold-like holding cord of the Lord's promises. Part of His provision comes from being in community with others—in a fellowship, church, or neighborhood. We are not to be isolated and alone in life; we are to support each other practically. "If someone is struggling under a heavy load, help bear that person's burdens" (Galatians 6:2 paraphrased).

The home ideally has two human keepers—father and mother who depend on the Lord God who is like a strong, solid rock underfoot. They are part of a web of community. When something goes wrong, and one parent is left alone, that body tries to fill in some of the gaps with extra support.

For all of us, the Lord promises extra help when we call to Him in weakness, failure, and need. Homes need God's help to survive.

5

∾

The Home's
Weight-Bearing Beams

Making a home that is a joy, comfort, and encouragement is one of the most important things anyone can do. The home *is* the basic building block of society. Home also shapes the individuals who comprise it—for good or for ill. It should not be a selfishly guarded, self-centered place.

Homemaking may or may not be full time, but it has to take priority over other things in our lives. Why?

Well, we all need stability of the right sort. Picture your everyday life as a tree, with your home as the roots. Roots are a priority for a tree. A home is a priority for life.

Of course, a proper home is a place. For some of us the place may be disappointing. Maybe the dream was of a white-painted house with a wide front porch, surrounded by trees and a garden. Perhaps the reality is a rather dark apartment over a noisy street. Often we have to do the best we can with what we have.

The design and construction of good homes, as far as living space is concerned, is one of the higher forms of human accomplishment. It is good for individuals and government to work toward developing better housing. In fact, in the Old Testament God displays an interest in decent abodes; He cared about safety and quality of life.[1]

We see a sure "fruit" of right thinking when people work for decent, satisfying living conditions for the general population. It is shocking to find a culture in which a few of the privileged live in luxury while most people do not have a clean water supply or adequate housing. This matters.

The Lord's parable of the seed planted in good soil and in rocky soil can apply to our homes as well as to our personal lives. Just as a seed can be "choked with weeds" so that it cannot mature, our home life can be "choked by life's worries, riches and pleasures" (Luke 8:4-15).

Having either a lot of life's worries or extra riches and pleasures *need* not keep us from turning to God and letting His love transform our lives as we become more and more mature. A perfect example is the response of many Africans subjected to that most terrible of life's trials—slavery. Even though they were under an evil yoke, great numbers of them turned to the Lord's light, life, and salvation. We still celebrate this experience in their music—the much-loved spirituals. History is full of stories of people who matured in hardship.

Jesus is saying that difficulties can choke out life, not that they have to. For instance, poverty, sometimes resulting from rich people's greed, and other afflictions often produce homes that have lost hope. This life-killing situation matters to God.

Christian churches and other responsible organizations can do something about such conditions. I know of one inner-city church that, instead of building a Sunday palace for its have-it-all members of society, financed the buying up of badly maintained city housing. They'd bring the buildings up to a good standard and rent out home space at affordable rents. Surely at judgment day such actions will receive their reward. God says He cares about our everyday lives—in this instance, our homes.

But going back to the parable, we notice a striking fact—the other kinds of weeds are riches and pleasures. We might not be acutely aware of this, as we live in a society of "too-much." We struggle to keep our body weight within healthy limits as we greedily gorge on too much too-rich food. We stimulate our senses with too much entertainment, excitement, information, travel—the list is endless. Likewise, there is a pressure to have too much of everything in our homes—the biggest and newest only will do, say the advertisements. We can lose ourselves in serving this luxurious home base, seeking to display our success through unnecessary show.

I believe both extremes are like the weeds in the parable— struggling with too little that is safe and decent and good in the home on the one hand, or suffocating under the weight of too much of everything on the other. By the way, trying to provide too much can cause considerable stress—a trap in itself. Or the perfect dream home may encourage idolatry. We can serve our home ideal (or body shape ideal, etc.) rather than God.

Rather than the extremes of great difficulties on one hand or too many material goods on the other, the balanced middle road is the good ground. In each century and culture this middle ground looks different of course. There is no blueprint for balance! What was unthinkable luxury for our grandmothers may be considered basic decency by our children. A middle road in London is different from one in Nepal.

Home. Yes, a place. A good enough, pleasant enough place "to put my feet up and thank God." When we walk in through the door, we are surrounded by an atmosphere. Although we see the "bricks and mortar" first, a home is really made up of the people in it. They either give it an atmosphere of love, joy, and peace or fear, loneliness, sorrow, and anger. This is a huge area to talk about. Where do we start?

Well, if you are living alone, the atmosphere is very much about your personal life. But most homes include a variety of people in relationship with each other. This is where atmosphere starts. I'll plunge into the question by beginning with husbands and wives. Of course, as in everything else, many of the principles can be applied to other situations. However, marriage has some unique aspects.

Husbands today receive confusing messages about their place

in the home and their responsibilities there. For instance, recent governmental measures here in Britain are seeking to ensure that any father, married or not, must by law support his child. And yet he has no say about whether his child's life is to be safeguarded before birth. He cannot stop an abortion, so he is powerless in that crucial area. These are conflicting expectations. Do we want fathers to be responsible for their children or not? Do we think they should provide for the family? Care and contribute? Have choices? And once again, the issue is not what *we want* at all. The real question is, "What is right?"

According to time-honored biblical wisdom, a father's unique contribution is to carry the final responsibility for the good of the family. This includes seeing that the family enjoys adequate provision physically, emotionally, and spiritually. It does not mean that he does it all or controls it all! The model has as its infrastructure a team of two people, the husband/father and the wife/mother. These two complement each other.

A lone parent struggles to cover the basics that two work hard to provide. It's a struggle even if that one person is in good health, and in this fallen, flawed world, single parents may have added trials such as sickness. In any case, the home must do without a mother, or it must do without a father. Both situations place unnatural stress on the lone parent in many ways. The price is *huge* for such parents. It is far from easy to cope alone with babies, toddlers, young children, insecure adolescents, and aged parents. Many would say, "Yes, I do feel that these cares and worries are like weeds choking me. I'm too tired to think, read, pray—too tired even to hope." Such stress obviously changes the home atmosphere and affects all in it.

The gift of a good husband/father in a human family is godlike, a reflection of the heavenly Father's care. Jesus says that as the heavenly Father knows we do need food to eat, clothes to wear, and so on, those of us who are in His care don't have to make these our ultimate preoccupation (Matt. 6:31-32). In the same way the family of a good protector/provider can be freed from the sick worry about having a roof that keeps out rain or enough nutritious food. *It is a good thing to be cared for—to have strong shoulders to lean on.*

The Bible doesn't simplistically say that the husband should be the sole provider for the home or have all the responsibility for protection and care. As in everything else, the responsibility is to be shared in various ways, depending on the individuals and the circumstances. In fact, until suburbia isolated homes from the working community, in most cultures men and women were "providing teams." Consider the wife described in Israel's ancient times by Solomon (Prov. 31). She buys and sells real estate, is involved in international commerce, and is pictured as a successful businesswoman. She is a strong, capable, vigorous woman who takes initiative. In fact, in this passage she comes out as the provider, and her husband has "full confidence in her." Proverbs celebrates such a woman's ability and the appreciation of her husband and family as well as the community's respect for her. (She achieves all this along with coping with the homemaking priority. Today she would be called a superwoman.)

But going back to the basic model in which the young family has the support and protection of a good father who is serving the family's needs, we see a precious treasure. This type of family is one of the fruits of the Judeo-Christian civilization we appreciate so much.

Because we live in a flawed world, life has lots of troubles. People face sickness, hard times, difficult circumstances, financial troubles, and many other challenges. A good team committed to the home will persevere through these and do their best to serve the well-being of each member of the family as well as of their neighbors and community. This includes the hard work of providing and the myriad of jobs needing doing every day. It means extras such as getting up at night for children or a sick person. Each of us is meant to be serving others. Christianity is absolutely clear about this.

The young family starts with a pregnancy. If the mother is in good health, it can be natural to go on working. However, it is important that the work be flexible and appropriate to the woman's actual needs. The days should not be so stressful that physical, emotional, and spiritual well-being are jeopardized. Usually she needs shorter hours, afternoon rests, and some days off.

Also at this stage it is vital that the mother-to-be includes homemaking in her life even if she hasn't previously. In the words of an old English expression, she is as "broody" as a mother hen making her nest. The pregnant woman should have fun preparing the home for her baby. Enjoying this task as a team draws the parents together. They may have to move to a larger house, and both will consider the options in light of the family's good. They should always try to respect each other's ideas and needs as well as the needs of the baby on the way! It is very wonderful when the mother is liberated from heavy agricultural work, commuting, over-crowded schedules, etc., and is free to devote energy, attention, and prime time to the home's needs. In fact, it is hard to see how our communities can survive if everyone has to use most of their energy for a salaried job. This is especially true as the pressure and pace of contemporary life increase.

Homes absorb immense amounts of time and energy. This effort is satisfying if one has a balanced schedule and can cover the essentials without too much stress. Essentials include the extras to the everyday round that is part of human life—the celebrations, reunions, disappointments, depressions, sicknesses, disasters. *Homes work best when someone is the contented keeper of the home life.* Homemaker is a good description. It really is worth giving full attention to this vital task.

This century's research has shown that it is a feminine trait to be interested in creating homes and caring for people. Dr. Erik Erikson's lifelong work[2] demonstrates this clearly. In his studies large numbers of girls and boys in controlled situations from a wide range of backgrounds all demonstrated similar patterns. They were given building blocks of wood, for instance. Almost without fail, the girls tended to create cozy home spaces out of the blocks, while boys constructed roads, towers, and rockets (mostly accompanied by much noise). Doll manufacturers cash in on the reality that girls still hanker for toys that are replicas of baby and home.

Tragically, teenage mothers-to-be who are pushed into aborting their babies think of these infants as just that. A few years earlier many of them played with dolls. To crush, to rape their mother-instinct like this is an abuse of all that they are. The pregnant woman, whether young or older, has a home within her body and emotions. She is sheltering and caring for her baby in that safest of abodes, the mother's womb.

Last year a young teacher in an urban secondary school was reading a poem with her English class. She was explaining the words, phrases, and meanings. The poem mentioned the womb as a metaphor for the first safe place, "the dawn of life's beginning." Suddenly a young girl of fifteen or so put her head into her arms on her desk. She was overwhelmed by grief. The teacher found out later that she had been pushed into having an abortion that had ripped into her very self—the home her body and emotions provided for her child.

Even as I write, I know that some readers will deny that there is a feminine homemaking instinct. And some would deny that abortion has severely abused women. When a whole generation has been injured emotionally, of course there will be a sort of general blindness. But I believe the truth is that our femininity includes our mothering instinct—a sort of homemaking desire embedded in our very being.

As I near my sixtieth year, I also observe my peers who scoffed at the idea of an essential feminine homemaking or maternal instinct. So many who achieved their goals in boardrooms or professions, at the expense of having a family, discovered as menopause approached that they were seized with a sense of loss. Their biological clocks ran out, and they grieved their lost chance for motherhood and family life.

The many single women I've known personally report similar struggles and emotions. They may be single by choice, or it may be just the way things worked out. In any case, childlessness frequently is significant to them. But none of them needs to be homeless just because they aren't married![3] Women such as Amy Carmichael and Charlotte Mason, who were both single and committed to a major work in life, created a home life for themselves and for those who were their "spiritual children." Women do not need to be married or have biological children to fulfill this deep feminine desire.

I believe it is vital for all women to exercise this creative and satisfying side of their makeup. Having a home is the basic pattern of life for everyone. Men may have a relatively weaker homemaking instinct; they also need a home base, so they may have to work harder to create domestic comfort if single. Many men I've known have made excellent homes for themselves. With no children to bring up, people can put their time and energy to different uses and develop other nurturing relationships. But the need to have a home remains.

When any woman becomes pregnant, whether planned or not, she already has a precious, unique child. The womb should be its safe home until birth comes at the end of term.[4] As the female body quietly fulfills its amazing designed purpose and nurtures this precious life, it is our job to see that the mother has the proper care, whether it is for ourselves or for someone else. She needs a wholesome lifestyle. She should maintain good nutrition and discontinue harmful practices such as smoking, drinking alcohol, or using other substances that will pass into that tiny, vulnerable body of her baby. The mother whose husband stands by her is in the best situation. It is not God's plan for us to be alone at this time. As time passes, acceptance of parenthood grows, and then comes excitement to see the baby at last. Then the baby is born.

None of us has an ideal blueprint for the addition of a child to a family. Our real lives give us more or less stress at this and all other times. And we all are made differently—what is hardship for one woman (such as too much work) can be comfortable for another. There are no absolute rules for all about details such as working hours, who does exactly what, etc.

It is wonderful for the mother to have that God-given provider and protector—the husband, the head of the family. In the biblical model the husband is like Jesus (and none of us, male or female, can match *that* example). As Jesus came to give His life to serve his flock, so the husband serves his family's needs. He attempts to provide as best he can, even though it'll be a tough and sweaty business because of conditions in this flawed world. As he matures, a godly man is less concerned with fulfilling his own ego and more devoted to enabling his family to develop their different gifts and potential.

Being the "head" of the family is not about fulfilling *his* dreams and desires but is about being responsible for the welfare of this little group—"my family." In the rigors of life and especially when disaster or trouble strikes, he is like the prow of a ship. That is, the heaviest waves hit him first and not his little flock. This is good, for even if his wife is going to end up like that superwoman in Proverbs, in real life there are many times when she needs his extra strength. For instance, when she's pregnant with a second baby, and the toddler has been up at night with a chronic cough for weeks, and she has pain in her lower back—then she'll be so, so grateful to have a "ship-prow" person. She'll be glad to have another "head" worrying about lots of details. In the course of life, a woman benefits from not having to exert all the assertiveness that is needed in situations that occur. If a neighbor's teenage son is drunk and starts breaking in, all wives *I* know hope it'll be when their husband is home!

When we are encumbered with caring for the very young or frail, then we especially appreciate a man about the house. Those of us who are single or widows are thankful for men in our neighborhood who can be called upon in need.

Thank God for proper men! Please, let us bring up our boys to be willing to take on this difficult responsibility. Today our sons and grandsons will have a more complex situation to serve. Our daughters and granddaughters will surely, occasionally or often, exercise other options besides the homemaking and family one. Gone is the day of the "happy little wife at home in her frilly apron and twice-dusted shelves." Today's men will have to take on full responsibility at times for the provision/career side and at other times allow or encourage their wives to also develop their potential outside the home's four walls. This process may or may not be something that earns money. Today home leadership is complex and requires various adjustments. If we use our present opportunities wisely, both as men and women, perhaps we can model more clearly what the New Testament intends marriage, home, and relationships to be. We know that will mean respecting and encouraging each other.

Jesus is pictured in many ways. Among others, He is our shepherd, our vine, our bridegroom. As our shepherd, He leads, guides, and cares for His sheep. This means He is always thinking of the sheep's good, not about fulfilling His personal agenda. People matter more than success. He gives of Himself, just as a vine lets the sap of its life flow into its branches. He gives valuable time and energy in small and big ways. He loves and respects His "bride," the church. He listens to what she has to say, and He understands. He allows *us* to make personal choices; He invites our cooperation. He does not bark out orders as we flawed persons tend to do when we are in authority. He steps back in appropriate areas; He lets *us* be creative and responsible in practical ways. He helps us get up and go on when we fall.

In the Gospels we see how Jesus related to a wide variety of people. He did not try to make someone into a different *kind* of person. Contact with Jesus makes us more and more ourselves—the best selves we can be. Jesus especially is known as a lover.

He loves little children.

He loves outcasts, sinners, scarred failures.

He looks into people's eyes and sees the lovely persons they are created to be.

"[Love] . . . always hopes, always perseveres" (1 Cor. 13:7). This book could be twice as long and not get to the end of telling what a wonderful shepherd, head, and friend Jesus is to us all.

A good head of anything enables life to flourish, be it a family, school, community, or church. Men and women are leaders in different situations, including parenting—one of the most vital leadership roles possible.

As we look to Jesus as a guide to what leadership or headship means, we know that although He encourages our individuality, creativity, and choices, He never swerves from the moral absolutes and truth that are the backbone of life. These give strength, shape, structure, and stability. He also always follows "the rules" He gives us to obey—rules that enable goodness, rightness, truth, love, and life. God is holy, good, love. "I am the way and the truth and the life" (John 14:6). "In him there is no darkness at all" (1 John 1:5).

Human beings are all far from perfect (sinless). This is why Charlotte Mason underlined the truth, given in the biblical model, that we are *all* "under authority," God's authority. All of us, including those in leadership, stand shoulder to shoulder as fellow human beings—husbands and wives, parents and children, teachers and pupils. The Lord God and His truth are the final guide. He is the final authority of us all. Everyone is equal under this headship, this Lordship—in God's sight there are no higher or lower human beings. *We all have His perfect directions to obey first. That is—if any other person's demands run counter to God's directions, we obey God.*

From the unborn baby to the most decrepit person in old age, each person's life matters to God. We don't earn this "right" to fairness through intelligence, health, or success. The Judeo-Christian teaching is that each person should receive a fair deal. Not only this, if someone fails to receive what is right, God cares. Repeatedly He warns those in authority who abuse their position that He notices. He is on the side of those wronged. We can appeal to Him as the "righteous judge."

Regardless of the office, the final authority is not held by a person, whether parents, teachers, husbands, wives, mothers, governmental officials, policemen, or kings. This awareness certainly changes the atmosphere in a home!

Another wonderful comfort when you have Jesus as your head

is that He sees leadership as a way to help you, a way to share your burdens. He is the kind of leader of whom you say, "If I come to him with burdens, or if I'm weary in a bad time, his help gives me rest" (Matt. 11:28-30).

One of the reasons we women have struggled so hard emotionally with the concept of headship is that in this sinful world we've been scarred by so many examples of dominating selfishness that uses us one way or another. And this is true not only of male leaders, we must hasten to add, but also of women leaders (including mothers). You can see this sad reality when someone groans at the approach of a boss, husband, mother, father, etc. In such a case there is the sinking feeling: "Oh dear, I'm at the end of my tether with more than I can bear, and now I have to cope with him/her on top of it all."

Jesus gives us the key to this experience. He says He can promise His help because He is "gentle and humble in heart." We fear pushy, strong dictates from people who won't listen to us or understand how we feel or see what we know to be true. We fear that we will be bulldozed. We shrink back from being used, from not being consulted or respected.

This Jesus assures us that His authority is considerate and thoughtful. It is "humble" and "gentle." This means that He is aware of the other person; He is other-centered. Humility is an attitude we must work toward; we don't find it easy. Then if we are wise, we'll know that we don't really know much either, as we recognize our limitations. Then we'll appreciate that even a four-year-old might know more, see more, be more accurate in a particular area than we can be. One reason the best leaders, including teachers and parents, are good at what they do is because of a humility that is real. They have genuinely "humble and gentle" hearts and not a strategy they put on.

This is the amazing model for leadership in the home, church, and society. In the home we are talking first about husbands/fathers in relationship to the whole family. Mothers are co-leaders; they are also responsible parents. The "Jesus-view" of leadership humbles us all, for none of us can model it properly. We all must confess our sin, pride, self-centered aims, lack of love, anger, blindness. However, just because we are flawed does not mean we can't be leaders! This is not the answer.

I started by saying that the family that is beginning to have children is wonderfully fortunate to have a good-enough *servant-leader* concerned for their good—the husband and father. Now it is a relief to have that sort of direction, love, and strong care. However, having a proper head or "prow of the ship" for the little family has a price tag. This person represents the Lord's headship in our personal lives. When we enjoy the advantage of being in a team under a leader, we must develop a cooperative heart, also "humble and gentle." We need to fit in.

In the biblical view, when we marry (one man, one woman), the "team leader" has been designated. The structure *has* a head or leader for as long as this family unit lasts—the husband. We've seen that this is not a hierarchy in the way we normally think of power structures—that one individual has more worth, insights, or strengths than another. In the family one person accepts the final responsibility for the welfare and good of each member. This is a privilege—and a burden too. In the "prow-of-the-ship" example, a prow gets battered by the force of stormy waves. In families where the husband has died or has abandoned his responsibilities in some way, the woman takes on the "prow-of-the-ship" position. She has to be the shepherd and will suffer a new hardship if the husband's headship was a reasonably good one.

In all cases, whether this leading care is taken by the husband or a wife who must act alone, it is never a personal rule, a tyranny, a dictatorship. The head is actually an "under-officer." He or she is under the rule of God's goodness, purity, and love.

So, for instance, when I as a mother was selfish or unfair in chastising a child or in my demands, I not only hurt my dear beloved child in serious ways, but I also "sinned against God," as the age-old confession says. In the end I'll face Him, not my child.

Being the head person, if properly taken on, is not a fun privilege, nor does it allow personal license! This is why the "flock" is made up of followers; they are to be a good team—they listen to the captain, follow the rules, play fair, and unite their effort to a common goal or purpose.

In each family, the strengths and weaknesses of the individuals are different. In one family the husband may handle a certain responsibility best, while in another family the wife is best suited to take responsibility in that area. For instance, in some homes the wife does the best job with the financial management; in others the husband takes this on.

Now for any team to work, its members have to agree to accept certain crisis decisions if the need arises. This is how a surgical team works. Consider a team working together in some state-of-the-art operation. Each member respects the others' areas of expertise. All members are necessary for the operation to succeed, and so they've spent time beforehand discussing how they can accommodate each other's directives (what does the anesthetist "command," etc.). After they've planned the operation, they start operating, all cooperating with each other. But if an emergency arises, the word of the head of the team takes precedence.

I also believe that team membership involves submitting priorities and plans to the team leader, as the followers display "meekness and gentleness."[5] This policy works well with mature people who are not doormats. They are confident in their strengths and honest about their weaknesses. Meekness enables a team member to follow the team's plan; each person is not doing his own thing. In the team model, one person, the team leader, draws together the various "threads" into a single unit. We are told to have a respectful attitude toward this individual, in whatever capacity he or she serves us.

In the biblical pattern, it is not a question of who wants what, but what is right. Mature people speak up and insist on being heard. Mature people, in turn, listen and are willing to give in if that is right. Such individuals can either lead or follow. They don't have to be the one in charge. They are glad to cooperate or stay behind the scenes.

If I'm right that it is feminine, healthy, and inevitable that the wife's interest in the home and its welfare differs from the husband's—if the husband is especially responsible for providing for and protecting the little family group—then it seems to me that there is a basic practical reality about having a head. That is, where the family makes its home geographically will depend on where his work is. To me this is usually a part of what it means to be a wife whose life is seconded to the head. (Where there is a choice of locations, this will be discussed and prayed about together with great care.)

If I'm right, it would mean that if, say, Jill, who is a doctor, marries Joe, who is a farmer in Dakota, she will follow him to the farm. She may or may not go on "doctoring," but usually marriage should not dislocate the husband's established work.

I know this is irritating for lots of young women today, but why? It is a simple truth for both men and women: We don't just marry an individual, but we also commit ourselves to different ways of life depending on who that spouse is.

Another practical everyday aspect for "the team" is to accommodate to the level of "things" the provider's pay packet can provide. Discontent and grumbling because of disappointments about not being able to afford everything (especially as portrayed in the media) is vile, both from children and adults who are being supported by someone else. In contrast, cheerfulness in the face of unchangeable conditions is helpful for everyone. In a sports team, this attitude is called "being a good sport." Note, however, that appreciation for the team leader does not rule out extra financial contributions from the team! The good leader though would want to ensure that the benefit of such help was in the best interests of the whole life in the home. If precious time and energy were used, for instance, just to provide vacations, new clothes, or a bigger house at the expense of the more vital everyday homemaking pri-

orities necessary for the family's welfare, this is where both the husband and wife should draw the line.

The attitude "We'll manage with what we've got" releases the
life-giving benefits of time, energy, and joy to spend on our homes
and communities. Life matters most, not material things.

Thus the guidelines given in the historical biblical view ensures
that we don't discard the "pearl of great price" for a "mess of pottage." The loud advertisements and the stress of trying to meet
their demands will kill home life if we comply. And this is not the
only blur before our eyes as we enter the third millennium. We've
been deceived into thinking that our worth has to do with success
or status. Both men and women are influenced by this false view of
our significance, which leads to a sort of slavery to achievement.

There is a sweetness in a well-lived life that escapes this confusing tyranny. It is a freedom from manipulative pressures to
push us into making someone else rich or seeking to make our life
worthwhile by being a "success" one way or another. A freedom to
be clear about what really matters in life. In our daily lives and our
homes, this means the freedom to walk in a middle, balanced path,
with self-confidence to choose what is best and right in our
circumstances.

Such a confident, balanced life is built on a "sure foundation"
with a strong infrastructure (weight-bearing beams). This stable life
provides the toughness needed to survive the storms. However, we
are not talking about a life of romantically unreal expectations. We
acknowledge weaknesses and personal failures and sin. True stability has the strength to be real, to ask for and truly give forgiveness, to start another day afresh. Whether we are men, women, old,
young, married, or single, we are glad to be able to come to such a
home, put up our feet, and thank God.

6

∾

Taking Time and Care to Create the Home's Atmosphere

Before the first baby is taken home, a functioning home life should be in place. In fact, the effort necessary to make a home and to establish good relationships is the priority after marriage. Unfortunately, this is just the time when advanced study, careers, church responsibilities, and so on leave many people stressed and rushed. It can feel like a battle to carve out any sweet leisure for the unhurried attention necessary to start life together in a strong, rich, long-lasting way. The ancient wisdom and godly directive given in the Old Testament[1] was that the young husband could not be drafted into military service for a full year after marrying. More important, he was supposed to "learn how to bring happiness to the wife he has married." In Hosea we see that the model bridegroom was never to be like a master ruling over his wife even in Old Testament days when believers had less light: He was not called her "master" but "her man." His attitude toward her is love. *Love takes time to be established between the woman and her man, and the man and his woman!*

Although it is rare for husbands or wives to face actual military battle in the first year of marriage, the intention of these directives is to set priorities for their first year together. The idea is clear: their home should be established and enjoyed before other major commitments distract newlyweds; the relationships in the home matter. These ties need to be built; good, strong relationships don't appear out of nowhere.

Another vivid Old Testament description includes the idea that home comes first in life. We see the couple sitting together under a lovely green vine, perhaps sipping their well-earned evening wine together. As there is no electricity to keep them up and going, the work has been done. The air sweetens. There isn't the frenetic distraction of a television screen—they talk, laugh, argue, hug, fondle, and enjoy each other. This is the sweet stuff of life that belongs to the beginning (and continuation) of homemaking in marriage.

The army officers are instructed to ask, "Has anyone built a new house and not dedicated it? Let him *go home*, or he may die in battle and someone else may dedicate it. Has anyone planted a vineyard and not begun to enjoy it? Let him *go home*, or he may die in battle and someone else enjoy it. Has anyone become pledged to a woman and not married her? Let him *go home*, or he may die in battle and someone else marry her" (Deut. 20:5-7).

It seems to me that long, traffic-laden commutes and the draining effect of too many duties can have the same effect as a battle. Many careers hinder the new family from laying strong groundwork for the new home, as they take too much time and energy. But not only careers are to blame. Although we need to be active in our churches and communities, over-volunteering must be curtailed. In this stressful chapter of history we are reaping the cost of such activism. Love and friendship cannot mature between people without proper space and time. These all-important components of life are squeezed out by the weeds of too much stress.

A vital personal life cannot develop either if there is too much hurrying to accomplish outside goals. We are in danger of being so driven that our inner life is hollow. Homes and relationships then are weak and fracture easily.

The Amish have enjoyed stable homes and communities. It's interesting to look at the ways some of their communities in Pennsylvania have achieved this stability. The children, boys and girls, grow up familiar with the running of farm and home. They not only take their place in helping with the whole range of chores, but both girls and boys become skilled in handling horses and in various crafts. Thus they are often experienced in homemaking long before marriage. Here you find young people who take an active part in a satisfying way of life at home and in a community.

Such homes are not merely functional "watering holes." The meal tables are beautifully laid out with homemade food. The gardens so lovingly tended beautify the immediate surroundings. There are fun celebrations to host at home or to enjoy going out to.

As children grow up, it is not assumed that they will automatically choose either the beliefs or the way of life. In practice in the communities I've read about, the girls seem to make up their minds sooner than the boys! These boys seem to enjoy a long spell of relative freedom to "taste" the contrasting society's way of life. Some choose not to follow on in their parents' footsteps, but they continue to be welcomed into the family.

Those who do commit themselves to all that being Amish means will soon be found courting an Amish girl according to custom. The first year of marriage seems to be a bridge for the young couple between their youth and the burdens and complexities of being fully responsible for the running of home and farm. They have a sort of postgraduate apprenticeship year together, first staying with one family for a time before moving on to others. They then see how things can vary and experience a wider range of relational and practical situations.

I'm sure that when snuggling up in bed at night, they make many a shrewd comment on what they observed! Sometimes they want to file away for future use what they have learned. Other times they may be upset or unimpressed. "We'll never do it *that* way."

These Amish people have a strong sense of contented identity. The girls evidently look forward to being able to engage in life as mothers and the careers of home and community. I don't propose that we copy their general way of life and choices, but it is significant to note the great care and attention given to this formation. A lot of thought is put into what will encourage and enhance the lifestyle and what would detract from it. This sort of thoughtful care is important for us all if homes are to survive, with all the pressures that detract us from everyday, ordinary life.

A balance between work and leisure creates an agreeable atmosphere in a life or a home, contrasting strongly with the atmosphere created by much rush and stress. One atmosphere tends toward anxiety and dissatisfaction; the other is more contented and peaceful. And here I will link up the question about how to create good-enough homes with Charlotte Mason's view of education and life. Homes and good schools should have the same qualities if we understand Charlotte Mason. They are both nurturing places. They are both about living a real life.

Many of us have been helped and impressed by her statement: "*Education is an Atmosphere, a Discipline, and a Life.*" This was her motto for the Parents' National Educational Union (PNEU).[2] I think it's also an excellent motto for homemaking. Revised, it would be something like "Homes need the right atmosphere, discipline, and life."

In 1903 Charlotte Mason wrote a paper on education for the PNEU.[3] The title of this paper too could be adapted to the subject of homemaking. It is actually "A PNEU Manifesto" with its subtitle "Studies serve for delight, for ornament and for ability." I would adapt that for this book and thesis to: "A Manifesto for Homemaking," with its subtitle "Good homes are good places to live and grow. They make possible and ornament a secure life that is vitally alive with joys appropriate to the personalities and abilities of those living there."

It is appropriate to adapt the section of the paper quoted in her biography as a key to her understanding of children's upbringing and home life, as education/development starts and continues here. I have to change only a few words; these changes will be in italics. Of course the original words apply to education.

The first effort of the PNEU, continued through ten years of its existence, was to impress upon its members the definition of *homemaking* as contained in our motto, *Homes consist of their* Atmosphere, Discipline and Life. By this we mean that parents and teachers should make sensible use of a child's circumstances (atmosphere), should train him in habits of good living (discipline) and should nourish his mind with ideas, the food of intellectual life. These three we believe to be the only instruments of which we may make lawful use in bringing up children. An easier way may be found by trading on their sensibilities,[4] emotions, desires, passions; but of this the result must be disastrous. The reason of this is that habits, ideas and circumstances are external, and we may help each other to get the best that is to be had of them; we may not however meddle directly with the personality of child or man; we may not work on his vanity, his fears, his love, his emulation or anything that goes to make up his essential personality.

Charlotte Mason is telling us about the bringing up of children. This is done at home first and foremost. Although I'll often be referring to children in the home, these basic areas apply to us all of our lives, right up to old age and terminal illness. The *Atmosphere* is life-encouraging to us or not; our home's *routines* either enable us to enjoy a balanced quality of life or not; and we either trudge bleakly and disinterestedly along life's path or enjoy intellectual input through books, nature, art, music, good relationships, and so on. These give us the spark of fresh aliveness mentally and spiritually that we call *life*. I have seen an elderly person whose life was drab and hopeless perk up with an improvement in the atmosphere, a better routine, and new interests in life. These are the areas this book is now going on to deal with in as much depth and breadth as possible. Getting this right is a real key.

A good place to start the discussion is with the baby at the beginning of life. What does a child *need* most of all? Charlotte Mason knew that the home and its parents were the most essential factor in a child's nurturing, growth, and life. She did not think that kindergarten could replace the fresh air of reality that exists in a home and the surrounding outside world. Why? Because a specially designed room with little chairs, toys, and so on is somewhat artificial. And a child's life is best started as it should go on—with two feet firmly planted in the reality of everyday life. A child should have permanent, ongoing relationships within the form and yet the freedom[5] that only a home can provide.

Groups of children need more control; they enjoy less personal choice or individuality in activities than is possible at home. If you are wondering why I say that, just think of a two-year-old following Dad into the garage "to fix the lawn mower" with him. Then imagine *ten* two-year-olds in your garage! And, importantly, for soul and language development, it is one thing to respond to all the sayings of one or two children every day and quite another if the child is a member of a pack.

Many people don't seem to realize how much children need peace and quiet as well as activity. Children at home without the distracting noise and stimulation of TV or video entertainment will tend to balance their own "free time." When they are tired and satisfied with all they've been doing, they will often settle to a quiet occupation such as imaginary play, drawing, reading, or even gazing at clouds in the sky. They can learn at their own pace, think their own thoughts, and concentrate on the things they enjoy personally.

This sort of a quiet growing time at home has form, as we'll see, and yet freedom too. A skilled parent who observes the child will learn what suits this child best and discover his or her needs. Nothing can possibly be a substitute for this advantage.

The home I am trying to describe has an atmosphere that includes both the cheerful sound of life and yet offers peace and quiet too. Although the home atmosphere is a stable, secure one, it is also flexible enough to change in response to the lives and needs of the persons whose home it is.

The atmosphere I'm going to try to sketch out actually thus depends on the next word in Charlotte Mason's motto—"a discipline." *That is, the atmosphere can be sure, confident, and balanced because the right sort of routines are in place.* Also, the atmosphere has the vitality and enjoyment of a rich life. But as I can't treat each interweaving factor all at once, you'll have to piece together all the elements and picture them all producing a helpful atmosphere or the opposite.

Atmosphere. It hits us when we walk into an apartment or a house. Maybe there is a chaotic atmosphere. Maybe it is sterile. It can immediately display the very "smell" of anger, cold control, or disrespect for children, the wife, the husband, the elderly, or those with special needs. In contrast the atmosphere can be one of concern, acceptance, and love for every person.

For those of us who are Christians, home life is the best testing ground to show how far we've advanced in producing the fruit of the Spirit. It is relatively simple to put on an act, of patience, for instance, in many public situations. We can display pleasing qualities at a church picnic, say, or even in the office, but the acid test of how far along we are comes at home. There we are tried. The "scum rises to the top" sooner or later.

Is there an atmosphere of love? Joy? Peace? Patience? Kindness? Goodness? Faithfulness in big and small matters? Gentleness? Mildness? That means an atmosphere where everyone is listened to and respected—everyone matters. Is it an atmosphere of discipline (where there is self-control)—where behavior is not "all over the place" but orderly, with people who are strong enough to keep their promises and follow through on their choices? In homes with children this means the sweet order of their having learned an attitude of obedience without having been crushed.

In Galatians where the fruit of the Spirit are listed (5:22-23), we are told that this goodness is the result of putting into practice God's commands and having His help.[6] As we are yet immature, imperfect people, none of us is able to achieve this alone or all at once. In other words, all of us need to have patience and perseverance as we keep trying to grow in developing spiritual fruit. This growth is part of looking to Jesus, "the author and finisher of our faith" (Heb. 12:2 KJV). The "atmosphere" of His presence was and is constituted by His genuine nature that is pure goodness, love, joy, peace, patience, kindness, and self-control. Unlike us, He was not overcome by failure and frustration when life got, as we say, "too much" for Him. When life gets to be "too much" for us, often the atmosphere around us becomes contaminated by hatred, discord, jealousy, fits of rage, factions, envy, sexual immorality, impurity, and debauchery (Gal. 5:19-21).

If you read that last list again, you'll see that these words could be used in describing a lot of today's videos, TV programs, computer games, and soundtracks. This poisonous atmosphere comes into every home in the land unless we make a choice to keep it out. If this is what fills any person's mind, it will also influence his or her behavior.

There are practical considerations too. If our lives are too stressed, it is hard to be patient, and we tend to be less peaceful. If people have not been listened to, they will not *feel* patient or loved. Furthermore, a person who is hungry and has not had a good meal at the right time will also lack patience. You can see that getting a good atmosphere is a tall order and that there is more to it than meets the eye.

We do need meals on time that are nutritionally balanced, homes where we can rest when we are tired, people who respect us and accept us as we actually are (this includes extending forgiveness), and a life that is satisfying and challenging too. "If everything were perfect," we sometimes groan as things go wrong yet again, "of *course* I could be patient!"

But people's lives weren't lived in perfect conditions in the past; nor are they now. And ahead troubles will surely come in everyone's life. We have to do more than wish for a good atmosphere! Furthermore, we flawed persons are part of the problem! (That is why it is wishful thinking to imagine that getting out of a troubled marriage will mean functioning better at home or in life—*If only it were someone else making this home atmosphere with me,* we think, *then I'd be able to do it.* That may be partly true taken at face value, but we ourselves represent 50 percent of the problems anyway.)[7]

Think of trying to get up enough willpower to change your worst habits into good ones! It takes more than we have in us to change and grow like this. The biblical picture is that we need extra power in addition to trying to obey the guidelines in our at-home everyday lives. We need an inner transforming help. This is why growth requires the fruit of the Spirit and is not the result of doing one's best alone.

Charlotte Mason thought a lot about the work of the Holy Spirit. She knew that we lack essential power and insight without His help—the help of God Himself. "I am the way and the truth and *the life*," Jesus said (John 14:6).

The source of life and the power to receive it come when we actually do as Jesus instructed: "Abide [stay, concentrate, give your full attention] in me."[8] Jesus described Himself as being like a vine and us like the branches. The sap of life rises through the vine into the branches and enables fruit to develop. But when we have become counted as His followers, when we have accepted His gift of forgiveness and promise of life—*we can still think and live in a way that is unattached to the vine.* Picture a branch that has to choose to stay stuck on. *Then* the sap will flow. Extra resources will build up that branch. This is what Jesus is asking us to consider.

Now part of this abiding means being focused on the example before us rather than being distracted and filling our eyes and ears with things that encourage what used to be called "our baser nature." Do you know what I'm talking about? I've found that some books, conversations, or films stir up resentment, impatience, or other sins such as bitterness or discontent. But other images or sounds we take in encourage the good, the pure, the life-giving.

Enjoying "the sight and company of Jesus" through careful reading of His Word, thinking it over, and prayer is the first way of abiding. God's Word is the primary source that speaks to us, changes how we think, and gives us practical examples as well as comfort and encouragement. There too we build upon truth as our understanding grows.

Charlotte Mason directed her students to this "sap": "In the discourse of the bread of life our Lord sets forth the general principle that He is the sustenance of His people, that whenever they manifest life in whatever direction, that life, that power and joy, is immediately derived from Him."[9]

When we read the writings of Charlotte Mason's friends that describe the joy that characterized her everyday life, we know that the source was not from an idyllic childhood or satisfaction in her circumstances, but it came from the Lord's feeding and her response to Him. When I had the opportunity to look through her books, next to her Bible stood the 1662 *Book of Common Prayer* with its daily "diet" of reading—the New Testament twice a year and the Old Testament once.

When following this reading schedule, one also reads through the Psalms every month using these in prayer as Jesus did. Someone who loved nature as Charlotte Mason did would enjoy in her imagination the sea, sky, and hills when these are extolled in the words of the Psalms, and she would give thanks to the Creator. This sort of daily time is more refreshing than anything else could be. It means "being a sheep in a pasture," not in theory but in practice. It means drinking the sweet, refreshing living water and lying down in the green pastures. This delight Charlotte Mason knew.

She influenced me for my life's good when I was writing *For the Children's Sake*,[10] all the while soaking up her teachings. At that time I was a mother with four young children, and I also had busy "extended-family" days from 9 A.M. to 3 P.M. in the large, bustling L'Abri household in Greatham. Ranald and I would have between fifteen and twenty-five people for lunch, and I was kitchen staff! Everyone who comes to L'Abri spends half of the day helping in practical ways. Thus in order for the "help" to clean and run a fifty-room Manor House, cook huge meals for up to forty or so several times a week, do the laundry, etc., I'd be teaching homemaking skills to people who'd maybe never peeled and chopped an onion, hung out the laundry, or cleaned a toilet. I tell you all this so you know that I'm not writing as one who has sat around romantically with extra time! I did have to be very focused so as to make our family and the creating of an "inner center" home based in our apartment my priority, my first concern.

It was possible to do this since the big manor house and its grounds made it very like an old-fashioned farming community. Both Ranald and I worked right there. As we were one of several families on the site, all of our children had a wonderfully rich life of undirected play together, with the security such a community gives. Ranald and I cared for our children ourselves. Only once did I ask for regular help with a child—a two-year-old (while I fixed the main meal), and that turned out to be a mistake! Caring for our children was not a job to be handed out; they were part of our life, and we were part of theirs. The families helped each other too by providing a meal here or a bed there, as between friends.

Anyway, as a young mom, I had a big problem—where to find time in which I could benefit from going to God. I didn't have good access to that rich source of power and light that changes needy mothers like me from the inside—change so that the family atmosphere is not created by acting a part temporarily, but issues from the improving healthy inner life of its adults. I was like a branch with a faulty connection to the sap.

I had the knowledge and belief all right. But I'd try to wake up earlier than I was able to comfortably. (We had babies and young children who disturbed our sleep. I was often starved for sleep.) When that early morning plan failed, I then tried to make time the last thing at night. That was no better. As a result, going to God was a duty, not a joy or a refreshing source of life-changing energy.

Then, as I prepared to write the book based on Charlotte Mason's teaching, I read in her biography that she planned her days so that the best time of each day was set aside to spend in leisure with God. That was after her afternoon walk outside, for her tea time was the time for personal leisure when she felt "quite fresh." Having worked hard all day and soon to start again, she'd look forward to this hour when she could give full attention to God and "feed on His promises with thanksgiving." Her biographer Essex Cholmondeley wonders when it was that Charlotte Mason "first began the lifelong practice of meditation,[11] giving to the gospel story 'that full gaze we call attention.'"[12] It was in an early letter (1861) that she described setting aside daily time for "half or three-quarters of an hour to Bible reading and earnest prayer." She goes on to call this "*seeking first the kingdom of heaven.*"

This practice is typical of Charlotte Mason, Amy Carmichael, and others whose lifework is significant and who were also thriving in their personal lives. They found a way to put into practice such directives. They planned their everyday lives.

We know that Charlotte Mason did not gallop through a reading to check it off a to-do list! Meditation for her meant that she'd pause when some idea or thought would strike her in the reading. She'd think it over, "chew on it," reflect.

This sort of slow reading also involves giving thanks for this or that promise or thought. This is a conversation, a relationship. Sometimes it means reading a shorter portion so that it can sink in. All in all, such a time is how we make God's Word real so that that "gold cord" becomes twined into our lives and homes. We have to practice to have it there.

This topic really belongs in the routines chapter, but it so affects the home's atmosphere, I must put it here. As Charlotte Mason so often wrote and said, only when we give "*full attention*[13] to the words of life" can the seeds take root, grow, and produce fruit.

As I read about Charlotte's time with God, "all the bells rang" for me. In a flash I saw where I'd been missing out and just what I could do. In my life as it was then, I saw that I did have about one and a half hours at my disposal after the L'Abri lunch, before school-age children came home. That was when I could invite a friend to have tea and enjoy each other's company. I asked myself, "Why can't I treat God in the same way as a friend for whom I prepare and put aside time? Just as when a friend is coming, I'll tidy up the family room sometime during the morning, lay a fire in the fireplace, see that flowers and candles are on the table and tea ready to make. My comfortable chair and footstool will be ready for me to relax in, and enticing paper with felt pens, play dough,[14] and other items will be laid out to keep any child around occupied quietly—so I can be free to enjoy listening to and talking to my friend Jesus—maybe letting sadness or joy sweep over us as we share something with the tea."

Well, I started to do just that, and I can tell you, it was a watershed in my life. I'd look forward to that quiet hour. It has been life-changing. Instead of a task to tick off the must-do list, these times have been the source of my personal peace, comfort, help, light, joy, and refreshment. Of course for me the timing changed to reflect various schedules. But I had a new practice, a way to live. Thank you, Charlotte Mason! Without knowing it, I and others were like shadows lurking in Scale How, also learning how to live!

Atmosphere. The one that is good is genuine, honest, open, true. And this means asking for and giving forgiveness, for we all sin. None of us gets it right; none of us is easy to live with.

Jesus put forgiveness at the heart of His model prayer for us, and His prayer covers life's situations. Perhaps forgiveness is the greatest single clue to a genuinely good atmosphere. Sadly, homes are where we so often receive and give the greatest hurts in life. Always we have to get on with doing the best we can with our still-plodding selves. The path to perfection is a long road; we progress slowly and never get there before we reach the end of our lives.

No. The key is being realistic and honest when we fail others or others fail us. An atmosphere in the home or in other situations can be healthy when there is forgiveness. To ask for forgiveness means admitting to having done wrong. "I'm sorry" sincerely said with evidence of a struggle to change shows us the way through. It takes true humility and strength to make this a way of life. Forgiveness allows reconciliation and hope as we make a new start together.

And what a difference it makes in the atmosphere! My father

had a temper that fitted in with the tough streets of his Philadelphia childhood—it would flare strongly. (And of course I inherited his anger.) But as a child I also knew that, if necessary, he'd say "I'm sorry" and mean it. He'd have the humility to acknowledge the wrong and submit himself to a little girl for forgiveness. He also took advice from his children, would listen, and didn't act as if he had all the good ideas. This always was a model for me. I knew that when the "I'm sorry" was said, the atmosphere could clear. So this is what I always tried to put into practice myself.

If, say, I'd shouted or punished a child more out of my own desperation or anger than the severity of his or her wrongdoing, it seemed right to say, "I'm sorry. Will you please forgive me?" The answer was normally a dear hug and a lovely light shining in a little face. Children are examples to us about forgiveness. They help us to try to do better. We shouldn't pretend it is okay for us to behave badly.

I think it helps to point out to young people that we, the parents, are also learning. We are all on the path together, side by side. This creates a different atmosphere too! It means that we are fellow pilgrims, and they help us even as we help them. I've had much insight and illumination from my shrewd, much-seeing children through the years.

We all have a lot of forgiving to do. Everyone has suffered wrongs that need to be forgiven and let go of. It is not good to let these memories fester inside like an infected hidden abscess. If harbored in us, they will feed a bitterness and anger that will poison us and the atmosphere we make around ourselves more surely than anything. Out of such inner "dis-ease" come bitter remarks that cut and injure others like death. The atmosphere becomes characterized by such things as cruel sarcasm, hopelessness, or discouragement. In this disagreeable atmosphere people blame each other constantly. Out of this grows, like rampant weeds, aggression, hostility, animosity, hatred. Then follows estrangement, separation, feuds.

The person suffering this malignant inner disorder of unforgiveness always seems to have a bone to pick and tends to think she or he alone has the right analysis and ideas. This condition leads then to selfish attitudes. There is ill (bad) humor, malice, animosity, unkindness. The list of terrible weeds goes on—brutality, hardheartedness, intimidation, spite. Such an atmosphere is likely to have little love in it and is severe, callous, tough, intolerant. This list makes us shudder and come to the conclusion that such situations are diabolic and hellish. Atmosphere. Writers such as Charles Dickens skillfully described it so we could almost share in feelings of foreboding.

I've gone on at length spelling this out because it is crucial that we are absolutely clear that goodness *matters*. It matters to God who is goodness that is completely pure. His love is unlimited, and the ugly words listed above are opposites to His character. We must not pretend to be good and sufficient in ourselves as we limp along, but be real and go to the actual source of life. This is the key to creating the right atmosphere.

Charlotte Mason had an understudy, her closest colleague and companion, Elsie Kitching. They worked together for years, and Elsie continued in the work after Charlotte died. Elsie's home was also at Scale How until her death in 1955 at the age of eighty-four.

She wrote a little booklet, "Children up to School Age and Beyond," and there is much in it that relates to the theme in this book. She said of atmosphere: "Happily brought up children learn gradually from the parents' own attitudes of sympathy, love, kindness; but such lessons must be unconsciously learned; they are part of the natural and proper atmosphere in which a child should live."[15]

This is why curricula and books that set out to teach "character training" may produce poor results. The traits being "taught" come across as a lesson, having nothing to do with life. Children need to enjoy kindness and unselfish love everyday like sun shining in their hearts. Then they will naturally grow to show the golden qualities genuinely "from the inside out."

Parents following Charlotte Mason's ideas will be reading books to the children that draw them into people's lives and situations where admirable, good, wholesome characteristics stand out. Children will want to be like the storybook friends they admire.

Kindness and love are like sunshine for all of us. "Love, joy, peace, contentedness" and so on are "fruits." They also are to be the description of the atmosphere in our homes.

7

☙

The Glory of the Usual or Jack of All Trades

Creating a home's good atmosphere and life has so many different aspects that it requires immense capacities. All giftedness can be drawn on for this task. Creative homemaking cannot succeed without the sort of time and attention that is given to other great achievements or professions of humankind. Not everyone is able to expend anything like the portion of time and energy on it she would like to. In this case, we have to choose what is most important and simplify unnecessary complications in our lives. Remember that nothing in this life is perfect, and small essential things make a big difference.

It is also important to say that each situation is unique—there is no one pattern for lives or for homes. For instance, I've told you that in the residential L'Abri Fellowship situation, Ranald and I worked together as a team in our home as well as in the absorbing L'Abri work. However, we each had separate and very different responsibilities too. As the wife and mother, I felt (and feel still) that the primary task for me was the home's continuing life and that Ranald needed to do the same for L'Abri and the church in which he was a pastor. That is, if a truly dire need arose in the L'Abri work or for the church leadership, I'd still carry on the family routines such as feeding a hungry two-year-old on time or reading a story happily together as if I didn't have a care in the world! To be dependable, the home atmosphere has to be as consistently regular as possible. And this means that one person has the freedom to respond to needs, give time, and serve. It is my personal opinion that this is one reason why it is inappropriate for a mother to have any responsibility that has to be an absolute priority over the family's daily needs.

Today the prevalent attitude is that the care of family and home is "menial," unimportant, a waste of expensive education and potential. Homemaking is seen as a mere detail that can be amply covered as secondary to a job or career, which is "real life"!

This gives the truth away—today's values are totally upside down from God's point of view. People and their everyday lives matter more than things or status. Serving others is the highest calling of all (apart from prayer)—serving them in ordinary ways, giving people what they need.

It helps us to clarify the Christian perspective if we turn to the early centuries when some Christian believers were applying their faith and the Scriptures to their actual everyday lives for the first time. What they said and did was such a stark contrast to paganism!

One such early guide (late 400s A.D.) was Benedict, whose life was steeped in the Word of God, both in thought and practice. He wrote a "Rule" for the communities he founded that remains valuable for all of us—in this instance, for homes and families. Of course we don't all subscribe to everything he writes about, but Benedict's wisdom on human relationships and life is based on biblical tenets that are always true and wise.

His chapter on "The Care of the Sick" is too long for me to quote in full, but here are excerpts:

> The care of those who are sick in the community is an absolute priority which must rank before every other requirement so that there may be no doubt that it is truly Christ who is served in them. After all Christ said: "What you did to one of

these my least brethren you did to me" (Matthew 25:36, 40).[1]
Make very sure that the sick suffer no neglect.

The next chapter is shorter; here it is complete:

Human nature itself is drawn to tender concern for those in
the two extremes of age and youth, but the authority of the
Rule should reinforce this natural instinct. Their frailty should
always be given consideration so that they should not be
strictly bound to the Rule in matters of diet. They should
receive loving consideration and be allowed to anticipate the
regular hours laid down for food and drink.[2]

What a contrast not only to pagan Rome or the barbarians but
to our modern world. This is our generation—with its hospital
incinerators that consume the youngest of all as we discard
unwanted babies, with its elderly who are not even given a small
amount of respectful appreciation, let alone be made a priority in
people's busy lives.

Of all occupations one might hold, it is the greatest privilege to
be entrusted with human lives in any way, in any situation. This
trust can include a wide range of services—engineering clean water
supplies, providing city services such as garbage disposal or courts
of justice—the list is endless.

But of all the ways we serve each other (including the privilege
of doing our heavenly Father's business—Christian work and service that can be life-giving), homes and community must be at the
top of the priority list. We must give the time, skills, and attention
needed for complex human life to be well cared for. This *is* God's
work; it is putting righteousness and love to work in actual lives
rather than speaking words only.

There is nothing in the serving occupations that is lowly from
God's point of view. Here is where the welfare of human life lies—
the very lives of persons that are so precious that Christ would die
for just one of them! He "lost His life" for others. We lose our lives

for others by being there to give a cup of cold water if a person is thirsty (a child running a fever who is trying to fall asleep). We can't give the needed drink if we are not there. We can't give it if the TV is so loud we don't hear the whimper or if "important" tasks stand in the way.

I've used rather strong language to show that the service people do in their homes and communities is highly valuable. Why do I feel free to claim that this is a priority? Why did Benedict write as he did for another kind of home (a residential community)? We write from the Christian view of who the person is in the first place. We are created with souls, personalities, minds, and bodies. Our everyday lives are just exactly where life is lived well or poorly.

As far as children are concerned, if their home life is not adequate, they are deprived of the opportunity to develop as God intended. This is like never giving them the possibility to eat food that will let them be healthy, never giving the attention and holding conversations that will allow their language to mature or their emotions to be satisfied. Not having a positive home life is a terrible thing.

And so I maintain that creating a home life is God's will for us—for the way He has made us. Caring for a family home is more than one person can comfortably achieve. A team of two does best—a mother and a father. In this flawed world this is not enough either—even with the third "golden" cord of the Lord working with us. We all need help from our neighbors and community too. And they need us.

It seems to me as I write that I see some raised eyebrows. "Susan is going overboard on this issue," I almost hear. But, no, I am not at all trying to fob off our inner need to call the things we have to do everyday important just to make some of us feel good. Nor could it be honest if what I'm saying gave others an excuse to use women or men as menial servants just for their own selfish comfort. That would be wrong.

We look to Jesus—as Benedict and all Christian believers in history did. Jesus is our example, the source of all our rules of life.

Some of the most poignant writing in the Gospels describes the time when Jesus was about to leave His disciples. When you are about to die and leave the everyday life you have shared with your loved ones, you go to the core of what matters. John describes a conversation at such a time with Jesus (John 14:1-4). Although we don't hear exactly what the disciples have been saying, we know they are troubled and scared—even full of horrible panic.

Jesus tells them not to let their hearts be troubled. He points them to something that will not change in the landscape: "Trust in God, trust also in Me." I am reminded of the time Jesus was walking on the waves. Peter went to Him, but was overwhelmed by his natural fear when he looked down at the churning "impossible" deep beneath him. But if he kept his eyes fixed on that beloved all-powerful face, he did not sink.

When we are actually confronted with overwhelming human experiences such as impending death, disasters, betrayal, or the stress of overwork, Jesus' advice is to keep your eyes, your gaze, your trust *in God*. Then He links Himself standing right there with them to this unseen God, the Father. "Trust in Me too."

Now we come to the comforting "ordinary," everyday side of His provision for them.[3] He is saying, "You can see Me now. I'll be the same when you can't see Me. You can still trust Me. Don't think I'll forget what you actually need. I'm the one who thought about picnics when you were hungry. I'm human too, and I know what hunger and fatigue are like—it matters. I'd stop so we could have a restful day off to enjoy. Remember how we'd go for a walk together and pick the ripened wheat kernels to chew as we ambled along, enjoying conversation, fresh air, exercise, and peace and quiet? The skies were so beautiful, and we'd enjoy the plants and the birds. Do you remember how I'd know when we all needed to stop and sleep after a hard day's work? Do you remember how I'd go home with you when you were worried because people you loved were sick or sad? I could help them, for I am 'the Lord your healer.'"

"Think of how the children's faces would light up when I sat down. *Here is a person who has time for me!* you'd see them say with their actions. They'd come and show Me things such as a pretty pebble they'd found. I found their conversations, bright eyes, and their little trusting warm selves so comforting in my grief-filled life. I'd enjoy listening, laughing, hugging them.

"Yes, I'm someone who is not above the details of our actual everyday human lives. You have shared this and the other side of our life together, and now you are terrified that I'm going away."

Then, like a departing parent comforting His child, He continues, "Trust Me now. I'm not forgetting you! Not at all. In fact *I'm going to prepare a permanent home for you. All you've enjoyed in My company here will be part of the home/place I'll be preparing for you all. Look forward to that sure home-going ahead.*" A home with all possible light and joy, but with none of the struggles or tears.

Later on He commands obedience in this chapter about life (John 14:15-21). In other words, pietistic thoughts and "airy-fairy" spiritual experiences are like vapors gone. Jesus asks us to apply His teaching in the everyday, in the ordinary. "If you love me, you will obey what I command."

I can almost imagine the forlorn look of this little flock of rag-tag people. They are thunderstruck. So He follows up with the promise that they will not be left on their own. They are to receive "a Counselor," "a Comforter," a Strengthener and Helper, a life-giving Enabler—the Holy Spirit. Jesus then uses a word that shows Him as the caring parent, for He says that this way He won't be leaving them "as orphans."

Charlotte Mason, that wise lover of children who also followed the example of Christ for everyday guidance and to know His truth, pointed to His words on the bringing up of children. She highlighted the commands that we are not to *offend, despise, or hinder* one of these little ones.[4] She says:

> Children should have the best of their mothers. . . . Is it possible that she should despise them? Despise: "To have a low opinion of, to undervalue"—thus says the dictionary, and, as

a matter of fact, however much we may delight in them, we grown-up people have far too low an opinion of children. If the mother did not undervalue her child, would she leave him to the society of an ignorant nursemaid during the early years when his whole nature is, like the photographer's sensitive plate, receiving momently indelible impressions?

Charlotte then goes on to explain that she does not mean that the child and its mother cannot ever be separated on a regular basis. In Mason's day, well-off families had a nanny who made the nursery *her* life's priority. A parallel arrangement today could be regular part-day visits to a grandmother or to an adult friend, playing in other children's homes, or attending a morning play group.

The constant society of his parents might be too stimulating for the child; and frequent change of thought, and the society of other people, make the mother all the fresher for her children. But they should have the *best* of their mother, her freshest, brightest hours.

Charlotte continues by saying that whatever arrangements are made for the child to be away from the mother, she should "keep a vigilant eye" on it all.[5] From this quote we must deduce that Charlotte Mason is telling us that the child, so impressionable, is of such value that the occupation of providing for her everyday life is of inestimable importance.

"You cannot serve God and mammon," Jesus said. In this context we see an excellent illustration. A career for status or success or power, a high salary, or a have-it-all lifestyle are the biblical "mammon." These are the values of the world. Other places in Scripture warn us that much effort for such goals leads to a result that is like straw, which blows away in the wind, as far as God is concerned. What will remain at life's end? What is precious to God?

We will not all have the same functions in life. But those whose main occupation is caregiver and enabler of a stable and rich everyday home life—these are engaged in one of the most important callings.

Do not think that women only have this privilege and satisfying work! Read the excellent book *Goodnight, Mr. Tom*[6] for a good example of a home and care given by a single man to a needy child. There are many other examples in books and in real life of male homemaking. Among our friends are fathers left to bring up families because of the loss of the mother through death. At other times, the mother finds work, and the father doesn't, and they have to readjust their "team work." Then there are couples like Ranald and myself who shared child care in the home more than is usually possible.

However, it seems that the feminine nature is happier than the male nature when juggling human life's ordinary, everyday basics with warmth, tenderness, and interest!

I warm to Paul when he is thanking men and women who battled by his side in the tough work of establishing the early church (Rom. 16:1-16). He mentions for appreciation another person who was special to him—the mother of Rufus, "who has been a mother to me too" (Rom. 16:13). Immediately a picture springs to our minds. A *mother!* How wonderful for the tough, old weary traveler. Other men and women had wrestled with him in ideas, prayer, and hard work. But Rufus's mother made a distinctive and welcome contribution to Paul's life. She was like a mother! That meant, as we say glibly today, she was "there for him." If he returned to her home at a late, inconvenient hour, her eyes would light up anyway. "Paul! Oh good, I'm so relieved to see you."

After the warm hug, she'd start heating food and drink. "I'm glad I have some of your favorite dish," the motherly woman said as she juggled caring for his varied needs, the way all mothers seem to do. In a few minutes his muddy, wet travel clothes were exchanged for comfortable old garments she kept for his all-too-rare homecomings. The fire blazed up magically, it seemed, and his favorite seat was soon near it. He sank back gratefully, rubbing his weary eyes as he began to enjoy her cooking skill.

"I'm always amazed at how you manage to have the best food I know anywhere—and your finances must make it a challenge!" The mother-like woman laughed comfortably; she was pleased to be appreciated. Their eyes met. "You look as if you have a lot on your mind," she'd say. Then Paul could unwind with the sort of conversation you can usually only have with a mother. No detail seems too small or unimportant. A recent stomach bug's misery can rub shoulders with a worrying situation connected to the emperor or to some great idea. It all mixes in comfortably together in a way that left Paul ready for the welcoming bed.

When Paul went on his dangerous way again, this caring, motherly person never quite forgot him day in and day out. As she was reminded of him, her prayers rose up on his behalf, "unceasingly."

A mother! What a treasure. Mothers are necessary when we are children and wonderful anytime. An individual like Paul appreciates someone "who is a mother to me," and as he says that, we immediately see her in a home setting. What are mothers in their craft without homes? What is a fire without a fireplace? Food in a basket from the market without a kitchen? Sleep without a bed? What is it like to have sorrow and pain and not have the comfort of arms to hold us? What is it like as a small child to have to do without either a mother or the home she and the all-important father make together? In fact, what does a child's life mean without a home of her own?

I may be wrong, but although we always have access to our heavenly Father, we can only have a mother's care when, like Paul, someone rooted in the everyday aspects of life will donate that to us. To me, this is what it has to mean to be a mother. (Fathers left to bring up children alone also fulfill this "earthy" role.) It is sweet to enjoy this privilege. All of us actual mothers or stand-ins succeed sometimes better, sometimes worse. No homes are perfect.

Many single women have given their lives to mothering. Amy Carmichael was one of these women.[7] She began serving as a missionary in Southern India at the same time Charlotte Mason was in Ambleside. At first Amy Carmichael was a village evangelist, traveling with Indian women. At this stage she was unpopular with most of the "ex-pats" (Europeans) because she made the Indian women her "sisters," her equals in the battle, just as Paul had worked with indigenous people from any background, both men and women. This policy was startling to the colonial British missionaries at that time! It was offensive too, as it had been to the "upper crust" of the synagogue and Roman society in Paul's day.

But then proper tea parties on verandahs had extra fuel for surprised gossip. "Guess what that Amy Carmichael is up to now!" She'd given up evangelistic work in order to make a home for frail baby girls and little children who otherwise were to be given to temples to be raised as religious prostitutes.

Everybody around thought this was terrible! Is it "spiritual work" to feed and care for a fragile infant? Is it "evangelistic" to be tied down to homemaking for a growing family of dependent children? Neither Indians (Hindu or Christian) nor fellow British thought so. They were equally horrified that she took on the practical side of being the mother. This was servant's work surely! Low caste and menial. A close friend said that "someone more suitable" should do this special work.

To begin with, it was lonely. No one else shared this vision. No others were ready to "lose their lives" in such a way. Amy followed the example of Jesus who bent down to wash the feet of His disciples. She prayed for others who would put aside the attractive occupations or lifestyles they enjoyed to "take up the towel" of this service.

Amy Carmichael persevered. She was committed. She never returned to her beloved adopted father in the Lake District nor to her home in Northern Ireland for a visit. A friend of hers has told me that this would have been "too painful," as she always deeply minded that separation. But the main reason was that mothers are essential to their children and homes; mothers can't easily leave for short periods of time, let alone for the several months a visit to Britain would have entailed.

Soon Amy Carmichael became "Amma" to all. The hundreds of children who eventually had their home in Dohnavur had a mother (an Amma) as long as she lived. They were not orphans. Amma often quoted a Tamil saying that captures the experience of all mothers: "Children tie the mother's feet down."

Amma wrote:

> We grew up from the first very simply, like a family. We were always, as it were, parts of one another (Ephesians 4:25 WEYMOUTH). In the ideal Indian family each member lives for the good of the household, and we worked together in this way and never as employer and employees. The children called the women "Accal" (older sister), English women when they came [were called] "Sittie" (mother's younger sister); and later brothers, Indian and English, [were called] "Annachie," which connotes a chivalrous thought of brotherly protection.[8]

A few paragraphs later we read:

> Before the children came, we were continually camping in tents, mud huts, or tumble-down old bungalows, and we never stopped to grow even a flower. But after they came, we had to make a home for them, so things were different. And because we know that beautiful things are dear to God (look deep into beauty and you see Him there), and that ugly, vulgar, coarse things are a jar, like a false note in music, we chose, when we had the choice, the beautiful, not the ugly. Someone, (the angels perhaps) had planted trees up and down the field for us. We cherished those trees. And flowers began to grow where only scrub had been, and gradually the place became sweet and green, almost as though it offered coolness. And the bare, red blot on the bare, hot plain changed to something pleasant to the eye and beloved, at least to ourselves.

This last paragraph is a clue. Amma made this her true (and "beloved") home; she did not take up the task of providing for the children as a "job." She, like Jesus, "came and *dwelt* among us." She settled down, made this her life and home. She gave her full attention to the children and the community. All must be as good as possible and beautiful.

And what of her home, the houses—were they like a bit of Britain plunked down in Southern India? No, Dohnavur was her Indian home. The children's Amma wore a sari just like other mothers. And she writes of the houses:

> When money came to enable us to do it, we used burnt brick and tiles.... The rooms are Indian, unfurnished, save for cupboards, brass vessels and, according to the nice upper class habit of the South, grass mats for beds: and the red-tiled floors are kept shiny by constant washing. Later on we found shells on the beach at Cape Comorin and water-worn wood like carved work by the river in the forest; and the children learned to dress their rooms with inexpensive loveliness.[9]

As Dohnavur grew to be a place of prayer, love, and everyday homemaking and later educational and medical work, the little cottage-like homes were happy, secure places. Each had (and still has) an Accal as the mother there. These Indian women totally committed themselves to belonging to the Dohnavur family. Thus the children enjoyed lifelong stability. Day or night Accal could be counted on. The Accal grieved, as all mothers do, when her children were in difficulty. She *loved* them. And the Accals wrote of having to readjust when one of their cottage family left or died. They were richly fulfilled in their lives dedicated to Christ in Dohnavur, serving a family of children in a home—laughter, fun, love, and warm hugs make this maybe the nicest occupation of all—motherhood!

Amma had the gift of writing, including poetry. Poetry often allows us to get close most intimately to the heart of another person. Never let it be said that only a biological mother or father can be a "real mother" or a "real father"! These words of a Dohnavur song portray the lifelong yearning parents everywhere have for their children:

Father, hear us, we are praying,
Hear the words our hearts are saying,
We are praying for our children.

Keep them from the powers of evil,
From the secret, hidden peril.
Father, hear us for our children.

From the whirlpool that would suck them,
From the treacherous quicksand, pluck them,
Father, hear us for our children.

From the worldling's hollow gladness,
From the sting of faithless sadness,
Father, Father, keep our children.

Through life's troubled waters steer them,
Through life's bitter battle cheer them,
Father, Father, be thou near them.

Read the language of our longing,
Read the wordless pleadings thronging,
Holy Father, for our children.

And wherever they may bide,
Lead them home at eventide.[10]

Amma has been a guide to me since I soaked up many of her books when I was a teenager, bedridden at home with rheumatic fever. I've found so many of her instructions ringing in my ears at this turn or that all through my life. Later on, my husband Ranald and I discovered Charlotte Mason's writings on the bringing up ´ ˈ ˑ dren, including education. These we found deeply enlighter

Then while reading a new book one day, I felt a thrill to find a link between Charlotte Mason and Amy Carmichael! The book was written by someone who had worked with Amma until her death and had helped lead Dohnavur Fellowship afterwards.[12]

The writer, Margaret Wilkinson, was at Cambridge University in the early 1940s when she first heard of Dohnavur. She started writing to Amma, and out of this correspondence grew a conviction that she should go to Dohnavur for her life's work. World War II was in progress when she finished her course, so she was not yet able to go out to India. After caring for her mother until her death, Margaret Wilkinson had a waiting time ahead until she could travel safely. What should she do to prepare herself for the Dohnavur family?

Amma knew, and the letter came that sent Margaret up to the beautiful hills of the Lake District. Margaret Wilkinson writes:

> Amma's book *Kohila* is the story of one of the first children brought to her, who grew up to be a nurse. In it Amma tells how she herself was led in the early days planning for the children's education. Writing of different people whose thinking influenced her, she says how the Home Education[13] series of books published by the Charlotte Mason College in Ambleside "was an immense help." This is how it came about that, some weeks after I arrived in London, the suggestion came from Dohnavur that I might use the waiting time doing teacher training at Ambleside. I applied to the college, and they agreed to take me for their one-year course for graduates on the understanding that if a passage offered to India, I could leave immediately.[14]

Naturally when I first discovered this connection, I was surprised by a special joy. The two women whose ideas and writings have shone out so clearly for myself and for so many others had a strong link "for the children's sake."[15] Charlotte Mason's ideas can be applied in any culture if the Christian infrastructure is used as the "skeleton," allowing local differences to give it shape and life. I was excited and thankful that Amma had been sent Charlotte Mason's books and that she'd adapted the ideas for her Indian children. Also reading this fact explained to me a lot about the Dohnavur home life and community, as well as the education of the girls there.

Amma naturally would have liked Charlotte Mason's ideas in reference to how to live life, what mattered, and shared areas of appreciation and enjoyment. Both women respected other people, including children. They recognized children's able minds and valued education highly, including for girls (unusual at that time). They both enjoyed nature and knew it well; both loved books. And they both had lives dedicated to God "for the children's sake."

Amma had written of the time before 1910 that "we often wished that Ambleside was not seven thousand miles from Dohnavur."[16] Far away from this Lakeland village, Amma was, in 1941, bedridden in a hot room. She loved "windows" to the outside—loveliness in books, pictures, letters—and of course she used her vivid imagination that breathed life into all.

Thus it was, we can be sure, Amma's thoughts often wandered to join the Cambridge graduate who'd gone to Ambleside. She would pray for Margaret, the preparation in hand, and for her life ahead that was dedicated to Dohnavur's community. She would pray for all in that "house of education." It would give her joy that Margaret loved hiking out in the hills and watching birds. Amma treasured the descriptive letters that arrived. Later on Margaret brought her appreciation for beauty to India. Then Margaret became Amma's "eyes" as she'd write daily reports of the wonderful birds and lush vegetation in Dohnavur's forest retreat when she was up there with the children and Accals on vacation. These notes went into that sickroom to share the refreshment of the much-loved forest loveliness. Charlotte Mason would have been glad that one of her teachers could share nature this way.

Amy Carmichael and Charlotte Mason both enjoyed life. They were thinkers, appreciating good books. They had settled homes and communities. They needed to prepare children and adults to live life well. In this pursuit they were practical and realistic. When Amma searched for advice in raising her beloved little girls (later little boys came too) and found Charlotte Mason, she was thankful. It was a philosophy of education, of bringing up children, that transcended any one particular culture. This was important. The children were not to grow up British, but Indian.

Margaret Wilkinson describes the nature-loving community she found and always enjoyed at Dohnavur. Her comments are interesting in two ways—first, as a "fruit" of the PNEU method adapted and applied for Indian children; second, as an example for us all in our lives. In 1909 Amma had written in her book *Lotus Buds:*[17] "We have one baby who collects poochies [Tamil for an insect]. 'Look,' she said one morning before prayer. 'Dear little five poochies,' and she opened her hand and five red and black beetles crawled slowly out, to the delight of the devout who scrambled up from their orderly rows with shrieks of appreciation."

Margaret Wilkinson puts this incident into the "whole picture" with her own descriptive words: "Amma goes on to say that, of course, the children knew the names of the flowers and birds and insects which surrounded them. She tells too of how they 'knew the habit of caterpillars.'" And Wilkinson continues to tell of the children's wonder at the amazing life cycles they knew through observation. She says that naturally, it was their mother, Amma, who'd taught them these things, "just as her father had taken her and her brothers and sisters out in the beautiful world around Millisle (Northern Ireland) when she was growing up and helped them to see the wonders it contained."[18]

Amma not only enjoyed and shared God's wonder-*full* world with her children, but she also wrote poems, songs, rhymes, and games for them. Margaret Wilkinson describes one singing game:

> We might possibly be entertained by the lizard game where a small girl kneels on a low bench and the other children sitting in a circle round her sing:

The lizard runs along the ground and then runs up a tree,
He turns his funny little head, and then he looks at me.
He wiggle waggles up and down, and then he looks at me.

While the one in the center wiggle waggles and makes marvelously lizard-like faces.

This is a glimpse of the real fun, liveliness, natural life, and happy quiet growing time the young children at Dohnavur enjoyed (and still enjoy today) at home and in their kindergarten and school. It was a life of genuine relationships, play, little tasks, stories, and wonder at the natural world around them. Hour by hour the bell of the House of Prayer would remind the Accals and children that the Lord was nigh; thoughts and prayers would dart toward God.

Amma wrote in detail about her cherished babies. An early book gives leisurely glimpses of the satisfying cottage-home life an Accal shared with the children:

It is time for evening hymns and good-night kisses. We have sung through the chief favorites, ending always with "Jesus, Tender Shepherd." "Now sing, 'Oh, luvvly lily g'oing in our garden!'" You point out to the garden: "It is dark; there are no lovely lilies to be seen; besides, that is not exactly a hymn; shall we have 'Jesus, Tender Shepherd' again and say good-night?" But this is not at all satisfactory. Tara looks a little hurt.[19] "'Tender Shepherd,' no! 'Oh, luvvly lily'!" Evu wonders if we are making excuses. Perhaps we have forgotten the tune, and she starts it:

Oh, lovely lily,
Growing in our garden,
Who made your dress so fair
For you to wear?
Who made you straight and tall
To give pleasure to us all?

> *Oh, lovely lily,*
> *Who did it all?*
> *Oh, little children,*
> *Playing in our garden,*
> *God made this dress so fair*
> *For us to wear.*
> *God made us straight and tall*
> *To give pleasure to you all.*
> *Oh, little children,*
> *God did it all.*

Then Tara smiles all round, and you are given to understand you have earned your good-night kisses. Evidently to Tara at least, there is a sense of incompleteness somewhere if the lovely lilies are excluded from the family devotions.[20]

Reading this tender account shows us the evangelist turned mother. Margaret Wilkinson says, "Amma wrote of herself and really meant it: 'My working life until the children came had been spent almost entirely in what is usually called "soul work," and I was the last person in the world to be of any use where bodies and minds are concerned. But I had to tackle both, and felt very often that "Jack of all trades, master of none" would be written on my tombstone—if I ever had one.'"[21]

Perhaps this gives us a good title for the mother, the parent responsible for the mix of everyday, humdrum "body needs" plus the wonder of unfolding minds and hearts responding to faith, hope, and love—the jack of all trades.

I suspect that Amy Carmichael, like other hard-worked professional people who become mothers, was relieved to suddenly have everyday joy and fun be part of her task. Here she was having to create a home that would be beloved to herself and the members of her family. It needed a heart and discipline of prayer (faith); a confident, cheerful, lively atmosphere (hope); and interrelationships that were genuine, tender, and unselfish in serving needs (love). It gave Amy time to sweetly kiss warm babes before cozy bedtimes while singing them favorite songs, time to "stop and stare" with eager children in the garden and the forest glades.

Like Charlotte Mason, she respected the children's own personal responses to the good and the beautiful; she communicated with their eager minds. And so we see her following a chattering group of little girls as they rushed gladly out into the lovely garden to play. They had only been kept a "little time" at their lessons (just as the wise Charlotte Mason prescribed, so they'd have plenty of "quiet growing time").

Amma wrote: "After a little time indoors we used to go out into the garden. It was wonderland to see the children. We never suggested questions and never answered any they did not ask (we had as much as we could do to find answers to those they did ask). But we, as it were, ran to meet their minds in welcome. It was a merry kind of schooling, and left many gaps, but it had some uses."[22]

Is it a surprise then that years later, when Margaret Wilkinson arrived in Dohnavur, and these little children were in their turn Accals and responsible adults in the Dohnavur family, she wrote: "Coming to Dohnavur more than thirty years later, I found myself joining a community of nature lovers. Her love of the beauty and wonder of God's creation had certainly passed to them. It had been one of the things in her writing that had drawn me to her."[23]

We have come full circle. Whatever the culture or century, whether a person is a biological mother or not, homes, communities, and everyday, humdrum living ("the usual") are an all-absorbing full-time occupation when undertaken with proper understanding and attention. Amy Carmichael writes that it is the love of Christ that could draw responsible persons to "such work." She says, "No money would have drawn these workers to us. Work which has no clear ending, but drifts on into the night if babies are young or troublesome—such work makes demands upon devotion and practical unselfishness which appeal to none but those who are prepared to love with the tireless love of a mother."[24] She continues a bit later on the page: "Yet we find that the work, though so demanding, is full of compensations. The convert in her loneliness is welcomed into a family where little children need her and will soon love her dearly. The uncomforted places in her heart become healed, for the touch of a little child is very healing. If she is willing to forget herself and live for that little child, something new springs up within her; she does not understand it, but those who watch her know that all is well. . . . May they be inspired by the constraining love of Christ and 'The Glory of the Usual.'"[25]

8

❧

The Infrastructure of Routine

Homes consist of their atmosphere, discipline, and life. Routines are part of the concept of discipline. The home life of anyone, whether it is someone with children or not, needs a regular pattern of life. People used to have more firmly established domestic routines than we do now. These patterns can be too rigid, of course. As in everything else, it is good to find a balance between the extremes. In this case, we need the stability of a regular life on the one hand, yet we must be free to adapt it or have "one-off" changes on the other.[1]

One of the keys of life is keeping the "frame" stable while adapting to our changing personal rhythms in smaller details. For instance, sometimes we do better with a few smaller meals or perhaps an extra rest after work, before beginning the evening at home. But there is a peaceful sureness about a life that has a "spine" of regular, basic routines that are realistic and balanced. This key area needs skilled management and compromise. Getting these practicalities right is one of the challenges for the mother (or whoever is coping with the household's smooth running). It can be satisfying to become attuned to various lives so that the clear, regular, basic pattern that gives continuity and stability can be adapted.

It is always important when viewing the "shape" of the home from its pattern-in-routines angle that the mother (or other caregiver) is counted in as having a personal life too. This may seem too obvious to mention. However, we human beings seem to be creatures of extremes. We so often find it difficult to find a balance in the middle. In this instance, we either tend to be too self-serving, *making our personal life the center stage* around which everything else is organized, *or* we are always figuring out what is best for *everyone else* and forget that we are to be served by the arrangements as well.

Maybe mothers get into the habit of forgetting to count in their own needs and lives when babies get them up at night regularly. They can come to feel that being a good-enough mother means always being like a personal attendant to baby, children, other adults, or the aged. Soon what the mother takes for granted is accepted by everyone in the family. They assume that Mom will do everything, even that she doesn't mind or matter.

This is wrong as well as short-sighted. One of the objectives in a home or community's routines is to ensure that those who bear the weight don't burn out. These people's well-being ensures the home's well-being. Another result of a good routine is that people have enough unified life, and yet there is free time too for individual work, fulfillment, and leisure.

If this were understood and homes were reasonably organized so that the "weight-bearers" had enough regular support or help for them to have work balanced by breaks, then we'd see less distress in homes. For instance, mothers at home full time with two or three children under school age are more likely to suffer depression than other groups of the population. It is sheer hard labor to always be on demand, supplying complicated family needs. It is draining not to have a change. This is where a good husband saves the day, and his help makes a huge difference.[2] Here also good neighbors and good ideas should help spread the load, not just once, but regularly enough to be counted on. It is going out of fashion to serve each other. But this is the cooperative ideal or model we are given in the Judeo-Christian Scriptures.

Thus in the home of a married couple, while the weight-bearing mother's needs are served, she in turn watches out for ways to be her husband's helper. He certainly is weight-bearing too. If they are following a traditional pattern, and he has been out at work all day, she'll try to ensure that he has a refreshing arrival at home. A listening ear, a hot drink or meal, the gift of some quiet and "space"—these are ways to make a practical difference. Jesus instructed us to be on the lookout always for ways we can serve each other—husbands and wives, coworkers, neighbors, and wider family.[3] "How can I lessen the burden for him/her today?" is the vital question.

This attitude is the right one *whatever* our everyday work-and-life roles are. We can switch tasks or work commitments as men, women, and/or friends, but we still need this readiness to assist.[4] Unfortunately today we are being brainwashed to look out only for ourselves. We mind being another person's servant.

It is not hard to work out the necessary basic schedule that covers our needs from cradle to grave. This schedule is like the thread on which all the beads of life are strung. We all need regular meals, sleep, times together, and times alone. Children need time for play. Organized play activities, passive entertainment before a screen, or virtual reality experiences—anything that came from someone else's mind—doesn't count. Children's play should enable them to develop the deeply satisfying habit of listening to their own ideas and imagination and acting on them.

All of us, whatever our age, stage, or circumstances, need unscheduled-by-someone-else personal time. This time is a vital "bead on the string." When people grow up with schedules that did not allow for such time and opportunity, we can see the results. These people often "are not in touch with themselves," which is a terrible alienation. Perhaps they graduate from college without personal interests that they've chosen and developed from childhood onwards. All too often they have read books only as an assignment, not for personal enjoyment. Perhaps they only went (and still go) outdoors as part of an activity arranged by someone else or for a sport. This emptiness, where a treasury of enjoyable relationships should exist, is a serious cause of many individuals not having a sense of personal identity. We can see the result too in people who do not have much imagination, creativity, or motivation.

Right across the spectrum of society as many people return

from work, they feel they must pass the time by flipping the switch to make their screens spring to life and give them a false sense of being engaged with life personally! They need to be entertained. Free time is boring, not an eagerly anticipated joy.

This was one of the reasons Charlotte Mason scheduled young children's days so they had the afternoon free to play outside or to spend plenty of time on a current passion—be it improvising on the piano, reading, dressing up, or acting in a play. She also knew that they'd grow up loving nature and its richness—it was their "playroom." For her this free time was so vital that she allowed no school lessons after lunch and no homework until the student reached the age of thirteen or fourteen.

A regular pattern of relaxation, rest, and sleep is necessary, or the person, both mind and body, burns out. Sleep restores and refreshes us every twenty-four hours. Every parent who has experienced sleep deprivation through a baby's needs or child's illness knows that the experience is actually torture if it goes on too long.

Modern technology has made destructive inroads into the vital area of restful interludes, threatening what is a beautifully precious "bead on the string of everyday life." Electricity artificially stimulates us all to a more-than-human tolerance of too many hours of activity. Gone is the reflective "winding down" at sunset. All too often glaring lights shine mercilessly even on the tiniest infants. Noises blare.

Why is there so much depression? There are many complex reasons, but one vitally crucial factor is failure to live "according to our frame" as the wise old Book says.[5] Going beyond our limits is also a significant element in the breakup of relationships, in the failure to enjoy a spiritually satisfying relationship with God, in some mental illnesses, and in lack of motivation and concentration at school and at work. The list is endless.

Human societies, homes, and people have always combined refreshing, restful times of the day with food, conversation, and fellowship. Although lunch might have been, say, a hunk of bread and cheese out in the field of work, the coming of the welcome daily rest time in every twenty-four-hour cycle was combined with needed nourishment. Everywhere on this globe meals together are a sort of daily celebration, a high point of the day. There is the sharing of news, voicing of concerns, fun, laughter, explaining of ideas, thoughtful discussions, and thankfulness for food.

In Europe until recently most countries had at least a two-hour dinner break in the *middle* of the day.[6] Of course, distances between work or school and home were short, and adults and children could enjoy a healthful walk back home for the delicious-smelling meal. As continental breakfasts are light, the potage (soup) beckoned. I never dawdled on the way home from school as the Swiss church bells rang out *midi* (noon)!

The bells still ring, and Swiss children under eleven or so still go home for two hours at midday for their hot meal. The Swiss dinner is a full three-course meal with good soup, often made of blended leftovers. Thrifty housekeepers never throw away so much as one cabbage leaf. No butter goes on the crusty Swiss bread (note: a low-fat diet with healthful vegetables).

Then the main meal of the day includes meat if it can be afforded, at least two or three times a week in my experience as a child. (And fish once a week too.) Eggs and/or cheese would be the protein base for other meals, which include potatoes and at least one other cooked vegetable in season. (People ate only what was around locally at the time—no long storage period, no chemicals used.) *Always, always* without fail, meals include a green salad—mixed greens tossed with a vinegar and oil dressing. Sometimes there is a second salad, grated carrot or celeriac being favored.

Finally comes a dessert. In my just-post-World-War-II childhood, this was usually an apple. The weekly orange appeared on Sunday. Items made with sugar were far and few between—and not just because of supplies. The Swiss have always been nutritionally aware. Last of all they have coffee. (Patisseries or pastries, if taken, go with a morning coffee or afternoon tea, not with a main meal.)

When I was a seventeen-year-old university student living

with a Swiss family in Lausanne, this schedule of meals was the sure routine for everyone. The midday meal was the center point of our day. We'd sit around a big old-fashioned table in the dining room, with Madame at the head. In the summer the table would be under the trees in the flowery orchard, complete with white linen tablecloth and our individual cloth napkins.

Of course, the discussion at that time often went above my head. The family members were intellectuals with wide interests. So I was fed and educated into culture all at once! At 1:40 P.M. the townspeople would stir and return to school or work.

Le souper was lighter, more informal, shorter. We might have a big bowl of freshly grated apple with flakes of almonds and raisins,[7] accompanied by chunks of brown bread and bowls of steaming *cafe au lait*.

In the earliest chapter of my life when I was a small child in St. Louis, the pattern of our family life revolved around the evening meal as the center, except on Sundays when lunch was the best meal of the week. I was fortunate because my mother had a flair for making mealtimes a pleasure and food nourishing (all on a low budget). I always appreciated and enjoyed her cooking as a child! She balanced the colors on the plate and the textures as well as food groups. I can still "see and taste" whole menus from early childhood. Harvard beets, mashed potatoes, and meat loaf. Macaroni and cheese with stewed tomatoes. Waffles, syrup, bacon, and orange juice. Homemade soups, homemade rolls, and fruit with cold glasses of milk. The table always was laid with care too—family meals matter. Candles lit on each side of a simple, low flower arrangement. In summer cool-looking fruit and ice clinking in glasses.

Today we talk a lot about how elusive self-esteem can be. Again this is complex, but if as a child you know you are a person that matters so much that great care is put into making your meals nice, then you tend to matter to yourself properly too!

When I thought of heaven when I was small, I always felt certain it would be just like coming home to one of my mother's special Sunday dinners. I knew that the Lord in heaven would serve us mashed potatoes, roast meat with gravy, and little lima beans and corn just like she did. In fact, I remember once having a tantrum of total frustration once at around five years of age when I confidently voiced this to my mother and said, "The Bible says so."

I still remember that careful look come on her face. It meant, as I expertly knew, that although she wasn't going to agree with me (could not, in fact, for absolute truth's sake), she still wanted to protect my ideas. She respected my thoughts and did not trample them down or laugh. (Thank you a million times, Mother.)

"Well, dear, that's nice," I heard, or something like it, "but the Bible doesn't actually say so."

"IT DOES TOO." (Stamp, stamp.) "I *KNOW* IT DOES. NANCY BARKER *TOLD* US IN SUNDAY SCHOOL."

Much later I realized that the long heavenly table I imagined, with Jesus Himself serving us as my mother did and placing in front of me a beautiful roast lamb dinner, did have a biblical basis. I must have heard of the "The Lord's Supper" and added the idea of "The Lamb of God" to it. I knew that Communion looked back to a real meal with Jesus and looked forward to the time when He said, "I have eagerly desired to eat this Passover with you before I suffer. For I tell you, I will not eat it again until it finds fulfillment in the kingdom of God" (Luke 22:15-16).

Speaking of examples, Jesus gives us a vivid model of how providing for physical hunger and also for the hunger in human hearts goes together. Again and again he spoke of food. He planned for it, provided it, and he stopped to eat with family, friends, and followers. He would talk, listen, relax, be satisfied. Is preparation of food only for women to think of? Why should that be true? Every climber of Everest knows that food provision is essential if such a project is to succeed. And so must every possible pattern of life be fueled. We must always have a time and a place for consuming food—not just gobbling it down mindlessly like brute beasts, but enjoying it as a community time together.

Jesus' example shows us that it is wrong to split off the spiritual needs of people from their physical needs. When you care about someone, you do not limit yourself to giving them words of truth for their eternal souls and satisfying their gnawing heart hunger with love and friendship. He shows us we must serve the *entire person.* Jesus gives water to the thirsty and picnics for the hungry. He was a "dab hand" at actually doing it, practical man that He was. He made fires and roasted succulent fresh fish (John 21:9). He broke bread miraculously so that there was enough for everyone: "I do not want to send them away hungry, or they may collapse on the way" (Matt. 15:32). He'd linger over evening meals one of the disciples' mothers had cooked, savoring the foods, enjoying the wine. If He'd heal a child or adult, His realistic next instruction was "to give her something to eat" (Mark 5:43). And when He was to leave us here in our everyday lives, he gave us a celebration meal to help us remember him week by week: "Do *this* in remembrance of me" (Luke 22:19). Do what? Eat together. Chew, swallow. Think about the real Me.

"In my Father's house there are many dwelling places (homes). . . . I am going away to prepare a place [home] for you" (John 14:2 AMP). In Revelation we are told that along each side of the river in the heavenly city are very special fruit trees (Rev. 22:2). When I was a child, I knew I'd just love that fruit. I still see every reason to look forward to the promised place ahead, although I know now my imagination could not begin to picture what it'll be like—it is too wonderful. But we do know that we are to have resurrected bodies as Christ did, and He joined his friends to eat after the Resurrection. He ate real food—in heaven *life goes on.*

C. S. Lewis certainly sketches such a picture of heaven in Aslan's Country. He, an unmarried academic for almost all his adult years, certainly was earthy and grounded in his awareness of real life. He and his friends, such as J. R. R. Tolkien, would meet regularly to discuss, argue, enjoy each other's manuscripts, and smoke their pipes in a pub in Oxford. They loved walking trips through lovely green countryside. The high point was the stop at a village pub and the welcome "plowman's lunch"—a chunk of cheddar or

Stilton cheese, fresh bread, and pickle relish—all this washed down with a pint of bitters.

The best pubs are usually ancient with a good roaring fire to brighten a dark day. There is a family kitchen behind the front room, and the cold, tired guests are welcomed by the savory smell of fresh home-cooked food—a daily feature for possibly hundreds of years. How can you resist a generous helping of steak and kidney pie steaming hot from the oven, served with fresh vegetables out of the garden? The guests, like the Hobbits, will "tuck in."

Of course, Tolkien and Lewis were university men, and Oxford and Cambridge have always known a thing or two about regular meals being essential in life's daily pattern. If you enter a medieval college court (with the buildings arranged around all four sides of a green lawn, just like the monasteries before them), you see immediately the three most important architectural features—the chapel, library, and dining hall, all holding places of equal respect. These are built so that their centrality in the community's life is evident. They have fine windows, higher ceilings than the rest of the buildings, and arched doorways. Even from the outside you see that these are the heart of the community.

We can do no better as we design the shape of our home life. We provide for worship and listening to God; we ensure that minds are nurtured and disciplined and given opportunity for expression in thought; we offer regular dining together.

If you could take a peek at Lewis and Tolkien each in their colleges not so long ago, you'd see them eating with the other fellows at the high table. This table is set at the head of the long wood-paneled medieval hall. Oil paintings are on the walls; candles flicker.

Below the high table at right angles are long wooden tables for the undergraduates. You'd find that the food is good, the cheeses excellent, and the wines superb. One reason Oxbridge[8] can be such lively fun is that the discussions/conversations can be excellent, while the basics of life are carried off with a flair.

Is this just for those who go to the ancient seats of learning? No, variations occur many places in most societies. Educational communities have been seen as a sort of specialized (or extended) home/village dedicated to learning (and originally for the worship of God). Thus it is typical to find chapels, libraries, and everyday communal eating and living areas there. Can we help a person grow (be educated) without each one of these components? No, in these crucial years of opportunity all three need to be "beads on the string."

Thomas Jefferson experienced these three essential components as an undergraduate in William and Mary, that fine old college in Virginia. He had an extra advantage there, as he was regularly invited to be part of a private evening dinner with some outstanding professors. The conversations ranged far and wide; this was an important part of his growth. Thus it was that later when he designed and planned the architecturally outstanding buildings for the University of Virginia, he understood that a community living together every day would be an important factor to consider. Farthest from his mind was the sterile misconception that you can fill a person's mind with facts and information while ignoring the rest of life, and yet get an educated, thinking person at the end of the process.

He designed the main university as a community built around a long, tree-planted, park-like lawn. At one end is the beautiful Rotunda with its library under the dome. Being a practical and ingenious designer, he killed two birds with one stone. He arranged the bookshelves so that they are out of sight behind pillars. Thus he created not only a fine library, but also a fine hall for feasts of celebration and special gatherings.

On either side of the lawn run the students' individual accommodations, one story high. Each student had his own front door to this home-in-miniature, with one room containing a lovely fireplace and good windows. At the back of each room runs a long walled garden planted with a rich variety of trees and plants. Here we find no students confined to airless, ugly rooms! After every few such terraced homes is a fine multi-storied house in the terrace. These dignified homes are designed so that the professors and their families will be an everyday part of the community. The first floor is a common room for the students to use as they are welcomed for meals, teas, lectures, discussions, and so on. Jefferson planned that in nice weather the lectures and seminars could take place in the shared gardens at the back.

Of course, he did not expect the professors to be able to provide all the meals! So he put the student dining halls (also communal eating) in several special buildings just behind the main quadrangle. He arranged for one of the halls to serve Italian food, another English, and yet another French. I do not know if there were any other national kitchens present, but he certainly thought education meant more than *reading* about other people! Again and again we discover that mealtimes are the key to the day for communities, families, and friends.

The sharing of meals has too often been neglected and is commonly now thought to be a trivial or less important part of home, education, or community life. I believe such ignorance is serious and has caused the collapse of one of life's foundations. It does not take up too much time; it is a thread that holds life together.

To every home come seasons of special stress when doing everything is too much. What is to be cut out? The continuation of the basic pattern of work, mealtimes, leisure, and sleep will be a key to whether this home and the individuals in it survive the stress.

A regular daily meal (or meals if possible) together is one of the top priorities. So is relaxation and sleep. Even in wartime or when painful disasters hit the family, it is worth a huge effort to keep this basic schedule going. In such circumstances, this health-giving routine and provision helps to keep us from falling apart. We ignore this essential fact at our risk; it is like pulling out the string from the string of beads.

It is frightening how this sweet fact of healthy life is being misunderstood today. More and more people think that grabbing something with calories, fiber, and vitamins in it is adequate. How wrong they are! Many homes are now no longer planned with any sense of communal rhythm. People act as if their homes are fast-food outlets with a microwave to cope with all the different schedules and a flickering screen to keep folk distracted while food is swallowed any old way.

Homes need a place in which to eat and a schedule that allows the time necessary for a regular mealtime. The place can be on mats on the floor around a fire in Nepal, a scrubbed pine kitchen table, or an oak dining table with silver candlesticks. It doesn't matter as long as there is room for everyone to sit down together. These meals spell home, should be as enjoyable as possible, and, most important, convey a rhythm of life.

Sometimes when you walk into a house, you see it as just an echoing house-shell. Other houses breathe the atmosphere and life of a home. Dining arrangements show whether this group of people enjoy a homelike life together or just lead separate lives and negotiate with each other on this or that when their paths overlap. There are several features of a home that people such as Charlotte Mason, Amy Carmichael, C. S. Lewis, and Thomas Jefferson would expect. The welcoming family table is one. In homes you expect this to be practically the most-used place of all.

Our family table was in the big all-purpose room in our apartment.[9] One side and corner of the room was the kitchen; another wall had a window. Opposite the window were two walls with a fireplace, bookcases, and cheerful original framed pictures. One was an oil painting by a local artist, the other by my cousin, also an artist. There were family photographs. The kitchen side was covered with beautiful paintings by gifted people—the children in the family. The couch and easy chairs could be grouped around the fire for story-reading and conversations, teatime, or leisure. There were good lights for individual reading, sewing, and art.

By the window stood the family table with a high chair pulled up to it for years. A good light hung down over the center. The round table could seat six cozily or be extended for eight, with ten possible by crowding.

The table was my luxury. I was endlessly thankful for it because it had been a "throw away" from somebody, and the top was cheap wood. For meals we covered it with a tablecloth—our everyday favorite was a red-and-white-checked cloth with red candles and flowers or fruit in the center. The luxury was that after meals, tablecloth folded away, I did not have to ever scold or worry creative children about spoiling the table. It was in constant use for painting, play dough, real clay, cardboard and paste marvels, games of all sorts, and ink pots for art or projects. It was the homework table, sewing center, Lego-land. You name it, our table was pretty much in constant use. By the way, this warmly humming hive of activity was here because it was the only heated room in the house for our use as a family. That draws a family together! Such room-sharing develops the give-and-take communal habits that oil the wheels of human relationships.

The family room was meant to be out of bounds for arguments. Our oldest daughter designed a little sign for each door of this room: THERE IS TO BE PEACE AT ALL TIMES IN THIS ROOM. Was there? Of course not! This was our *aim*.

The above description is only how one family arranged life's requirements within the room they had. (We now have a different arrangement of rooms as we live in another home.) I do not think this would be a useful model necessarily for anyone else; we each have our personal circumstances with advantages and disadvantages to work with. But, whatever our resources, limitations, ideas, or lifestyles, we should plan a central place "where we'll eat together." It is good to place the table (unless you are Asian and eat on the floor) in a pleasant, enjoyable area. Windows and light are factors. So too is warmth in cold, raw, damp climates. That is why the cheerful, cozy farmlike kitchen makes a gloriously friendly eating/living place! In hot climates, cool and darkened is welcoming. It's important to have air—ventilation—so that it is not stuffy.

There should be higher chairs for the smallest and comfortable chairs for everyone. The elderly enjoy a supportive chair. People sitting around the table should have the comfort of pillows behind their backs if that helps them, and they should not have light glaring in their eyes.

If there is a table to protect, invest in a good insulated covering to go under the tablecloth. Sometimes we prefer a cheerful wipe-off cloth, preferably not plastic. There are good designs on treated cotton, and I like non-iron table mats. The English have beautiful wipe-off mats that are used in the best dining circles and never have to be laundered!

We all sometimes enjoy special meals when extra care is taken in just setting the table, as well as in preparing the food. I've always aimed for a good effect without having to spend a lot of time. (I've been a working mother for thirty-six years.) It is amazing how quickly some holly, ivy, and red candles cheer up a red-and-white-checked cloth. Or a flat white sheet for a tablecloth can look superb with a simple bowl of flowers with brass candlesticks on either side and white tapered candles. (With the lights out or dimmed, you can't see whether it is ironed or not.)

Children love the fun of creating different table settings. I'd sometimes take five minutes to cut place mats out of birthday or Christmas wrapping paper. In the table center a child's creation from Lego or cardboard can have pride of place. Children can arrange some little extras round it—space men or little dolls or animals. For a celebration they might like to make place cards for each family member and the friends. (Of course this table has space for friends!) Such a tiny effort can bring cheer on a rainy day and encourages a dreary-feeling child or family no end.

Children love to cook with you. Bread-making gives them dough to shape again and again. If they've reasonably clean hands, it'll do—baking kills the germs. Four-year-olds can be "dab hands" standing up on a chair at the counter next to you. They'll beat eggs in a bowl, mix in flour, peel potatoes slowly, or chop carrots. Two-year-olds love washing up the plastic non-sharp things with a waterproof apron on. Three-year-olds can sort clean silverware into their compartments.

I believe that early working together in interesting (and tasty) food preparation is essential for a person's whole-life welfare. There is something so reassuring, "rooted," real about it all. I'd put the baby reclining seat safely up on the counter for the youngest. They love to see the water splash and enjoy the nursery rhymes you start saying and singing as you go. By the time they are toddlers, they will enjoy sitting on the counter to see for shorter or longer times. By this time they'd be singing the rhymes or saying them with you. It's all very cozy and satisfying.

This is a bleak, fallen old world. Life has real pain, disappointment, and evil. Whatever lies ahead, the best preparation is a childhood with a core of everyday calmness/well-being that is given substance by a cheerful, comforting, satisfying, and full-of-hope kitchen. "The kitchen is the heart of the home." An old and wise saying. The sunshiny stability of the early years tends to be carried on into the rest of life, dispelling shadows.[10]

Anyway, as meal preparation nears its end, often several people have come into the kitchen asking, "What's for supper?" (Maybe the most-asked question in the home.) The early childhood fun of helping means that by age seven or eight, children are ready to be part of an efficient cooperative family work team.[11] One of these children may have been by your side setting the table, making the salad, anything. This is so often a warm, friendly time together. Questions pop up about all sorts of subjects, or maybe an opinion is debated hotly. Sometimes it's been peacefully quiet; sometimes music or an interesting program on the radio is shared. Visiting adults feel more at home if given a job to do too. Elderly members of the family come into their own as they expertly join in.

In our life's chapter now as "older" persons, this is a time Ranald and I often like to share. A television screen has no place here, for *we are the ones living life*. We're seeing and hearing each other or relishing some peace to think our own thoughts. We're savoring the smells, giving appreciative attention to the textures. There are craftsmen at work here both in food appearance and caring for human relationships. I think even the smallest kitchen should try to have room for a comfortable chair. Someone worried, sad, or merely tired out will gravitate to this person-orientated heart of the home. Such a one will probably want to be sipping a hot or cold drink in a mug.

And so to the table. Anticipation is running high. Sometimes one member of the family is disappointed; tuna casserole is not his or her favorite, but lasagna day will surely come around again. All have learned that there is one shared menu (unless there is a medical exemption), and, as in all other areas of life, sometimes our personal preferences are gratified, sometimes not. That is life. We should learn to accept it in a matter-of-fact way early on. Children know that Dad and Mom have favorite foods too.

The atmosphere should be cheerful without being noisy or chaotic. Here at the family table children learn to listen to others and wait their turn to speak. Here they learn to "eat nicely," whatever that means in their culture. A good family or communal rule is: "If you can't say something nice about the food, say nothing at all." Sometimes the hum of conversation dies down after grace is said, as everyone concentrates on satisfying hunger. A warm togetherness around the family meal table is really what fellowship and communion are all about. This is the time to take turns and each tell about the day's events and for everyone else to listen. Ideas crop up, questions are asked, there is debate. Community/family meals have a rule—only one person talks at a time.

Ah, how one looks forward to this satisfying regular part of life! Talk about growing in confidence! It is such a pleasure to have the whole family laugh at *your* joke or listen to what *you* think or did, because it matters. Nothing can replace this day-in, day-out pattern. NOTHING! Here you "donate yourself and receive the other."[12] Relationships are forged around the table. It is a vital part of life.

Children are not the only ones at the table who should be minding their manners. It is we, the grownups, who are the examples of pleasant self-control. If we're upset with a child or other adult, the mealtime peace is too precious to be shattered with recriminations. Table conversation is an art that includes interesting "telling"; it can be stimulating with debate or discussions about ideas, but it is never a time to attack another person. It is not a time for lectures, sermons, or prejudice.

The more difficult subjects we must communicate with each other about should be dealt with more privately, one-on-one, or as family councils NOT held at mealtimes. Mealtime conversations should not be used to make someone feel bad or angry. This is basic good manners. One of the bad habits we fall into is showing our lack of respect for people in our family this way, especially for children.

Of course, real families and groups of friends or communities are not perfect in this key matter, just as we fail in so many other ways. It is terribly easy to fall into bad habits within the home! And this is true whether it is a traditional family group or another small community home such as a household shared by university students. "Familiarity breeds contempt" conveys a symptom of our human weakness and sinfulness. We must lean hard against this tendency and consciously practice respect with our nearest and dearest.

All that I am writing about as we've walked into the dining room is an example of the fact that atmosphere, discipline, and life are intertwined into one. Elements of all three aspects have been twined together in these paragraphs. May something I've said entice you toward making the effort to establish life-giving patterns in your everyday life at home, at school, or in a group to which you belong.

I've chosen a literary illustration of eating together as a part of abundant life and an illustration from the Dohnavur Fellowship in India:

> "Here we are," said Mr. Beaver, "and it looks as if Mrs. Beaver is expecting us. I'll lead the way." . . .
>
> The first thing Lucy noticed as she went in was a burring sound, and the first thing she saw was a kind-looking beaver sitting in the corner with a thread in her mouth, working busily at her sewing machine. . . .

"So you've come at last!" she said, holding out both her wrinkled paws. "At last! To think that I should ever live to see this day! The potatoes are on boiling, and the kettle's singing, and I daresay, Mr. Beaver, you'll get us some fish." . . .

Meanwhile the girls were helping Mrs. Beaver to fill the kettle and lay the table and cut the bread and put the plates in the oven to heat and draw a huge jug of beer for Mr. Beaver from a barrel which stood in one corner of the house, and to put on the frying pan and get the drippings hot. Lucy thought the Beavers had a very snug little home. . . .

You can think how good the new-caught fish smelled while they were frying and how the hungry children longed for them to be done and how very much hungrier still they had become before Mrs. Beaver said, "Now we're nearly ready." . . .

In a very few minutes everyone was drawing up their stools . . . and preparing to enjoy themselves.[13]

Among our Dohnavur customs is a happy way of keeping birthdays and coming-days. (A coming-day is the anniversary of an arrival). . . .

The room where the one to be feted lives is dressed with flowers (flowers have always meant much to the children . . .).

On great coming-days there is a feast for all in the group to which that one belongs. . . .

The food is simple enough. There are a few delectable extras, such as payasam, a sloppy concoction of rice and palm sugar, or homemade honey cakes, or balls of a nutty and oily nature, something not tasted every day, and these luscious delicacies are thoroughly appreciated, sometimes with open abandonment, often with weighty seriousness. . . .

But one year we had to be very careful. The feast was to be ordinary food with the cheapest of twisted hard biscuits to help out, and we feared that the children would be disappointed. It was not so.

"If we may have it all together, and strings of flowers over our heads, and decorations (of flowers of course), that makes a feast," they explained. And we found that it was so. (The setting—children cross-legged on the ground with the "decorated celebration table" laid out on a cloth. The plates—banana leaves!)"[14]

Last of all, the following illustrations show "the example of life" for us all to emulate at home, in our communities, and even on the road:

> As they approached the village to which they were going, Jesus acted as if he were going farther. But they urged him strongly, "Stay with us, for it is nearly evening; the day is almost over." So he went in to stay with them. When he was at the table with them, he took bread, gave thanks, broke it and began to give it to them. Then their eyes were opened and they recognized him, and he disappeared from their sight. (Luke 24:28-31).

> Early in the morning, Jesus stood on the shore, but the disciples did not realize that it was Jesus. He called out to them, "Friends, haven't you any fish?"
> "No," they answered. . . . (John 21:4-5)

The disciples cast their nets on the other side of the boat at Jesus' command and hauled in a huge catch.

> Then the disciple whom Jesus loved said to Peter, "It is the Lord!" As soon as Simon Peter heard him say, "It is the Lord," he wrapped his outer garment around him . . . and jumped into the water. The other disciples followed in the boat, towing the net full of fish, for they were not far from shore, about a hundred yards. When they landed, they saw a fire of burning coals there with fish on it, and some bread.
> Jesus said to them, "Come and have breakfast." (John 21:7-9, 12)

9

❧

Of Beds, Balance, and Books

God created twilight. The home sighs with relief. It is time to lay down tools and come in from whatever labors and efforts have filled the hours. Time for tired little children to have the mud washed off, to be kissed and listened to—time for everyone to pause as the evening meal signals the satisfying day's end!

During my early childhood in America, our visits to my grandparents' little brick house in Germantown in Philadelphia always followed a pleasant routine. It was fun. Grandmother's house smelled and looked different. The dark, never-lived-in front parlor was a museum piece even to me. The light white-and-gray kitchen was where home happened. There stood the big central kitchen table for food preparation and eating; there, the rocking chair by the radio. (My grandfather and my dad, as a teenager, had made the first radio on the block—a "cat's whisker," I was told to my puzzlement.) There in the kitchen also stood the gas stove in blue enamel with gray and white flecks.

And there my grandmother reigned supreme with her sharp cleanliness and assertive control. She was proud that she was the first to have her wash neatly hung out on Ross Street every Monday morning. The kitchen and home made up her world. I knew that while my grandfather was still alive, he had been expelled to the basement to sit and smoke his pipe, comfortably relaxed in his old chair by the furnace. Not a bad hideaway for a tired thinking man!

As far as I can tell, her grueling childhood had left her no tenderness for her man.

I knew I was like him in some ways—we both adored my grandmother's homemade chicken soup and applesauce. (The soup was really homemade, including the noodles. The sauce she'd get from a can and put it in a pan on the stove to look like the real thing.)

These were cozy memories for me. Little children should not be heir to past sadness and tensions (which I now know had been aplenty in that kitchen, as where all human beings live together, especially when they've suffered from hard childhoods).

For me it was a room that smiled with companionable hours spent cooking and enjoying simple food. The evening rite consisted of wiping off the table and washing kitchen plates. (I don't remember a dining room meal with dining room best plates.) For me the warmth inside contrasted with the cold night outside as Grandma got out the checkerboard or Parcheesi game, and a happily satisfied little girl anticipated a long evening at that kitchen table, peacefully trying to beat her grandmother. I think she loved it as much as I did. I'd still play with her years later when I was a mother of two myself, after she'd moved into two rooms in my parents' home.

Of course, if I was visiting during the hot Philadelphia summer (no air conditioning naturally), twilight did not spell the cozy kitchen but held other delights. It was time for the neighbors to settle down on their front porches for the evening. Porch swings would squeak, and gossip would extend from porch to porch (Grandmother and friends were experts at exclamation points). Ice cream would appear with cold drinks. We youngsters in shorts and T-shirts would play around the block in the friendly twilight. If we were lucky, we might get to ride our dad's old wagon down the hill. As the dusk deepened, hide-and-seek or cops and robbers would be played with exciting abandon. But maybe we'd drift away from the porch more thoughtfully and fill a jar with fireflies. We would gaze at their mysterious flitting light or up at the stars.

Such memories of actual experiences are the stuff that gives our inner core its shape and life—our personal history. We weave our thoughts, feelings, choices, and activities into the rhythm of days, evenings, and nights. Work, study, play, leisure, relationships, solitude, interests, thoughts. We are participants in the "dance of life" and know we are involved as a separate person who is part of a family and community. If we are believing Christians, our Lord God, King, Father, and Friend is at the hub of the wheel, at the center of all of life. The regular patterns stabilize us in life through thick and thin. When disaster strikes, we hopefully go on "automatic pilot" and carry on the basic rhythm. Even when we are suffering a broken heart or are "plowed up" with anxieties or burdens, this habitual "tick-tock" that keeps going helps us every day. We may stare out woodenly into space at the twilight "sit-down" time, but even that pause does refresh too.

And as it is for us personally, so it is for the family. The carrying on of the basic routine saves us as a group from falling into confused fragmentation. Fragmented life patterns cause a downward spiral, as age-old wisdom knows. So in Jewish and other strong families and communities, when there is a death, for instance, good hot meals are brought in by neighbors (or used to be). The physically, mentally, and emotionally exhausted adult returning from the hospital or the scared children opening the door after school are thus greeted with the reassuring aroma of homemade chicken soup, say, and a good meal to follow. It may be a neighbor putting you to bed, but you know her, and you've had a good supper, bath, and story just as usual, so the routine carries you along its stabilizing way. Adults need the food and normal routine as much as the youngsters do. Everybody resurfaces better into well-being when such age-old wisdom is being lived out.

When I wasn't away on one of the rare visits to my grandparents, evenings at home were different. My earliest memories of going to bed early are absolutely delightful. My mother had stenciled a curving line of leaping deer across my wall; how I loved the bedroom I shared with my big sister! The grandmother in Philadelphia had made me a quilt of multicolored, hand-woven wool squares sewed in patchwork cheerfulness with my initials embroidered in one corner: S. J. S. I pretended this "counterpane" was a land of many-colored fields and green forests.[1] My pillowcase had been made by my other grandmother (the saintly missionary one). The material had blue stripes alternating with flowery stripes, and a ruffle all around. In that day of white sheets (deliciously sweet-smelling and welcoming, having been hung on the line to blow in the sun), a patterned special pillowcase and my very own bed cover made me feel surrounded by caring love.

I'd willingly go to bed in this welcoming place, especially as I knew I'd next have the "Best Time of the Day"—my mother reading to me out of storybooks. "Please, just one more!" came my plea. She was a most obliging, pretty young mother, and often I could get quite a lot of extra "mileage" from her. Usually I'd beg for some poetry too.[2] (Mind you, the saintly grandmother would read for even longer, especially when you had measles.)

But only my own dear mother, after kneeling for our prayers and turning out the light, would sing to me. It is very special for a weary little child to have this lovely bedtime routine. And the songs brought the Lord Jesus close to us in comforting strength, assurances, and safety. I wonder how old I was when this routine stopped? I think by the time we left St. Louis when I was six— although the songs went on in times of sickness.

Mother always sang the songs in the same reassuring sequence. "Jesus bids us shine with a strong, pure light," "This little light of mine," "I'm so glad that my Father in heaven, tells of His love in the book He has given." On and on she sang, and the stars shone into infinity ahead. Somehow in my infant mind I knew I'd be shining one day like a "jewel in His crown"—Susan, a jewel. Whatever naughtiness or hot rebellion had ruffled the day, it ended with harmonious resolution and with being drawn into the warm circle of God's love, with the knowledge that I was treasured by Him. And in the sleepy world I seemed to drift in, I was joined by "all the little children in the world; red and yellow, black and white, all are precious in his sight." Jesus loved us all and everyone. Sleep came.

When I grew up, married, and had children, it was mainly Ranald who held the "Beloved-Singer-to-Children-at-Bedtime" place. When it was Daddy's turn to pray with a child, that child would also have the enjoyment of his much-loved repertoire of choruses. When the children were very tiny, he would rock them in his arms and soothe them with these. But a bit later, they'd be cozily tucked in bed with the light off. As well as giving a child a wonderful routine, it arms them with emotional and spiritual strength for seriously challenging adult trials ahead. I remember one of our children, being sorely tested while living and working in a remote, dark Himalayan valley with her husband, saying that in some of the hardest situations it was these songs that would come back with light, cheer, comfort, and hope.

Both in my childhood and later on when Ranald and I were bringing up our family, everyone at home would gather right after supper without fail for The Story. In our home our little ones (usually until five or six) often would have had their nursery tea before the family evening meal. By the end of the day I'm afraid several of our youngest interfered with the sort of civilized meal I have previously described. Some toddlers refused to eat, made the conversation together impossible, or even threw food. Older children and parents minded this, so such "tinies" would have an earlier routine involving a meal they liked, maybe at a low table by the fireside or in the kitchen. This gave them their own little conversation without needing to be quiet while an eleven-year-old asked what a homosexual was or whatever. Sometimes they had several favorite story books read to them while eating. (A firm favorite.) Two in particular, who were close together in age, were pretty troublesome. So I'd pop them in a nice bath where they were distracted with water play that absorbed them after all other concentration had worn away through a busy day of play.

Both of these children (and most of the rest) always loved applesauce, yogurt, and wheat germ. I'd mix a big bowl of some such healthy concoction and, calling it "birds in the nest," would spoon this in—first to one, then to the other—using only one spoon. The children who had this special treat all loved it. I found it a peaceful way to get tired little ones fed and ready for bed. They'd emerge with damp curls, satisfied, dry, and warmly clad in little warm over-pajama sleep suits, ready to play calmly by the fireside while the big ones sat up for grown-up supper. Then the little people were more fun for a tired dad to read to or sing songs with at the piano (a never-ending joy for the children and now for their children too).

Whatever method or plan had been used, our youngest children were usually in bed between 6:00 and 6:30 P.M. This is a traditional British nursery routine; it is pretty tried and true if you don't use naps after two or so. The schedule leaves the adults and older children a bit more peace for a meal they can quietly enjoy or for their reading time.[3] Another advantage is less aggravation for weary adults who try to get worn-out little people to be more self-disciplined and orderly than they are developmentally able to be.

Children also enjoy a welcome sense of pride at "graduation," when they are deemed old enough to stay up and join the main meal. Then they think of it as something special while they try to behave "like the big ones." Children always like goals they can look forward to and steps they get to as they grow. They do better when allowed plenty of time to really be ready for the next step up with its privileges and extra demands.

Of course, this nursery plan is not the only good pattern. It is an arrangement that has worked in *some* British families and for us most of the time. Another beneficial plan can be found in the north of England when the whole family sits down for an earlier "tea" (hot, cooked food) at 5:30 P.M. or so. Scottish families and many American families also follow this practice. It also has its advantages—warmth, fun, and closeness. *It is very important to find a pattern that fits your own life at each stage.* Ideas like this are like a cookbook. You say, "Oh yes, I'd like to try that," or "No, that wouldn't work for us. My children take a good, long nap, and I need one too. Then they can be up to see their dad in the early evening. He has to come home late, and we like to eat together."

Anyway, however it was arranged, when the meal was over and small ones tucked up, everyone old enough would be eagerly looking forward to another chapter read aloud from the current book. When I was more than seven years old, my dad read to us all every night. He had the frustrating habit of counting out a certain number of pages and refusing to read extra! I remember listening to the stories when I was between the ages of eight and twelve in a Swiss alpine village called Champery. There we'd light a fire in the tiled wood-burning stove and rejoice in its warmth, especially after a day in the snow. (The rest of the chalet was unheated at night, including our frosty bedrooms.)

How I loved that living room! My mother had made plaid curtains. There were shelves full of wonderful books lining the walls below the little chalet windows. With shutters closed, curtains pulled, fire crackling, we'd settle down. Often the grownups (my parents) drank tea; we children had steaming hot chocolate. Sometimes there was popcorn from America, or on Sunday treats such as homemade orange rolls.

Together we'd "go" to Yorkshire to *The Secret Garden* or to the Home Counties to laugh together over *Winnie-the-Pooh* or *Alice in Wonderland*. (My mother definitely read *Winnie-the-Pooh* and *Alice* best of all.)

When Ranald and I had children over five or six, the much-loved ritual continued. There was never a question of older teenage or college-age children who were at home opting out. Quite to the contrary, it was one of their pleasures. They'd look forward to visiting old storybook haunts and friends. The Narnia tales were read around four times over the years, and these improve with later savoring like a rich, old wine. Twice Tolkien's Lord of the Rings, several times Laura Ingalls Wilder's Little House on the Prairie series, and all of Meindert DeJong's books were repeated too. Many others are much-loved favorites also, and two or three years or so after a reading, the family would decide that the newest graduate from "nursery bedtime" should hear a particular book. And of course in listening to the reading again, an older child is more mature in understanding and appreciation.

This gloriously satisfying hour together, day in and day out, came almost without fail at home, on vacations, when we had just moved, in happy contented times, and in sad, distressed times of family life.

When there is general upheaval going on, this normal routine is a helpful rhythm. Depression sometimes lightens as people lose themselves in the story. A dawn of interest and even some joy thus entering into a mind can help dispel darkness. Sometimes the spirit of the rebellious child or the ruffled adult gets soothed. Selfish introspection can be turned into concern for other people who lived different kinds of lives, those dealing with other circumstances.

My mother knew that my dad had had little tenderness or cultural opportunities in his immigrant-like family. So she thought that reading aloud together would give him "mind pictures" and tender understanding to fill some gaps as well as enrich the children in the family. And so it did. Dear Dad. He had a big soft heart, and when he reached the touching bits in the story, his voice would press on, only slightly shaky, while tears would course down his cheeks. We children learned a lot about compassion this way. We learned that it matters when other people hurt or amazing joyful things happen.

I've seen a wide range of adults coming to L'Abri have the eyes of their heart opened, so to speak, in the same way. They become aware of other people, times in history, attitudes, and communities. Books such as those by L. M. Montgomery, Meindert DeJong, and many others can almost furnish adult minds with a sense of having been there. More than that, emotions are touched. Such books help us chart new and better paths for our lives.[4] Such reading leads on to other good literature. This education-into-life goes on to bigger issues, and the complications of adult life are tackled.

With teenagers read *Brave New World* by Aldous Huxley, for instance. The book will encourage a lot of discussion—especially as the listener suddenly realizes there are strong links in the story to the current debate about genetic engineering. Books by the Brontes and Charles Dickens can work well with fourteen-year-olds, starting with *Jane Eyre* and *Tale of Two Cities*. Literature shared is an enormous rich field to be harvested.

Then there is the fun, humorous element in reading aloud. The right reader makes *Winnie-the-Pooh* a delight.[5] There are lots of wonderfully funny books. Can there be anything better than gales of laughter shared in warm togetherness—laughter so hearty that you're out of breath? For older listeners read *My Family and Other Animals* by Gerald Durrell (warning—either omit expletives or read them as part of text, whichever is comfortable to you). The family member or a friend who has a wonderful gift of reading in different accents, tones, and sense of drama can bring great richness to the story. By the fireside whole communities of strong characters emerge and live. Meanwhile the reader grows in confidence and ability.

Discussion, interests, and inspiration will grow out of such a reading-together pattern. Books *must* be chosen for the listeners' enjoyment. Avoid like the plague anything that moralizes or preaches. Avoid textbook-like listing of facts. It is *living* books that work.

Children's books that are well written are a delight for life. Of course, there is also a rich supply of adult literature, biography, and history that we find refreshing. The choice is ours! Listeners will be able step by step to enjoy more advanced or classical works. Whereas a book may seem too dry or hard to tackle alone, when you hear it read aloud well, it is enjoyable after all. Older children who could not enjoy reading, say, *Jane Eyre* or *Tale of Two Cities* on their own will, if you persevere through the first chapters, "get into the story" and enjoy the book a lot. Of course you need to know your children's readiness, and the reader has to be enjoying the book and be expressive too. Just like food served at the meal, some enjoy one story more than others. But as we choose books with enjoyment and quality in mind, this will not be a problem.

Children who came to stay as part of our family for three or more months sometimes found this routine strange at first. I'd try to help with bowls of popcorn or mugs of hot chocolate. In our family, if you were old enough to stay up for the story, you were old enough to sit still and listen quietly, having settled down into a comfortable position.

However, soon the children would be "hooked" and begging for "just a bit of the next chapter. It is soooo exciting." Children coming out of some distress benefit especially by this cozy together time. It is emotionally comforting to become part of the family group, drawn in by listening to the same story. I've watched children who had not been able to concentrate before and saw their dull eyes clear and light dawn on their somber or restless faces. They would start listening with rapt attention, rather the way a starved creature concentrates on eating. Such a child might be held on a reassuring lap and can relax into the warm closeness. This is good.

Another fireside activity is reading aloud any letters to the family from afar. Sometimes an older child wants to read a composition or poem he or she has written. Others bring an item from a newspaper or magazine to share.

When there was extra time, we used to read poetry. I have always enjoyed reading it, and children would soon volunteer to read poems they liked too. Sometimes our family schedule and the children's interest allowed more than the reading from the main book. We could start the session with an interesting history narrative (also from a living book). Missionary and real-life Christian experience books should have a place here too. In my childhood this type of book was saved for Sunday evening reading times. My worldview, sense of other cultures, and priorities were influenced by Isobel Kuhn's interesting books about Christian light coming to the Lisu.[6] I also remember at an earlier stage feeling I'd tramped through Africa with David Livingstone. Later, with our own teenagers, we all were transfixed by *The Small Woman* by Alan Burgess.

For at least three generations, and probably more, our family has been influenced by *Pilgrim's Progress* by John Bunyan.[7] One generation after another, we share this experience of seeing life as a road to be walked. It is good to visualize, as my mother did when she was a child, the burden of sin and guilt that rolled away at the cross. Even when going through that final river of death, a pilgrim in the book named Hopeful had said, "When thou passest through the waters, I will be with thee; and through the rivers, they shall not overflow thee." As one by one we came or will come to this ford ahead, we can "take courage" as Christian did—and find as he did that "the river was but shallow." Yes, it is a great preparation for life to hear as a child "all the trumpeters" whose glad sound welcomed the pilgrims on the other side.

When I was a young child, my love, respect, and interest in the Bible increased when my dad read *Sunshine Country* by Kristiny Royovej (translated from the Czechoslovakian as Cristina Roy).[8] Another book inspired the same wonder, *Mary Jones and Her Bible* by M. E. R. (author's full name unknown). Both of these books stand out in my mind. I still feel as if I too had tramped barefoot for miles to secure the greatest treasure—a Bible. I imagined also finding the amazing story in a cave. Before listening to these books being read, I'd taken the much-quoted Bible for granted.

In times of stress, sadness, or depression, whether one has been brought up with such books or not, the reading of children's books together or alone can be comforting and positive. Many adult books (or other art forms such as films and plays) add more burdens by telling of other people's miseries, and that can be just too much for our sagging emotions. Several of my friends and I take out well-loved children's stories to give us refreshment when we are struggling one way or another. We all have our favorites. We've enjoyed these children's books and may return to them or to some familiar and loved literature. Elizabeth Goudge kept a volume of Jane Austen's by her bed. (A good idea. I also sometimes return to Elizabeth Goudge's books.)

Charlotte Mason instructed the young women leaving Scale

How for their first job to have a book always on hand to read. Reading was a habit for life. Most would have felt limited reading only one book at a time! They would typically be reading whatever held their interest—literature, travel, history, poetry. Others also would be reading up on birds or plants; interests were varied for them—geology, geography, scientific research, music, art history, various cultures, books in other languages, essays, plays, Christian books, myths, exploration, ideas. With such resources and interests, Charlotte Mason knew her young teachers would not easily "dry out."

Indeed, I know several of these women who are now between seventy and ninety years of age. Without exception they are lively people who exhibit a love of life. Having an eager mind, well fed by good reading, balances the dull side of the everyday. They enjoy nature, are craftswomen, and have rich, lasting friendships. Some have been married, others not. They all put down roots, had homes, and were/are active members in their communities. Some continued in education as teachers; others were full time at home with families. Their lives, although varied, share similar health-giving qualities.

Joan Molyneux (now with the Lord) told me about the little school where she was principal. The students were evacuated to a country house during World War II. Her face lit up as she shared how she had created a home for the young pupils. She described how the children would come downstairs every evening to sit around the fire with their mugs of hot milk. They and she were drawn into Narnia's magical land together, rapt and satisfied. (The books were just coming off the press.)

Some of the other Charlotte Mason-trained teachers were missionaries, or their husbands had jobs that took them to difficult places. But they all knew that home life came first with its routines providing a stable pattern—however much the family moved. Many would teach their own children; they'd wait for exciting brown paper parcels of books to arrive from the PNEU office in London. The children brought up like this are not at all rootless.

Another teacher, Marion Berry, who had had a distinguished professional life as the headmistress of a PNEU school, didn't stop living "for the children's sake" when she retired. Near her was a residential "home" for children. She gave her time to the youngsters on a regular basis. Her account of these emotionally and educationally deprived children is not romantic, but it presents a good example of the best in the PNEU school brought into a home setting.[9]

Berry's book also shows how children can be rehabilitated with love and attention. She wrote, "My first customer was David, in care all his life, a stolid, uncommunicative twelve-year-old, who for a long time never gave me a flicker of encouragement. He didn't believe in ever uttering the simple words, 'Thank you.'"

David could not read or write much at all. They struggled along together, but with *his* choice of poetry. Berry described the boy's selection as always "a delight to me although he read it in his own wooden way." His reading improved, but it was "not much joy." Then, Marion writes, "Not much joy until I said it must be my fault for not having the sort of books boys like, and his eyes turned to scan my own bookshelves. *The Kon-Tiki Expedition* was taken out, and things began to look up. With two pages from me to one from him, he thawed out a little."

Later we read of Michelle who "needed more help with her reading and writing."

She used to say she'd been thinking about *Watership Down*. Her face, when I suggested reading a special book for her, was full of such incredulous delight that I never grudged my trips to a far distant library to keep her going on a course of Rumer Godden.

I haven't lost my memories: I can still see people in my cozy little sitting room—Stephen ensconced in a small fireside chair utterly entranced with *Watership Down*. I did most of the reading, and he took up the final two paragraphs of each chapter, managing passably well. Sometimes the whole hour was spent like this; sometimes I sensed one chapter was enough. On one occasion, "What next?" brought the answer, "Game of Scrabble with 'Moonlight Sonata' on the record player." Once they had got to know my range, I let them choose what to do. I can see Alex on the floor by the fire making up her mind which song to have, "*Sur le Pont*" or "*Au Clair de la Lune*," singing softly to herself as she puts on the record. And Jimmy streaking in at the front door, and by the time I've turned on the hall light, he's got two chairs drawn up by the fire with a copy of *101 Dalmatians* on each. We read the statutory chapter in the usual way. He snapped the book shut and went to the bookcase saying, "Now poetry. Two each," handing out large anthologies. We rearranged ourselves at the table and got on with the choosing. He seemed a bit stuck.

"What's the matter? Can't you find one?"

"The trouble is I've got *three*."[10]

Who benefits when we have a rich home life in our "cozy sitting rooms" with or without a fireplace? *We* do, whether we are married or are single like Marion Berry. We then can extend this life to other persons (whether family or not) in hospitality. This is the model of a fruitful life.

Having discussed the place of books, reading, and interests in all of our lives, I'll return to the happenings in our apartment at the time when children of different ages were growing up. After the story, the "middle" children would go to bed one by one. Embroidery or drawing might be out. Usually people started leaving the fireside, one to get on with homework or music, another with something else. Sometimes one or two lingered, talking. Youngsters just home from college would stay on to tell Mum and/or Dad what their first term was like. Occasionally a thoughtful discussion or an argument carried on. Another time the chat would die down right away, as one person was deep in a book, and another leafed through an illustrated library book. Someone else would write a letter. One child or several might be playing a game with their dad. They sat poring over the Stratego or Scrabble board. Many evenings Dad left for more work (maybe a meeting of some sort).[11] Perhaps several young friends would be making a merry noise around the Pictionary game, or just one friend would come in to work on a homework project.

Children would attend Cub Scouts, Brownies, or Guides once a week, and older children liked to go play outside again. Teenagers drifted away to join L'Abri students "downstairs." Long volleyball games on summer nights were fun; in winter it was music-making, chatting while sitting around in the library or big kitchen while somebody strummed a guitar, or playing a game of charades in the living room. These fun evenings in the community satisfied older "children," and they didn't have to be going out to teenage parties and so on. Home and community were too lively and interesting.

While those of us living in smaller homes in less close-knit communities don't have all this communal life, our situation has other advantages.[12] We should cultivate a richly enjoyable life individually or together both at home and by following up interests and friendships outside the home. We can enrich that smaller circle too by inviting in other people, including some who are different. A lonely young person just starting work in a new city enjoys visiting a home, for instance. You can picture him making cookies in the kitchen with a couple of teenagers and settling down afterward to a Monopoly game. Another guest might be missing her piano back home, and soon her improvisation fills the house; one of the family's children gets out her flute to play along. Life should bubble up like a spring of water in our homes, and that life takes many forms.

Two or three times a year we've borrowed a VCR for anything from a weekend to a couple of weeks and rented a few interesting or fun videos. Because this activity is unusual, it's a treat to enjoy together. We've found that we are so spread out in age and interests in our home that a TV really does not work, although there are some interesting programs. Once when we were on sabbatical, a friend rented us a TV. It was fun to sit down after the current small

fry were abed and enjoy Olympic skating or a documentary on the
history of flight. But for everyday living, with such a range of interests and few enough hours for the family's life together, it was too
intrusive. One person or another wanted to watch "just this one
thing." Having it available squeezed out more valuable ways of
spending time.

Just as we would not let our families swallow contaminated
food, so we should not let youngsters (whether younger or older)
just sit and watch whatever comes along. Much on TV lacks value;
even more is poisonous. It pays to be choosy about anything on a
screen. Our minds can be contaminated or even destroyed, not just
by the content of programs, but also by advertising, although many
European countries have TV channels without advertising. As we
watch, we open the door to this influence. Advertising is brain-
washing people, especially children and young adults, into wanting things they don't need. It also makes them fearful that their
"image" is wrong. Those selling their wares aren't concerned about
viewers' welfare. On top of this, "just watching" is addictive and
dulls bright minds. It makes us all lazy—we lose our appetite for
reading, for conversation, for real life with its engagements that
demand energy, thought, and creativity.

Apart from that short spell on sabbatical (and one other brief
six months), we have not used television at all at home. But I have
a friend who made a different decision about TV than we have. This
friend watched chosen programs with her children as part of some
evenings at home together. They then would discuss what they'd
seen. She felt this had been crucial for her children to understand
the world around them. It was a way to be "in the world but not of
it." These children too have grown up healthy in mind and life.

Without the addictive intrusion of television or overuse of passive computer entertainment, the family has more time to enjoy
and develop personal interests, be creative, read, laugh, talk, know
how they feel, play games, cook, develop craft skills, be sociable
with friends, and do volunteer projects in the community. It is a fact
that these screens are so full of alluring color, movement, and atten-

tion-grabbing entertainment that they are addictive. They lure people away from living friendships, community, books, nature, and hands-on activities. Entertainment is an area where *self-discipline must be exercised and choices must be made.*

Marriages too deteriorate from the influence of so much artificiality. The other problem is time. Hours can be gobbled up, leaving little space or time for companionship. This is one of the reasons why relationships today are losing their "glue" and enjoyment. All of us need time to enjoy each other and life together, time too to grow through the rocky moments with conversation and prayer. Those couples on front porch swings knew a thing or two! While watching the kids out playing at dusk, they could talk, sharing joys and worries. This way couples built intimacy, which could include leisurely physical affection. Holding hands and strolling along in the sweetly scented early dusk after work was refreshing. Another favorite was lingering over a candle-lit supper after the little ones were abed and the older ones out playing basketball.

The art of giving attention to each other is being lost as our eyes click onto yet another video that is all too like the last one. Gazing into the fire, enjoying a back rub, or resting and listening to music while stroking the loved one's hair—that is the sort of thing I mean. You can see where such evenings take the married couple—happily off to bed a bit on the early side! Come on, folks, eat your heart out! Life can actually be simple and sweet, even in our rushing age that smells too often of diesel fuel. Let us slow down a bit! We're not programmed to *have* to choose to waste our time looking at or playing at "virtual" life rather than investing ourselves in flesh-and-blood relationships! It is our real life that matters.

Also choices that give us our own "real" time provide those of us who are not married space for building satisfying friendships or for enjoying life in our own company.[13] Those single persons whose lives illustrate the points I've made in this book would have stared in disbelief at the outrageous idea that leisure and life patterns at home are more for married people than for themselves. What a curious thought! During all of our adult lives, this home-based "off-work" time is sweet and life-giving. Lots of us cherish solitude. Those of us living with others seek it out—and go to our rooms to be alone and quiet, maybe with books or music. Others sit down to write to friends or take a reflective stroll to get rid of the day's tensions.

Jesus needed to balance the busy "people-days" by going to a quiet place to pray, to be alone with His Father. When we are suffering from too much work or the hubbub of lots of people in our days, it is so sweet to withdraw in peace and quietness. For those of us who know Jesus, this can be our most recreational place. There we find ourselves in green pastures with sweet water to drink. These considerations and choices are for all of us. They do not depend at all on our age, occupation, or marital status.

Some find quietness while they iron, sew, paint, or do woodwork. Others enjoy music-making or an evening alone doing some baking. It is vital for us to have the leisure to recharge our batteries, sometimes alone, sometimes with friends. Surprising as it may be, the physical side of housekeeping can be soothing after a day in front of a classroom, at a computer, or making rounds of hospital beds. It is a question of balance of course! An executive who has been working at mental tasks all day finds a change in washing the supper dishes, mowing the lawn, or tackling a pile of ironing while favorite music plays on the radio.

I've found that if I'm upset (and maybe angry), scrubbing a floor on my hands and knees can get that energy all out and leave me relaxed and ready to go on again. People who go to work in the morning might think of the everyday tasks at home in this way and find them as relaxing as some leisure activities they would have to pay for (or get even more tired driving to). As household gadgets and prepared meals have become the norm, we are sometimes ignorant of the possible balance menial, ordinary tasks could bring to our lives.

In line with the principle of *balance and change*, we all should find it health-giving to alternate mental work with this sort of unwinding, hands-on physical activity or vice versa. Rushing anxiously at breakneck speed as we do a job can put our blood pressure up and leave us in knots. If we are overwhelmed because we've tried to fit into a day more than we can cope with, our activities change from a pleasure to yet another agonizing duty.

In contrast, if we want to enjoy what we're doing, we'll give the task our full attention. That is the trick. Watching and enjoying the wood as it shines brighter. Admiring the colors of the vegetables. Smelling the sweet laundry off the line. Giving thanks for the ordinary, appreciating it. These can be such a joy. Of course, if a person has been doing housework all day, it'll be a balance to go out sometimes for a lecture, a swim, or book club discussion. The principle is the same.

Another positively health-giving occupation around the home is gardening. There is something amazingly satisfying about giving growing things one's attention. Really get into it. Feel the earth between your fingers, smell its sweetness after the rain. Wonder at the cool green grass under your bare feet. Relax under a tree and gaze at the pattern of sun and shade. Plant seeds. If you've had a personal disaster, try gardening—there is healing in it. Ask for advice about soils and plants so you choose easy-to-grow plants in your local conditions. When shoots and plants appear, they bring hope up with them. Plant bulbs in the fall. The English love drifts of daffodils. In small or paved yards, invest in big tubs of petunias or geraniums. When there is space, plant interesting shrubs. Plant trees. If you can, try to cultivate native wild flowers. Meadows need grazing really, but try to reintroduce flowering weeds if these are disappearing from your local environment.

Enjoy birds. Attract them with feeders offering peanuts, seeds, and other foods. Put out water in a bird bath. (An old garbage can lid will do at first!) One of the most wonderful "bird reserves" I've ever seen was in the yard around a friend's home in suburban St. Louis. It is a veritable Garden of Eden on an ordinary plot of land. Up and down the street are sterile patches of identical lawns. But here eyes and senses are delighted by a home surrounded by flowering borders, vines, trees, shrubs. A variety of food for birds is put out in many ways. In the living room when you look out, you want to linger in this beautiful place. American birds are fantastic. They seem immense and like some extraordinary exotic fantasy to English eyes: bright red cardinals, huge blue jays, overgrown robins. Here is plenty of God's wonderful creation to enjoy with rapt attention, all in a tame, "boring" suburb!

It is a real tragedy that so many homes are barren of life. While trying to describe the evening "leisure routine," I've moved bit by bit into *leisure at home generally speaking*. We are talking about rich, enjoyable, desirable life. And it is good—friendships, fun together, solitude, craftsmanship, hobbies, reflection, thoughtfulness, prayer, passionate enjoyment of creation. It is enjoyable sometimes to go to bed early. Hot baths or showers are refreshing. Peace. And all this life is at home.

So many of today's homes, whether we are married or single, are increasingly barren, boring, colorless places. It is a terrible deprivation for us all. Life need not be like this! "Taste and see that the Lord is good" (Psalm 34:8), we are told. Also we can say, "Taste and see that our everyday home life can be good by God's grace." We need not be distracted, gobbling half-tasted food, irritable, and needing constant entertainment. We need not long for better relationships as if they were caught by chance by the lucky few.

The birds in a city such as St. Louis are marvelous. Sit and watch a humming bird come to the wonderful lily-like flower in a pot outside the kitchen! Children are full of fun; the sky is full of glory and light. Oh, turn off the noise—you may find that a song rises up out of *you* on the evening air. Be still, become peaceful, practice enjoying beauty and life. It's worth it.

Make your one-room apartment, trailer, houseboat, hut, city or country house . . . a *living home* all your life.

10

✧

Contentment, Thanks, and Enjoyment

Each bead on the string of routine has its simple place. The time I get up. What is best for us to do at this moment? For many of us, it is essential to our well-being not to rush into the day. The beginning of the day can be a "green pasture and still waters" time. If we start the day in a chaotic way, we're already surrounded by an inner and outer sense of not having fitted into anything ordered. We can feel swept along and at the mercy of a fast-moving stream. We so easily lose the sweet result of making choices about what is most important, when that priority can fit in, and how essential responsibilities can be attended to calmly with our full attention. All of us laugh ruefully, having experienced days full of a swirl of activities like an uncontrolled flood when we're not able to enjoy much of anything. In such situations we are also distracted by the jostle of the things we *aren't* doing and only keep half an eye on what we *are* coping with. The unattended things seem overwhelming as their demands surface into our minds. This adds to our stress and confusion.

Lists can help us plan our days. This tool is especially useful if we clarify what *must fit in*, what we'd *like* to see fit in, and *what can be pared off* a too-full agenda. When we do such planning, we need to include our daily tasks, regular commitments, work, and projects; but we also need to provide the ordinary but vital everyday

slots of time for life's basic pattern. In other words, don't forget regular meals, time together, time alone, relaxation, exercise, sleep, and
so on. *This is the framework into which you'll have to find time for whatever else is on your list.*

I've quoted Benedict's rule once or twice so far. He was planning a community's life pattern and then filled it out with wise life-
giving content. As he based his rule on the authority of the
Scriptures, its ages-old wisdom and simplicity guide us with principles for planning life uncluttered by the confusing too-much that
surrounds us today.

It helped me no end to think on his advice to first of all set your
necessary basic pattern of the everyday, and only then can you
decide what, when, and how all the other demands can be fitted in.
He clearly emphasizes that the basic routine won't keep changing
apart from appropriate flexibility when age or health demands it.
This regularity is health-giving for body, mind, spirit—for the individual and for a group such as a family.

Routine gives us continuity and stability. If the routine is constantly having to be altered because of extra things to do or other
people's demands, we must think again. The basic healthful
rhythm of life and its "discipline" are being eroded or damaged.
Sleep and rest should be adequate so the person does not burn out.
Too often we are like little pathetic trees all shriveled up through
straining to keep up a fast pace for long hours. How *can* such trees
bear fruit? How can *life* flourish? The "trees" that are us also need
life-giving "sun, fresh air, and proper food." And the "seedlings"
(our children) are even more sensitive to deprivation.

Benedict's monastic communities made up of committed men
or women were productive. These Christian believers spent hours
daily in prayer, worship, Bible reading, and reflection. They were
also influential workers. Their farming skills changed agriculture.
Their learning led to a culture that produced schools and universities. Their care of the weak and sick led to hospitals. They altered
the pagan European cultures. Of course, we might say, as they did
not marry, they could have more focus in life than a married per-

son can. This *is* true, but it is more than an illustration of some possible benefits of celibacy. The Benedictines are a historical example of people who took time to live balanced spiritual, physical, and intellectual lives; and yet they were enormously productive and influential. (See *Seeking God: The Benedictine Way* by Esther de Waal.)

That is the lesson here. We tend to think that the ordinary is of less importance than the spiritual or areas of work/productivity. Too often nowadays people feel that taking time for the ordinary everyday aspect of life and home is a waste of time. Benedict certainly had goals, and those who joined him had also made a choice about the sorts of things they'd include in their life. But they pursued their goals and projects in addition to a balanced everyday pattern of community life, not in place of it.

Practically this meant that each person was refreshed by having ordinary needs met. For instance, sleep and rest had a proper place, with provision for care in times of ill-health too. People were not only allocated enough time for sleep, but comfort was considered (the bedding was to be adequate).

I like Benedict's provision for an early afternoon rest time, as they got up very early. He thought it was important to say that these people in shared dormitories should not disturb each other. Thoughtfulness mattered. Not only this, he was always aware of how one person differs from another in details. There is flexibility. Thus he says that while one person will drop off to sleep, another will be quietly reading a book.

The Benedictine way of life altered European cultures, including England's. The traditional English way of life is undergirded with Benedict's balance and attention to everyday life. On this green island we have traditionally kept the ordinary going in its satisfying pattern. (And this pattern is believed to be the basic discipline in a child's life and education.) Benedictines came here with the Normans (around A.D. 1000), and their centers of discipline and life became life-giving examples that the culture slowly followed. Balanced everyday life became more and more generally adopted in homes and villages. Like the tick-tock of a cultural clock, this life was rooted in God's worship and His Word on the one hand and in a livable pattern of human activities on the other. This balance gives a unique sense of well-being and glad atmosphere to traditional British life that has stood the test of the centuries.

Children's lives have been fitted into this balanced pattern that allows them individuality and yet develops home and community roots. In Britain creativity and inventiveness have flowered on the "trees of people's lives" when people have this stability. The caring attitude to everyday life includes one's surroundings. The British are known as gardeners and animal lovers. The ordinary was celebrated, enjoyed, tended. Is it any wonder that life flourished, often so beautifully? This was the culture of our Charlotte Mason, the admired C. S. Lewis, and the balanced pioneer Amy Carmichael. They so take it all for granted that they may hardly mention the subject as such. But it is always there, as strong and life-giving as a tree's roots, as the earth, the sun, the rain, and the oxygen.

Those of us who are Protestant will remember the improvement of the *re-forming* that started in a major way right here in Cambridge. It is no accident that it was young monks (the forerunners of our present-day students) who would gather with excitement in a pub near today's King's College to read and discuss the new books arriving from the continent, along with the Scriptures—in English at last! They were meant to be the sort of people who were committed to an entire lifestyle that honored God and His Word in everyday life. Thus they were eager for all purifying and clarifying of the truth they had inherited.[1] So we all must be, whatever our generation or Christian background. All organized groups springing out of God's Word of truth become contaminated by at least some lack of understanding or purity, or they develop the scabs of legalism. Reforming is needed again and again. But there is the great danger of thinking that we should throw everything away that went before. A lot can be lost this way. Jesus spoke only of pruning away the *poor* growth.

As the monks gathered to read and discuss, seeking something better, at last the ordinary folk of Cambridge could join in. Now they too could appeal to the source of God's Word themselves; it was in English![2] In Cambridge, in all of Britain, in Holland, and in France—as the Bible was translated, God-fearing folk "came into the picture" in a new way. This point is beautifully illustrated in Dutch Reformation art. Suddenly *everyday life* is celebrated in painting—a mother in a kitchen courtyard with a child; a woman pouring milk and setting out the daily bread; a still life of everyday food, fruit, and vegetables; a couple together; a living room with people of different ages enjoying music and talk.

We who may be termed "religious people" are in danger of floating away from rootedness in the everyday. Spiritual interests or religious work can become an escape from the humdrum, something apart from our bread and butter, something more "beautiful" or "important" than homes, work, family, and neighbors! When that happens, our thinking tends to become irrelevant to ordinary life.

That reforming time in history brought God's Word back into real-life focus. People saw as they read that their homes, farms, and trade-based lives had a place in God's design. They and we are not wasting time by giving these areas our time and attention. We are meant to work, sleep, rest, walk, talk, and eat to the glory of God. They also saw that they too could possess God's Word by understanding it themselves. Their thoughts and feelings too were important. Ordinary men and women gained an exciting new sense of liberating worth and beauty in their everyday and spiritual lives. They realized that the Scriptures include a pattern for living for married men and women as well as for the celibate. All of life came under the purview of the Bible, enhancing the value of it all.

Many learned Reformers were like Thomas Cranmer, who in 1549 finished the first English prayer book. They continued to value former wisdom, words, and beauty as long as these conformed to the original biblical teaching. They did not throw the old out; they attempted to purify doctrinal statements and directives so as to make clear the scriptural infrastructure of truth.

Lives lived by the deepest and simplest faith in the Son of God often glorify the medieval sky. . . . [But] there was abundant need for a reform of worship by the time the Reformation crisis actually came. There was need for a great simplification, a great removal of elements totally alien from the teaching of the New Testament, a great return to true ideals of Christian light and liberty, and a great revival of the common use of Holy Scripture.

Did not a Hand greater than human guide the hands which were so reverent in their touch upon the past, yet so resolute to build up, for the present and the future, only what should be true to the Bible and wholesome for the soul?

I have studied many Forms and Orders of Worship—ancient, modern, eastern, western; and I deliberately believe that the English Prayer Book is the nearest approach to perfection of them all, with its union of daylight truth with reverential humbleness, of immemorial treasures of the past with provisions for the life of the present hour.[3]

The Benedictine influence remained to give health to the continuing culture. The traditional English way of life is very human and is home-and-community based. The heroics that make a person miss out on regular sleep, rest, leisure, interests, meals, and worship are seen to be destructive.

Take a British day as an example. There are refinements to the three meals a day. This is the culture of tea breaks (which now can include coffee). Unable to wait until the evening mealtime of leisure, the British lighten the afternoon's effort with its own little pause. Surely *this* is the pause that refreshes! Teatime for all is a sure space to stop, be refreshed, talk with friends, or enjoy some quiet. Remember that this break was Charlotte Mason's best time of the day—and she saved it for the (Benedictine-like) choice of Bible reading and prayer. Teatime was C. S. Lewis's favorite time too. His usual plan was to read/study/write all morning, have lunch with congenial friends, and then take a good, long walk until tea. At tea he would enjoy conversation and then go back to more of the same work as in the morning until dinner again with friends. Evenings were for leisure reading or a jaunt to the pub for a pint and discussion.

Teatime! In English communities—whether they are schools, hospitals, universities, or homes—a place and time is provided for such breaks in the work schedule. More often than not, a mid-morning teatime slot is included in the day too. And, yes, this *is* one reason England has been a great nation. It is false to think that the more you push into each day, the more a person will learn, understand, or produce. We are not machines. Regular reflective pauses give us time to think, have new ideas, integrate understanding, or be drawn to new congenial fields of action or thought.

Traditionally in the great universities of Oxford and Cambridge, lectures start at the decent hour of 9 A.M., giving students plenty of time for a leisurely breakfast. (And for the Christian Union people, time for proper full attention to the reading of God's Word and prayer alone or with friends.) No heroic 7 A.M. classes here! Plus, it takes only a few healthy minutes on foot or bike to get from your room to a lecture. (Ideally, no time- and energy-consuming monster of commuting to rob the day of its balance.)

After a morning of lectures, in the recent past the afternoon was kept free of scheduled academic requirements (apart from occasional tutorials alone or in a small group with your tutor). This is still mainly the case. "Well," some will ask, "what *are* these high achievers doing with this time?" You will probably find them on the river rowing or on their college playing fields engaged in a sport. Educators recognize that students need a balanced day. After concentrated brain work, it is time for the body to move, time for fresh air, team challenges. If students went on studying without a break, they might only cram in facts and information rather than be educated as the whole persons they are.

It is a good sight to see students coming from the playing fields with their minds and bodies refreshed in clean, sweet air. They pass by my window as I type, healthy and chattering young folk. They

will repair to their rooms to have a pot of tea or coffee as they settle down to their books again. In my student days when rooms
were heated with gas fires, we girls would be invited into such
rooms at this pleasant hour. The boys would have brought in bread
or crumpets to toast on long forks in front of the fire. The kettle
would hiss. And we'd take on the world in lively discussion. The
topics (and our minds) would be enriched as we listened to each
other. One person saw things from her scientific point of view. She
would pause to take in the historical perspective from her friend.
A Christian might add an element that would change this: "If the
biblical view is true . . ." We'd become interested in books or lectures new to us and outside of our own studies.

Conversations such as these at tea, dinner, and tutorials are
part of the person's education. Children and young persons are not
educated to be like a computer storing facts that can be regurgitated
at the push of a button. (The computer performs better at this anyway.) No, they and we all need time to digest ideas and relate them
to other disciplines. They and we need time to think. It is ques-
tionable whether a person can be called *educated* without such individual formation.

Why does this book about home and its life keep bringing in a
wider educational view? I believe that good education and life at
home overlap. Education starts and should continue in the home
life until we die. The little baby born into a functioning home with
loving parents (or a parent) starts his education as a person immediately. The early stages, especially for the first three or four years,
are the most formative of all.

Today there is great pressure to turn babyhood and early
childhood into a formal educational time, involving institutional
learning as in a school. I believe with Charlotte Mason that a good,
rounded everyday life at home is the most comfortable and the
right place for the little person so full of potential. Babies and little children benefit in many ways from an unhurried-along first
chapter spent at home with a parent (or grandparent, etc.). Here is
the special closeness, the bond of love and lifetime commitment.

Here is the order of routine, but with the space and time for the child to make choices. Here our individuality is discovered, is expressed, and it flowers. We aren't one of a herd—we can be ourselves at home.

At home, as emotional needs are satisfied and the child is nurtured, language develops naturally. Within the relationships, life is "named," and questions soon come too. The child thinks his or her own thoughts. Children are interested in everything, eager to try "doing it too." No, there can be no substitute for a good-enough home and the parents who make it possible![4]

After several years of home life, children are ready to join larger groups for a few hours a day. They can benefit from focused teaching of skills and are eager to spend more time with their friends. Schools are not necessary, nor are they necessarily efficient in providing a next educational step. But they were and are a good idea! Someone knew Hebrew, Latin, reading and writing, or accounting and was willing (or eager) to impart this knowledge to children. Parents busy at work and at home were glad to send their children off to learn together for a few hours.

Schools can be modeled either on a home or a community (such as the Benedictine example), or they can look and feel more like factories. It is a terrible thing to treat a wonderful, individual, eager little person as if he or she is a component or a mechanical cog in the wheel of the economy. In the all-too-usual factory approach to education at all stages, the person is seen as a vessel into which facts are poured.

In this machine-like organization children are expected to conform to the "norm" for their age. An example is a little boy who developmentally still needs lots of running about freely out of doors—happily experimenting and using his imagination for play. He enjoys stories that are read to him and has lots of questions. But he cannot yet discern letter shapes or words. If he is forced to sit down for long hours and told to be "good"—and that he is "bad" or a failure when he cannot and does not learn—this is a sin against him. Charlotte Mason said, "Children are born *persons*." They

march best when the drum is adjusted to their individual development and needs. They are not all the same, nor should they be.
People do best when they are in small enough groups *to be known.*
We need relationships. Thus I am extending the need to make balanced life-pattern choices at home to schools and other learning
communities. *This is the age-old wisdom we are forgetting and neglect-
ing at our peril.*

I have been talking about balance in life. Perhaps never before
has the ordinary, balanced, sane, and enjoyable life been so at risk.
The tree-trunk-like stability of commitment is vanishing. People are
more and more drifting in and out of lifestyles and relationships
according to how they feel. Rarely now do the hard, clear questions
"What is right?" or "What is true?" give people the direction to
plow on through disappointing or unhappy times. Many have no
road map to follow in life.

The map that is true for all of life gives it direction and also provides an individual with a sort of "inner skeleton." People can
know who they are as persons and what life is about. Without any
map at all, let alone this reliable map, individual lives have about
as much shape as a blob of jelly. The society these people form cannot know its own mind. On top of this, more and more routine life-
giving daily patterns have been demolished. It is as if an enemy is
out to utterly destroy our life in every way. One of the ways a tor-
turer destroys a person is to deprive him of adequate sleep, leisure,
solitude, or friendship, and of course food. This fact has been well
understood in all cultures. Sadly it is fairly normal now for people
to fail even to begin to provide themselves or their children with
these basics. People expect to live in constant stress.

In L'Abri Fellowship[5] our days are governed by a clear routine
that includes "sit down around one table" regular meals with discussion, conversation, and cooked, nicely served meals. Everyone
is expected to join in, listen to each other, and stay during the course
of the meal—in other words, basic family living. At a L'Abri table
we share our various cultural heritages; the differences are fascinating. But whether we are European, Asian, or African in origin,

family/community meals are common to us all. Of course, there are differences. For instance, in some Asian countries, conversation happens after the meal, not at it.

In the last few years, many of the people (mostly between eighteen and thirty-five years old) arriving to be part of L'Abri's shared life are unfamiliar with the universal patterns of life together. Some even think that formal meals with discussion are a strategy in some program or another! I've had educated people stare in disbelief when they heard that whether they are with us or not, this daily pattern remains exactly the same for workers and their families in L'Abri. We are finding people therefore who grew up without basic family living.

In the last years statistics have reflected this trend. More and more children every year no longer sit down to daily meals around a family table. Their nutrition suffers as does their all-around development as a person. Sadly, there are also many who are not experiencing a home of abundant life either. Adults can be so busy with career, tasks, projects, and so on that they regard life-giving activities as messy and time-consuming. It is easy to feel that the less effort at-home living takes, the better it will be!

In the last chapter, I outlined only a few areas where life springs up and is shared in a home. Home life is, apart from book-reading together, variable, depending on individual interests, the situation, time available—all sorts of things.[6] I did not write out the examples so that they could all be copied. I'm only suggesting possibilities. Some homes have more music-making than others. Some families enjoy woodworking or metal work; others are enriched by an uncle who knows and loves the stars. Such a person wraps up a wonder-filled five-year-old and takes her out to gasp astonished at the night sky. He gives that child a legacy for life. Areas of life we love often emerge early on through the influence of someone who is naturally enthusiastic with rich enjoyment. There is too much to include here. We are not machines. Life is built of relationships—to God, to ourselves, to other persons (known through an actual relationship or through their books, buildings, or paintings, for instance), and to the created physical world.

If we as a society and as individuals give up the pattern and balance of everyday life, if we stop having the time for the "mess" that living makes, we disinherit our children (biological or otherwise) who are following us. They, unlike our forebears, will not have the opportunity to mature and broaden through experiencing community. Little children are coming "home" to sit up at a kitchen counter and have food shoveled in, like a car drawn up to be filled with gas. According to statistics, many children spend the mealtime sitting in front of a TV or computer screen, while plied with store-bought snacks or convenience foods. Nutritionally this fare is a disaster. It tends to be over-salted and full of saturated fat. Children spurn the vegetables and fruit they really need.

But health is only the first cost and maybe the least. The sense of being knit together into a community of people cannot come to these children. They cannot have a family's attention as they describe their day or discuss ideas. They don't learn to listen to others. Manners mean developing courtesies, and these are neglected. I have been told that young executives in London sign up for expensive courses to teach them table manners for their jobs. They feel vulnerable, not knowing how to behave. It is not natural for them to relax in a group at a meal.

Many families now only plan for a "life" that a child has to be driven to. They are ignorant of home-grown activities. After school children may go back into the van, be restrained,[7] and be driven (already weary) to an organized activity. Although in itself the activity could be interesting or good, on top of the day at school, the child has less and less of his or her own time free from being organized. Children can thus lead lives that are as stressful as an executive's.

In contrast, at home two children may decide one afternoon to make music at the piano while a third runs into the garden contentedly. They are not machines. They should not be constantly programmed. Another day, one of the children may be weary. He feels like curling up in an armchair to read or color in a sketch of airplanes. Adults also should have enough time to unwind and to follow their personal interests. This is part of the abundant life.

I believe that at every stage of human life we should be fitting into a home-life pattern—that is, a routine that is regular. *But* the child should also be able to make personal choices about how to spend his or her time too, in the early days, through adulthood, and later in old age. This balance is vital, and we are losing it.

More and more life is being accelerated until we rather fragile beings are not fitting comfortably into the whirl. Suicides and depression escalate.[8] Contentment with one's day, home, work, leisure, and relationships is disappearing. Little children are too often restless, and many are even drugged so they'll be able to concentrate. This is an alarm going off, or it should be seen as such. What are we getting wrong? A lot. Tragically the sweet, natural, not-too-much, not-too-little life that suits our frame (as the Bible calls our capacities, our limits) is being lost.

The sad thing too is that everyday routines are increasingly seen to be restrictive rather than life-allowing. Making things worse are the pressured, machine-like pace of life, the sterile living bases (they are not really homes), and the computer program-like design of "education." All these factors combined mean that we see large numbers of people coming from all continents who have been deconstructed. They have lost the habit of enjoyable, livable life. They drift, not even going to bed when they are tired. Wearily, they overstimulate their nerve endings with another full-color video. When they do go to bed, they can't relax or sleep. A medication is used for by some for relaxation; others use alcohol; others use sex. Bleary-eyed, they rush to get going the next morning. ("Is it morning?" they wonder. "When is the next weekend coming up?") Over-taut, under-contented, dissatisfied, they plunge on their destructive way. In Christian circles people will ask, "Why don't I experience a relationship with God?" Often they, we, have pushed and overstimulated ourselves to the point we aren't having an enjoyable relationship with *anyone*—let alone God. Meals are missed, hours wasted in a semi-comatose condition.

Am I exaggerating? No, not really. We all recognize this syndrome. Surely little children have to be losing out most of all. Tender, new little creatures, all ready to thrive in a stable life-giving home routine! They are treated like machines mentally, in a way not according to their frame physically, and they will be ridden over roughshod spiritually too. They cannot realize their potential, as we glibly say. They are living, breathing, made-to-love, made-to-be-righteous persons who eagerly stand ready to make relationships of all kinds.

Not giving them their heritage is, I believe, a terrible abuse, and it will result in lost lives. This lostness and confusion is first individual and then societal. Strong police forces, endless morality training in factory-like schools, all the programs that can be devised—nothing, *nothing* can replace the sweet content of a home where we can come back, put up our feet, and thank God.

As people think over how to spend their lives, time, and effort, all too often the only message they hear is that having a "good" career is why they've been educated. In this way they seek status, financial gain, or power as an acceptable life goal. I've heard of many women being belittled for choosing to devote themselves full time to family, home, and community life. "Well, what are you going to *do* when the children are old enough to go to school full time?" is a typical question. "*Do?*" Have we not heard, have we not seen that human life is a gift, a treasure worth tending?

Is it actually more valuable to push a pen on paper or buttons on a computer than to be expert in human life and its care? Is life more worthwhile because there is never time to pick wild blackberries and make a fruit crumble? Are *things* really more important than *people*? Will the warmth and wisdom of the expertise of caring for each other be handed on? Isn't this an amazingly interesting and complex life vocation on the one hand, and yet clear on the other?

I find it so. To me it seems an enormous privilege to be what my children call "Mum." I've found each stage full of challenge and interest.

Preparing a home to receive our first child,[9] I went to Lausanne and carefully bought fabric to make the room cheerful and home-like for her. I had fun planning the baby's care. We needed a dresser top with a pad for changing the baby and a chair where we'd both be comfortable and relaxed as we enjoyed breast-feeding. Nearer the time of delivery, I prepared a thermos so I could have a hot drink too in the middle of the night.

My sister, who was in America at the time, sent me a book by Adele Davis, *Let's Have Healthy Children.* I became interested in nutrition. I found that many health problems were related to nutritional factors. I carried on with the study of food and health; this knowledge was invaluable in providing healthy meals for family and L'Abri students. As I've always run on a low budget, I've been able to prepare meals that were nutritional yet inexpensive. Food preparation is a fascinating and useful hobby. As food is so universally appreciated, cooking is a field of expertise that gives a lot of rewards. There is the satisfaction of helping people to a more robust health and giving them pleasure.

It is satisfying to know enough to give tired, little children a healthy "nursery tea" with muffins or pancakes made with wheat germ and stone-ground whole wheat. Whether they are my children, my grandchildren, or other children, it's fun to see them enjoying it so much and know that every ounce is health-giving. I like to see them crunch down on freshly cut apple wedges with pleasure, just as I liked them when my mother made them for me. These efforts assure me that I am fairly expert in an essential area of life.

Older children clamor for the homemade yogurt many of us regularly make. They have all downed gallons of it through the years—with honey or homemade applesauce. College students return home to favorites; it is "job satisfaction" to see their eyes light up as they come into the kitchen and find their favorite home-made cinnamon rolls.

By now I'm not reading on food and nutrition so much, but I

still keep my eye open for new research. I try new ideas in cooking too—an area I never tire of. (Although I've sometimes wished the family could be put on vitamin pills for a few days so that a project could be finished!)

I've also become really good at speedy preparation after years of cooking. Not for me pie crusts (saturated fat, and it takes time). My family enjoys hot fruit crumbles instead.

Then while expecting my first baby, I started reading and learning more about another area that takes any amount of expertise—the human being. Babies, children, people—who says *they* aren't fascinating! And that is your business if you are a home and community caregiver. As we seek to serve human beings, we can read, study, and observe in order to grow in related knowledge. The field is broad, deep, and of great interest. It includes the spiritual, physical, and personal (emotional and intellectual) sides of human life. It includes both the individual and society.

Could there ever be such a fascinating vocation? When I was expecting this first child, my helpful "big sister" also sent me a thick book encouraging me to relax, enjoy my baby, and build up expertise as a mother of a family. This book was invaluable to me, as it strengthened my conviction that it was worth taking the time to learn about this unique baby, both in theory and practice. The book encouraged me not to let details such as having a picture-perfect home hamper me. It helped me see that having a balanced-enough day for myself was essential, such as napping myself while the baby napped or settling back and letting the baby suck as long as he wanted too while I rested.

This book also went on at length about the family as a community. It helped me to see my task as more than just giving my baby individual care for a certain length of time. I needed to think about the needs of each family member and about how adding a new member would work out practically in all our lives. The book portrayed this baby fitting into family life.[10]

I lapped this attitude up. Although I kept to the basic L'Abri pattern in my "job," I knew clearly that the baby and family (including myself) came first in my priorities. This book portrayed the mother's responsibilities and work as highly valuable, and yet maintained that she should not become the family drudge. I realized as I read that there would be various ways of doing things.

I enjoyed finding out all I could about the coming baby's needs. And when she came, I used her as my royal reason for all sorts of pleasant ways to spend my time. Because my dear baby loved nursing for so long, comfortably sucking on after the milk was perhaps not even a trickle, I had lots of time on my bed enjoying her, just drifting in and out of a relaxed state.[11] I'd prolong this delicious task with stacks of reading and cups of tea. In short, I made the most of the opportunity and excuse a baby gave me!

With subsequent babies the nature of these times changed. The new baby would be nursed, and it gave the current toddler a chance to be cuddled in the other arm while sitting on mother's bed next to her and having extra stories to listen to.

But don't think that nursing a baby kept me on my bed or in a quiet chair if that is not exactly where it suited me to be! One reason I continued nursing so long for each of four babies (eight to eighteen months) was because it is so easy, can be done anywhere, and can satisfy a hungry baby immediately in trains, planes, at a L'Abri discussion, out on a family hike to a remote beach, etc. I'd wear a loose top, pop baby under, and most people were none the wiser. (In any case I was glad to demonstrate easy child care.) Naturally, the baby's health physically and emotionally were also considerations. But nursing is not a big deal. A child thrives and enjoys a similar bond with the mother who bottle-feeds, if necessary. This is true as long as she usually is the one the baby snuggles up to contentedly.

Yes, the full-time mother or parent occupation is enjoyable as well as valuable and interesting! Because children need a regular, gentle routine and life, we who serve them also reap benefits. Who would not like a job where you can sit barefoot in the shade of a tree on cool grass in the home garden or a park, enjoying a summer afternoon? What a job! And then homemaking is one of the few occupations/professions with such variety. The child and family changes; there are new challenges to rise to. So in addition to a health-giving stability (of routine and life), the job is a fascinating kaleidoscope of experiences too.

This book is far too short a space to extol the varied areas of knowledge and understanding I've explored as I've been privileged to be a caregiver and people-server. As an occupational therapy student in a small college in Oxford, I had already enjoyed the field of human design and function, both the physical and emotional makeup. Such interests go with the homemaker's profession, this vocation. We don't have to read about all the areas related to our occupation. However, as we become experienced and knowledgeable, we also value what we are doing more and more. This in turn means that we encourage others to put prime time, attention, and gifts into serving "the glory of the usual." Homemaking should receive its due honor.

It is commonplace at this time in our history for the occupation of full-time homemaking or serving-people-and-community work to be sneered at, called menial, uninteresting, or drudgery. This is almost incredible when you stop to think about it! Making a home is hard work, often using every fiber of our being and all our energy and emotional capacity. But so do other worthwhile professions. It is also rather strange that only the drudgery side is seen when our job has been facilitated by washing machines, electric stoves, and other technology.

The devaluing blow to homes and communities comes at a time when people, both men and women, see their worth more and more gauged by their success in career, academic work, and/or earned income. This evaluation is, not surprisingly, the other side of the materialistic age's coin. More and more people suffer a sense of personal worthlessness. Parents and friends push people to enter the arena competing for earned worth. Persons push themselves beyond their limit.

Sadly, we as believing, practicing Christians can also easily be swept up by this all-prevailing attitude. Note that we too may see the "usual" in life, the ordinary, as worthless rubbish. Christians can be made to feel they must be super-active in church or mission-related areas every spare minute in order to score points as "successful" Christians. People worry that they don't perform as well as an evangelist or a Mother Theresa. Or maybe they expect a spiritual cloud-nine experience all the time. Once again we have to say that this is an area in which balance is needed.

There are two dangers. We can do *too little*, or we can push and be *frantic activists* whose little "tree" of personal or home life is withering up. A big practical help in getting all this right enough and workable has been that mothers were liberated from various areas of the rat race, including battle-like schedules, to be contented keepers of hearth and home. Homemaking was usually seen as a valuable and necessary contribution to society. And indeed it *is* "full-time Christian work."

One casualty of the confused work patterns (that see house-keeping and child care merely as chores) is domestic peace and contentment. This is a terrible loss for us all. Contentment often falters when mothers full time at home are consistently plagued with the question, "When will you get back to *work* again?" The return to office or job is thus perceived to be a "real" job, not like being a drudge at home.

How different from this attitude was the contentment I read about and experienced myself—first as I enjoyed early childhood with a mother who found fulfillment in her home and family, later when I had the joy of seeing what it was like myself. Perhaps this fulfillment and *contentment with the usual* is one vital ingredient in life that is missing these days.

Contentment comes when we accept our own or our situation's limitations. The truth that nothing in life is perfect is always with us. Of course, we actively seek creative ways to change ourselves or a situation when that is appropriate, and we use creativity, problem-solving skills, thoughtfulness, and common sense.

However, to be contented, we need to look at what we do have (not at what we don't), give thanks, and cheerfully make the best of our marriage, children, house, and each day, season, and chapter in life. We learn to enjoy the ordinary elements in life and see them as precious. This is one of the keys to life. Some people find it more natural than others. But we can cultivate contentment; we can encourage it in ourselves and in each other. When we are believers, we should pray for it.

Contentment, giving thanks, enjoyment of each day as it is—these together are a pearl of great price. This attitude gives health and life. It is good.

11

❧

Choose Wisely and Leave Time for the Daily Rhythms

There is a danger in reading about the way one person, family, or group does things and what they've experienced. Each one of us and the lives we lead are as different as snowflakes are unique. Yet we all have certain things in common. So we need to clarify to ourselves and to each other what should be the same for all, if possible, and yet see how different these commonalties can look when worked out in real life.[1]

In this book I'm trying to do both. I've used God's universal reality as the big picture and explanation of all life and creation. In this worldview each person's life, although no longer perfect, has inestimable value. We don't have to earn worth; we are each one precious. God has created us to have a relationship with Himself—with a future that transcends the seen world and death. This reality is contrary to today's materialistic evaluation of individual persons, their worth, and their everyday lives. If true, this view explains *all* of life and reality.

Our society is currently going full speed ahead in devaluing human life. No longer is a tiny unborn child seen as precious; it has no legal protection. Increasingly, this has led people to think that those who are defective should not be allowed to live. This grim attitude is a reminder of the extermination camps in World War II.

There too life was extinguished—the aged, the imperfect, along with the Jewish people. Many were denied their right to life.

With such attitudes prevalent today, how can we expect young adults to sacrificially cherish dependent life? They are hardened by the crass demand that whether a child lives or dies depends on the mother's *wanting* a baby just then or on the baby being without problems. Unfairly, the father has no say; he is prevented by law from protecting his unborn child's life. This human baby is no longer respected as having any intrinsic right to life and care.

What a strange, distorted society we have become! While abortion goes on in one medical department, another will be trying by any means to supply a consumer's demand for a child as a possession. Any sense of a baby's life being a most sacred trust is disappearing. Gone for most people is the knowledge of *God's* approval and design as we protect, serve, and nurture a child or children, whatever the personal cost.

All this leads to an attitude that is damaging to the children who are "wanted" and who do survive the first days of life after conception. Even God-fearing believers can be trapped in a utilitarian view of the child (and then of other persons). We increasingly demand that our progeny fit the vision of "what we want." We say, "I want a boy and a girl." Also, "They must be totally healthy," or "I can only have a baby when *I've* finished five years' work." And then, "They should look attractive to me and later on conform to my plans." This leads, for example, to the damaging insistence that a nonacademic child be guided toward college.

Obviously such attitudes are not new in human thought, but the way we are treating human life, generally speaking, is rubbing off on us all. This behavior partly explains another startling fact. In the last decades as developmental science has clarified how *important* the first years are for each child's future intelligence, welfare, and wholeness, we have had a parallel *decline* in respect for society's most natural and best full-time caregiver—the mother who devotes much of her time to this task. We have now reached the place where people actually feel pity for a mother "stuck at home" with two or three youngsters. Her hard work, skills, and growing wisdom are devalued. The entire human community then loses out.

While there is less and less respect for full-time parenting as one of the most valuable services rendered to the human race, our culture has also devalued any careers associated with early child care or education. We seem to be prepared to spend a big wedge of the national budget on social rehabilitation programs, health clinics, and so on (all terribly costly), while failing to attract top-quality persons to early child care. Caregivers are often low-paid members of society: This reflects little integrity, for we know how vital these years are. I've known young people at the end of their school years who have been officially advised: "You can do better for yourself than go into nursery or early childhood education." I have been ashamed to hear Christians advocating this ungodly view. Are we crazy? Schizoid? Do we plan to produce whole nations of disturbed or poorly educated adults?

As well as our confusion about children's lives needing to be convenient to us, we have the expectation that our marriages should suit us too—immediately! This is all unreal. None of us or our lives are all that good, satisfactory, or perfect—not our spouses, children, or anyone else either. We will be disappointing to each other in big or little ways in many areas. For instance, jobs could always be better. If we are Christians, we'll find we'd imagined church would be an exception, and it isn't! This demanding attitude leads us to dissatisfaction, discontent, grumbling, complaining, and sometimes giving up. As we discard this and then that, we are throwing away our own life's opportunities. We are left with sawdust.

We won't always like the choices we've made. We won't always like our resulting situations. We dream of a *pot-of-gold life* at the end of the rainbow! This tendency is like waiting for something good to happen and forgetting we need to put in hard work, effort, and time to obtain the results we'd like. Instead we need to watch for small successes along the way and develop patience, skill, and wisdom. Bit by bit change can come with prayer and perseverance.

When we recognize the upside-down trend of thought and action in our cultures now, perhaps we'll begin to see how the opposite view was able to produce in so many people's lives contentment, joy, fun, enjoyment, and a proper pride in the worth of their lives. When people generally accepted their everyday rooted life with its limitations, responsibilities, and challenges, they actually ended up much happier and fruitful people. Such rooted acceptance and active response still works today.

God's commands are the way to life and goodness. In them are love, safety, and satisfaction. People who try to follow His commands and fit into His design aren't constantly whining, "This is not what I want!"[2] Satisfaction means *carrying through with the situation that is our life, just where we are.*

Biblically, *serving each other is one of the highest priorities in life.* And in God's sight children are to have our special consideration. Their welfare is more important than designing a new rocket or computer, for instance. Faithfulness to a child's life and other promises made (such as in a marriage relationship) are counted by God as reflecting His pure character, trustworthiness, perfection. He tells us that *these* are the things that are His will for our lives. Joy, peace, and thankfulness (the opposite of grumbling, dissatisfaction, discontent, complaining) are fruits of the Spirit and also evidence of a person who makes the best of life's ingredients, gets on with the job, and daily looks out to enjoy the "good bits." *This is how abundant life flowers.*

While one person is always miserable about a husband with an unreasonable temper and a cramped house, another with the same and worse glories in and enjoys the sight of trees outside the window. Her eyes shine as she describes watching a sunset. Abundant life bubbles up like a spring of pure water in all sorts of lives. Blessed are those who learn to enjoy what is good in *their* everyday. They are happy who learn to appreciate the value of the good-enough job they are accomplishing in their own humdrum, flawed life. Glad are we when we don't fret about what cannot be changed at that time. People such as these paint beautiful living pictures in the frame of their lives.

The way to build up contentment is to go ahead and accept the result of unchangeable circumstances, including poor choices and their consequences—and make the best of it. I say, "Okay, this is my life, spouse, child, area to live, body. I'll work with it." It is very like preparing a creative meal out of the limited ingredients you do have instead of fussing over what you don't have available. Instructively, cooks with few ingredients have often been the most creative. (There are a few situations in the home where God's Word certainly gives us an open door for leaving. We don't have to put up with everything. I am not talking about those things.)

I want to address the reality that we'll have to adapt ideas and ideals to fit who we actually are and what our lives are like, while carefully keeping what is morally essential for human life. After digressing to attend to this necessary subject, I'd like to return to practicalities in the home and in bringing up children. Probably because so many people have lost the "inner skeletal structure" that God's truth gives to our lives, they have lost confidence in their own common sense. To make it worse, more and more of us no longer live in settled communities with the wisdom of tried-and-true traditions. We may have no one to whom we can turn for advice. So we tend to turn to books, listen to speakers, or attend classes that tell us exactly what to do in every part of life.

As I am a Christian, the ideas and methods I'll mention will be ones I've heard of in Christian circles, but such directions are sought for and produced by all ideologies. Jesus said that we are not to create burdens for other people to bear. I have been sad to see that some of the "Christian" instructions, instead of helping us in our own lives, discourage us by telling us we have to do things that in fact can't work for us. Of course, *we are never to tamper with God's righteous commands.* They are best always—the only good—the Ten Commandments *and* all of Scripture. But many of the practicalities in life are personal choices or cultural; these do not involve God's commands. In these there is freedom for people who wish to honor God's design.

As an example, look at full-time mothering. Some women have been told that to be a "good Christian" or a "responsible mother," they should never go out of the home to work. Others have decreed that contraception should never be used to space children.[3] Still others are sure that they are God-instructed to proclaim that all children should always be educated at home. Others say, "Never! Children from believing homes should always be in a Christian school." A different group of citizens believe that "being in the world and not of it" means your children must always go to the neighborhood school, whether it is good for them or not.

But in real life we all face different circumstances. Detailed choices must be made individually. It is no good staying at home to parent full time if the family goes hungry! All such directives are extra to the biblical infrastructure or principles.

The subject of homemaking by a lone parent is a good place to illustrate a variety of choices while still leaving "the beads on the string" at home. Obviously each person needs to adapt a basic plan so it can fit his or her own situation. Maybe a mother will not have the luxury of an everyday walk with her toddler, for instance. Maybe she won't even be able always to feed her infant herself or rest enough after a birth to be strong and well.

In these circumstances, some more difficult than others, *choices need to be made*.[4] I've had friends who, single-handed, have brought up children well enough, with warmly welcoming homes. They planned how they personally could best manage in different ways at different times. Some choices are individual: A solution in real life cannot be ladled out like soup. All of us in every stage of life need to keep the basic "tree trunk" of daily life stable and yet adapt and choose creatively in details. This principle is for all of us.

Some of my single friends were able to stay at home full time with their children. Although the ones I've known who did this had to then manage on a low budget, they decided it was possible for them and worth it. Money is not the only problem. Being alone with small children around the clock is terribly draining unless you are part of a neighborhood or community network of friends who help each other.

The single parent will find it helpful to have the child in part-time care two mornings or afternoons or so a week from early on. The child benefits by getting used to trusting other capable, kind, and friendly adults. At around three years of age, children benefit from the company of other small children who can play together in a group. A well-run play group two or three mornings a week is ideal for any child and parent in my opinion. Some mothers run self-help groups in their own homes on a regular rotation for four or five children.

It is important also regularly to have a trusted baby-sitter so that the parent can go out and enjoy his or her friendships and interests. Remember, in any circumstance the home is to be the dependable fabric of life. This means that both the parent and the child must be woven into the fabric. No one person is the center; each life matters. All children have too much weight to bear if a parent's essential welfare is sacrificed for their sake. If we dry up or go to pieces, we aren't much good anyway. Children do best when the adult needs are met in the home life and routine. We can never do everything that we'd like to for a child, family, or home. So we need never feel guilty at taking basic time and resources for ourselves. Our well-being is vitally important for theirs.

It is especially important when these choices are being made to keep in clear view the framework that makes a home and life work well. Thus, when we think about whether we should or could change things so as to be able to go to work part or full time or take on volunteer work or other activities, *we should make sure the basic fabric is covered first*. By this I mean a routine of regular meals together, appropriate bedtimes, and rest or leisure for each member, including time together and individual time. Essential too is the weekly day off from labor or the work routine (the Sabbath). This day should not be destroyed by being turned into a "waste can" full of home jobs!

The younger the children, the more they benefit from a full-time parent or other committed person who loves and values them. On the other hand, other people are actually as refreshed by part-time work as by adding leisure activities. Some of the time away can be work in this case and still count as a "break." Children in trustworthy hands and a good situation certainly don't mind what the parent is doing while they are there!

In fact, many parents who have a perfectly stable relationship with their spouses also choose part-time work for one parent for the same reason: They enjoy it and return ready to put more energy and interest into the home, or the extra income is necessary. When we can do so, we should ensure that such part-time commitment actually enhances our lives and does not put a strain on the energy and time needed to enjoy homemaking. For instance, the job should not require long hours. If we spread ourselves too thinly, we can end up not doing anything well.

Then there are many people, either single or married, who have to continue with a full-time job in order to supply even the basics such as lodging, food, heat, and thrift shop clothes. If we do feel it is right or necessary to choose work, then how a child is cared for is a huge concern.

Children under ten need as homelike an atmosphere as possible. Sometimes they can stay in their own home, and their caregiver comes to them. This arrangement can be ideal if the caregiver is mature and able to create continuity in the home atmosphere and day's routine. But with immature or uncommitted caregivers, or those who stay less than five or six years, the arrangement can be destructive to the children's welfare. (The traditional nanny devoted her life to a family of children from the first child's birth onwards.)

Sometimes grandparents are gladly willing to give up their leisure and give the little ones a daytime home of love and care. It is worth it to find an apartment and job near such relatives! Grandparent care is an age-old tradition that can work well. I've also met an inner-city aunt who loved not only making her apartment the daytime home for two or three nephews and nieces, but she home-schooled them too!

It is sometimes possible to locate a mature woman living locally whose life's work of homemaking is so much a part of her that she will add a child or two and be able to love and care for them as an adopted aunt or grandma. Many women who need financial help but who themselves choose to be full time at home undertake this job as their choice. As in all arrangements (including a mother at home with their own family), this option can work out superbly or terribly. Just read Dickens for examples of the latter! A small child is vulnerable.

I've talked with a woman who has a highly skilled job related to art. She married and was glad when she became a mother. She has been able to combine children, homemaking, and her profession comfortably. Near her workplace (a short drive from home) lived a motherly woman who opened her heart and home to the woman's children from babyhood up. As the work was virtually next door and flexible, the mother could come in and out as needed, even breast-feed the babies several times a day. These fortunate children never had any other caregiver. They are part of a secure and home-loving family. The mother's work can be left off for a few days when a sick child needs to stay at home. When the little ones started school, the mother could pop them on her bicycle to take them there before going to work herself and then collect them in the afternoon too. She has energy enough for both work and home. It has worked well.

I have friends who are mothers and also medical doctors. These women have made choices different from each other's—good ones for themselves, their homes, and their families. (Obviously the same sort of plans can be made in any area of work.) Some have made home and family their full-time occupation. It has been utterly satisfying. A few of these mothers home-schooled their children; others have sent children to school.

Then there are doctor-mothers who have worked part time. Several became school doctors and only worked for a couple of days a week. Another friend worked part time in women's health clinics. One has always corrected medical exams at home as her medical work. Once I met a top specialist who decided that she did not want that pressure as a wife and then as a mother. She gave up the status that went with being a consultant and took on a less prestigious job in a local hospice. It was a job that gave her flexibility and could also be part time if needed.

In contrast, I knew another mother, a top oncologist, who did carry on. She had her working hours arranged so she could be at home with her one little girl when she was not in school.

We all have different levels of energy. We must not try to do something just because someone else can cope with it. What works well for one parent or family can be a disaster for another.

As Christians, when we have these sorts of choices to make, we start with commonsense considerations and prayer. We take time, staying open as we listen to other people's wisdom, to understand ourselves and our situations clearly and biblically, whatever others think.[5] If after we follow plan A, we see that our family members or ourselves are more and more stressed, irritable, or not sleeping well, we should pocket our pride and think and pray again. Perhaps we'll decide we've learned something important and will back down from the whole arrangement. Or maybe a few small changes are all that is needed.

An important point—we cannot tell other people what *they* should do about making such choices in their lives. I know of a long-respected missionary society that has a history of fine Christian work. They had a policy that a missionary director told families what to do in such situations. The parents had no choice. The mother was always to be a "full-time missionary." That policy is reasonable and important as long as the idea of being "full time" can be lived out in different ways. But, sadly, the organization mandated that parents send each and every child to faraway boarding schools, regardless of local circumstances, the child's need, or anything else. Although some children not only coped with this program but thrived, others have been scarred for life.

I feel that it is especially wrong to be orphaned in Jesus' name. The choice of children's schooling is exactly the sort of decision parents need to make themselves. They are close to and responsible for each child in a unique way. They cry out to God for their children's welfare as no one else does.

For a second reason this mission society's policy is troubling. Surely in a pagan or post-Christian culture, modeling a Christian family is of vital importance. Living out Christianity is powerful and should demonstrate what is being taught to children. The family is the natural place to start. Homes are also where hospitality can be given, and hospitality is the basis for much Christian evangelism in the New Testament. Here in the home we find the relationships we are told to build up; here we find a place to practice love and demonstrate what is right.

For those of us who respect the Bible and look to it for guidance in principles, 1 Timothy is important. The main subject being addressed is church leaders—thus the passage is about Christian work. We find husband-wife teams responsible together for church groups meeting in their homes. Chapter 3 says that the wife is an active member of the team. She needs certain traits to be able to fill her position. Such wives must "in the same way . . . be women worthy of respect, not malicious talkers but temperate and trustworthy in everything" (3:11). What the husband does at home matters too. A deacon "must manage his children and household well" (3:12). So husband and wife are working together professionally as church leaders, and also as parents, homemakers. Both aspects of their job matter in the new Christian outposts. Both aspects are part of their Christian work and witness. Both these areas are included in how they serve Christ. "Those who have served well gain an excellent standing and great assurance in their faith in Christ Jesus" (3:13).

In chapter 5 we come to a discussion I've found fascinating and full of clarifying light. The subject is widowed women, believers, who in that society were freer than others to serve the Lord in special ways. This is not a new concept in the New Testament. In the Gospels we find Anna, a widow, who had dedicated her time to prayer daily in the temple. She prayed for her people and awaited the Messiah.[6] She obviously was also in contact with other active local believers. She was known in many circles. One of the great moments of scriptural drama occurs, of course, when she and Simeon, both aged, are rewarded by personally getting to see the salvation of the Lord.[7] He was a priest dedicated to daily service in God's house. But Anna, because she was widowed, had been free to choose to fill her days with prayer too! Their service and its reward is made parallel. It is fascinating to note that she is afterwards the one who is in touch with people in the community. She is the one to go and tell them the good news—the first evangelist.

In a similar way, there is in the book of Timothy a group of widows who could do what we'd call full-time Christian work as they were free of other ties. It seems to be a combination of prayer and what we'd call personal and community work. Surely there is no reason why such women should not serve this way if they are suitable; new Christian communities badly need the services of mature, believing women. Two verses here grab my attention. "If a widow has children or grandchildren, these should learn first of all to put their religion into practice by *caring for their own family* and so repaying their parents and grandparents, *for this is pleasing to God*" (1 Tim. 5:4, italics mine). We find that if there is family to care for, that is a priority and pleasing to God.

The next verse pertinent to this discussion applies to everybody in the church—men, women, old, young, single, married, widowed: "Give the people these instructions, too, so that no one may be open to blame. If anyone does not provide for his relatives, and especially for his immediate family, he has denied the faith and is worse than an unbeliever" (1 Tim. 5:7-8).

Strong words indeed. They should make each of us ask what we must do before God in order to "provide for our relatives, and especially for [our] immediate family." This last is addressed to men and women, as most of the Bible is. There are exceedingly few places that address only men or only women, and this epistle has several of the few gender-related instructions.

The next instructions to the women who are widowed throw light on all women's lives. Here we see a practical feminine slant. What is included in serving family and neighbor in love? What does God mention? We find an answer in the next description of women who are over retirement age (here 60—1 Tim. 5:9). Which ones qualify as examples? Those that have been faithful to their husbands and are well known for their good deeds. These are listed as bringing up children, showing hospitality, washing the feet of saints, helping those in trouble, and devoting their time to all kinds of practical everyday good deeds.

Such a life is not a self-centered and nuclear-family-centered "suburban" woman's life. Nor is it a pretty Victorian life of ease. On one hand the widow gives herself to devoted prayer, on the other, to all practical community services, so to speak. Counseling; pastoral work; emergency services; nursing; care of the aged, orphans, the troubled in society, or a missionary's needs; welcoming the refugee and misfit or stranger in difficulties—all these jobs and more were among those done by these women at different times in different situations! They would listen, answer questions, teach— all sorts of things on top of managing a well-run household as the first priority.

Of course, none of the women who are our examples did *all* of these things! I'm sure that when the babies were coming thick and fast, caring for them and their homes was plenty. But by the time they'd reached sixty, between them they had plenty of scope for their gifts. They'd become the wise experts of the human community and individuals. We know from the New Testament that some women had gifts of teaching in the community and church as well. They also prayed publicly and worked with Paul and others to build up the new groups of believers. Others were businesswomen who supported the church with their profitable enterprises.

The New Testament always portrays the Christian church as a body—some people have one designed "best place," some another. All churches, societies, cities, and times in history can use the uniquely feminine work of caring for people's and society's needs, but not at the expense of the home. The youngest widows aren't necessarily to skip the stage in life of being responsible for a home and the everyday task of bringing up children. They are advised to marry in this passage and context. Among other things, home-making provides the training for more complex work. In other discussions Paul gives different advice to the unmarried, saying that they do well to stay free of everyday cares and not to marry![8] This advice, incidentally, provides a good example of the complexity involved in a person's choices and our individual responsibility to choose what is right for us before God. Sometimes one course of action is right; at another time or for another person, another choice is appropriate.

In 1 Timothy 5 the argument is that some of the younger women may at first get carried away with altruism and *promise* to serve others practically, thinking that they don't need to consider their personal desires. The warning here is that it is best not to make a commitment we will find hard to keep. Paul reminds us that we might start feeling our "sensual desires" again. These are not wrong; God created our senses—in this way, a woman's desires draw her to a man and marriage, just as a man's draw him toward a woman. The Bible never says a woman's place in marriage is only to fulfill her husband's needs. No—while she is to serve and fulfill him, he equally serves her and is to learn to fulfill her needs sexually and in all the other ways.[9] The wife serves the husband, and the husband serves the wife. Both serve the children.

Anyway, here we have a wise caution toward well-meaning younger persons making spiritually motivated promises not in keeping with their actual makeup. These younger women are advised: "I counsel younger widows to marry, to have children, to manage their homes and to give the enemy no opportunity for slander" (1 Tim. 5:14).

It is also worth noting the warning that reminds us of the old proverb: "The devil finds work for idle hands." The danger warned against here is that when women don't have enough responsibilities or lack self-discipline, they may gossip or become busybodies, "saying things they ought not to." A godly feminine goal[10] is to be other-centered and serving, but to be professionally confidential about it. When you become involved in the lives of your family members and of those around you, secrets and personal confidences come your way. We respect other people when we are mature and never treat their struggles as something to be talked over or told to others as news (not even passed on as a "prayer request").[11]

When one is a counselor, doctor, teacher, lawyer, or a pastor, professional confidentiality goes with the position. The keepers of home and community are instructed to do no less. They too are supposed to be able to respect boundaries, not overstepping by making up other people's minds for them. Planning for others is never on the agenda. We help other people to come to their own decisions.

Missionary work is not the only calling in Christian work men and women have. Closer to home for most people are the requests to help in a local church congregation or local mission projects (such as crisis pregnancy centers and so on). It is right that all of us share these responsibilities. How and what we do is once again a matter for individual thought, common sense, and prayer. In this area also we can receive a lot of pressure to neglect our basic home-life routines. On the other hand, we hear and see a lot of propaganda telling us that our personal comfort and safety are priorities; we should *never* stretch ourselves. Both extremes are wrong. The choices we have to make in paid and unpaid work are not simple. It helps to remember that we cannot do everything we'd like to *or* are asked to do. It helps to "remember our frame"—the real person that is tired out after a few hours of work at home or elsewhere, the real person that needs sleep, rest, food, etc.—and a home that needs care and time.

This chapter has been first of all addressing questions individuals have in trying to best provide for and care for their own family of children. A single parent will be facing extra emotional and practical challenges. These parents can be made to feel guilty no

matter which choice they make! I've heard people wrongly criticized for staying at home full time and not being productive
enough financially. Then I've heard others criticized for having
somebody else care for their children so they can study, have
breaks, or work!

Then the chapter addressed some questions relating to
Christian work. Caring for life at home (with or without children)
is Christian work. It can also be the "facility and staff" for the wide
range of all people-related work, which is also "full-time service."

The general effect of taking on any extra work outside the
home is the same whether it is paid or unpaid. We need to keep
checking to see that it is according to our personal capacity (or
"frame") and that the home has the attention due to it.

The home is to be like the house safely built on a rock, because
enough time and resources have been devoted to everyday, ordinary life. This house is stable, with continuity; it's sure, dependable,
and built on the only true foundation—Christ. The prodigal child
cannot return home unless the home carries on whether children
are there or not. Jesus cannot comfort us when He says that He goes
ahead beyond death through the Resurrection to prepare a place for
us, unless we understand that such a settled vision of life is good.
We cannot give this our abstract approval, as to an idea; *we are
meant to demonstrate abundant life in the place where we live now—our
everyday lives.*

Single. Married. With children. Without. Old. Young. We all
face our own particular choices. Our lives have a particular pattern
and should be at least a pale reflection of His life. Our "places"
should be a bit like His place.

Although there are many other areas to discuss, we'll return to
the care of children when a parent or both parents work. When
making choices, it is of the utmost importance to remember that the
sweetness of home life cannot be purchased. Having many things[12]
does not make a good home or make people happy. On the other
hand, poverty is a terrible life-destroying enemy. God makes it clear

that He hates the effect of poverty in people's lives. He also hates injustice, the cold wind of indifference, and lack of love.[13]

Most of us need to work to provide enough money for a secure home. In the traditional family, the husband has been the main provider. Adequate, healthful housing is a basic need. On the other hand, today we are led to believe that we need more than we actually do. It is definitely not worth all the stress and the disadvantage of not having an at-home parent just to provide extra rooms, a big yard, and so on. There is a lot to recommend the frugality of a relatively simple lifestyle. It can be character-building to have to share rooms, for instance. Having less, with good planning, can mean fewer complications in life!

Possession of material goods has to be one of the areas for individual, thoughtful choice. A bigger and nicer home has its benefits, of course, but is it worth so much juggling of time and energy that there is never enough left for abundant life to flower from home's routines? The price is terribly high if it means constant stress.

Many other "needs" are perceived needs only. Although it may be right to put in hard work for various reasons, buying an impressive car or always having new clothes is not a valid reason. Although such material things are certainly not wrong in themselves (and we can be thankful and enjoy them when we are among the few on God's earth who have such luxuries), still it would not be right to sacrifice our home life and well-being for their temporary use. *Things* are not our eternal possessions! Nor is the status of a "successful" career. All these things are short term only; they will rust or wear out, or thieves will steal them—and then we die. Jesus said we are "fools" to make things or position our priority.[14]

In contrast to the foolishness of piling up possessions in this life, Jesus said that God's judgment is upon us all when we put stumbling blocks in front of "little ones."[15] In other words, smoothing the path in front of children is worthwhile. Letting little children grow up in the care of constantly changing adults is definitely an emotional and intellectual disadvantage (or "stumbling block").

Jesus always puts people's good first; things are only to serve people's needs or are gifts for life's enjoyment.

When I, at fifty-seven years of age, remember Jesus' example, a chill shadow is cast over my heart. I recognize that I am a sinner, and this has harmed others. On top of this, I did not always make wise choices or have the right attitudes toward children in my care, my husband, my wider family, friends, and neighbors. It is the same for all of us fallen persons (and one good reason for midlife crisis). Jesus has told us to love the Lord our God with all our heart, mind, and soul, and then our neighbor (including family). We have all failed and need God's forgiveness and other people's. The Holy Spirit is promised to us to help us in our lives and in the carrying out of our good intentions.

The *Book of Common Prayer* (mentioned previously[16]) has a general confession for every morning time of prayer and for each evening. Through the centuries such a prayer of confession has exposed the need of individuals for God's forgiveness:

Almighty and most merciful Father, we have erred and strayed from thy ways like lost sheep. We have followed too much the devices and desires of our own hearts. We have offended against thy holy laws. We have left undone those things which we ought to have done; And we have done those things which we ought not to have done; And there is no health in us. But thou, O Lord, have mercy upon us, miserable offenders. Spare thou them, O God, which confess their faults. Restore thou them that are penitent; According to thy promises declared unto mankind in Christ Jesu our Lord. And grant, O most merciful Father, for his sake; That we may hereafter live a godly, righteous, and sober[17] life, To the glory of thy Holy Name. Amen.

Part of the response to the confession above is:

Wherefore let us beseech him to grant us true repentance, and his Holy Spirit, that those things may please him, which we

do at this present; and that the rest of our life hereafter may
be pure and holy; so that at last we may come to his eternal
joy, through Jesus Christ our Lord. Amen.

Unless we are at the end of our last illness, there is always time
to put this into practice in the "now" of everyday. I know of a
retired missionary who lived in a residential home for the elderly,
who actively kept up with caring for others until the end of her
days. As well as a life of prayer, she had time to give, to listen and
respond, to brew cups of tea or write a letter for someone who
could no longer do so. Just as when she'd been a "missionary" in
her younger life, she found plenty of spiritual need-related work
here too. She read books, including the Bible, to people. She carried on.

If by not choosing a high-pressure job or lifestyle, we have
more time to remain healthy and balanced ourselves, serve our
home, bring up children, be good neighbors (be "salt and light" in
the community), we should consider that seriously. Why sacrifice
taking care of human life for the trinkets of extra possessions or
prestige? On the other hand, this very service to other people can
mean hardship.[18] We must, in any case, take care to live within our
small human limits.

These considerations are not for women only. Many men find
that they must say no to a promotion, job transfer, or demand if
they are to do their part in home and community life. It is clear to
many working men and women that their time and energy are in
danger of being totally absorbed, with nothing left for at-home relationships or responsibilities. Single persons of all ages should allow
enough time for their lives at home. Good communities are made
up of everybody. We all face choices.

A good husband is not only concerned for his children, but he
also considers his wife. Several years ago, I met a physician who
chose to stay in a neighborhood family practice so as to be able to
design a more flexible weekly schedule than he could have had as
a specialist. This schedule gave him good time at home every day

and in the local community. He did not want to be like his father who had been a virtual stranger at home, leaving early, coming home after the children's bedtime. In contrast, this physician wanted to know and enjoy his little children. He and his wife also desired to be part of the community, which included their church. He scheduled his week so that two days a week he took on the home's care. It was then that his wife was able to finish her commitment at the university. She was refreshed mentally and could develop her talents. It seemed a balanced plan. Since then I've seen other such arrangements work.

In fact, at L'Abri something like this worked well for Ranald and myself. He enjoyed being his children's main caregiver for a couple of hours at a time on a regular basis. I'd benefit from leaving what seemed like "too abundant a skirmish of life" in our apartment to lecture, lead a discussion, tutor, and, when children were older, go away to speak at conferences.[19] When we had a sabbatical, he asked me to teach him to cook too, and he irons beautifully. (This he enjoys, as I do.) These days he shares more of the house-cleaning too.

Together we participated in the education of our children, both when they went to school and in the years when one or another was fully educated at home. He and I both read, discussed, and sometimes helped with homework, whether the children had other teachers or not.[20] Ranald assisted in musical subjects and engaged the children in music-making. I oversaw much craft-related work and specialized in helping our dyslexic children with reading and writing. Ranald helps with Latin; I do the French.

We've certainly had a clear division of labor. I've enjoyed being primarily responsible for the home's daily routine, atmosphere, and life. Generally speaking, apart from the meals and story times, putting children to bed and days off together, Ranald fitted in the extras as he could. He was a pastor or elder in the church for many years, as well as being responsible for the L'Abri work in a more total way than I have been.

Among our acquaintances are a very few couples where the

wife has temporarily or permanently had the main bread-winning job in the family. Other friends have sadly "lost" their wives (or husbands) through death. Some men seem to adapt well enough to being the main homemaker when they have flexible jobs that can fit in. But in the main, it is very feminine to be creative and capable at home.

When we start to juggle other responsibilities along with making a home, what must not be sacrificed? In times of crisis, such as a flood or when someone is dying, even the most basic must sometimes be neglected. But beyond that is another level of essential well-being that should be aimed for.

First of all, *we need a home base* that is of sound construction and keeps us protected from the elements. It should have light and air and be as pleasant as possible. This home needs at least an efficient cooking area and a pleasant place for the dining table. It may be that the main "living" area is here, and if so, the room needs a relaxing and welcoming grouping of comfortable chairs, couches, and lights for reading, conversation, and other activities. Asian cultures show us excellent ways of utilizing smaller spaces. The Koreans heat the floors, so this comfort welcomes parents and their children as they spread out mats and have plenty of roll-away, sitting-comfortably-together space! A Korean mother surrounded by children, books, toys, or homework on a colorful rug looks so cozy!

Then we all need sleeping space. In the West we are accustomed to a separate room for the parents, and this seems to us a good idea—in fact, a necessary idea! Children after puberty should have a separate room for the two genders. Typical row houses and cottages have three bedrooms—one for the parents, one for girls, the other for boys. This is surely a basic model! Nowadays we expect a bathroom with hot water. One will do perfectly adequately for a family of up to six or eight people. In such instances an extra toilet downstairs is a help.[21] Of course, if either parent works from the home, it may help to have a room for an office. (Rooms can do double duty, if necessary—bedrooms are often wasted space during the day.)

It is wonderful to have even a small yard. Little children find it satisfying to have a place for their sandbox and swing. But it would not be worth it for children to give up the serenity and enjoyment of a "not-too-full life" with an at-home mother just to provide such an extra. Far better than a garden and a harassed parent juggling too much stress is an apartment with a relatively relaxed mother's care and the fun of going out to the park with her every afternoon.

When I was visiting a young grandchild in an apartment in an American city, I saw many good ideas put into effect. A sandbox on the balcony. A homemade cardboard walk-in playhouse in the living room. Every day a walk along sidewalks to parks to play, including time to pick up pine cones and sticks. Time to climb, jump, and explore. Also in this city were good libraries for children and a Discovery Museum. There a child had a wide variety of extra play and space possibilities to expand the apartment's range—climbing up and sliding down, dressing up, an art room, science hands-on fun, a train set, etc. There was also a nearby swimming pool and just a short forty minutes away (with Daddy on weekends) were forest trails and countryside. The family went on lots of hikes. The apartment home worked well used like this.

All persons do need an adequate home. This includes those of us who are single, of course. Then we all need *enough time for a home-based routine*. This routine should be balanced so that necessary parts of the day, such as getting dressed or packing a school lunch, are not frantic.

There should be *regular meals together daily*, at least one. The preparation of food is part of home life. So is the friendly enough-time-for-each-other atmosphere. *Chores should usually be shared.* Even my non-domestic father used to wash the Sunday dishes with his children, as did many of my friend's fathers who were pastors. Nowadays most fathers are much more part of the home team—a good thing. The main thing to remember is that we serve each other.

Many of us have come to realize that *reading books aloud* in a home is not an extra or a luxury. I would always want to see reading together a part of the daily schedule. Some *personal daily reading* belongs in life too. (The mind must be fed.) Christians will set aside time for "chewing the cud" as they *think over God's Word and pray.*

Adequate rest with leisure and regular bedtimes should be part of the routine. Adults should have time for little children at tuck-up time.

There should be time for these daily rhythms.

Except during emergencies there should be time for some creative occupations in a home—time to arrange flowers, paint a room or a picture, or make curtains or bookshelves. Time to make the home (especially if it is one person's one-room home) a place where he or she "comes home and sighs with relief." So the home needs to be reasonably tidy and clean too. *Home should be a pleasant place for us.*

Every person's weekly schedule should have a day of rest from work (the Sabbath or Sunday). There should also be personal time for at least some satisfying interests for each member of the family or community. Many busy people find that if they examine their week, they spend an alarming amount of time watching TV or videos. They would discover that they feel more alive taking a walk and giving it their full attention—smelling rain on dry ground or freshly cut grass, gazing at cloud shapes, listening to and noticing birds. They would learn how satisfying it can be to read a good book or perhaps study a subject such as art or architecture with interesting (and free) books from the library or take a course. Most of us would enjoy joining a group to discuss literature and poetry or to learn a skill such as quilting, needlepoint, carpentry, or furniture restoration. Others join great and little choirs or orchestras or put on plays with local drama groups.

One of the reasons Jesus says it is a bad thing to be poor is because it squeezes out life. We can be poor in finances or poor in free time or energy.

If you live a high-demand, stressful life, try to see that the basics stay in place. And none of us should ever forget the place where we are remade—our source of life, the Lord. He promises a life-giving sap for each one. He especially cares when things are in a terrible state too.

"Come to me, all you who are weary and burdened, and I will give you rest" (Matt. 11:28). It would be folly not to be sure of this essential time in the daily schedule. We find it in a quiet place and moment, with God's Word and our full attention.

"Here I am. I *am* weary (confused, low, happy, etc.). I come."

12

☙

Early Days, Vital Days

It is a good choice for a mother to stay at home full time during a child's growing years. Not only does the child benefit, but also our communities will be only echoing housing complexes if there are no more parents at home all day. The art of everyday living is fast being lost. When Mom (or Dad) is at home, hopefully someone is there to listen when children have something they want to talk about. Meals can be produced on time, and friends find a welcome too. The elderly enjoy sharing home and community life while they contribute wisdom, perspective, and history. In our traditional communities of the past there was more time for all than we have nowadays.

When enough time is spent on home life, time-consuming activities can find a place. For instance, children are then able to play complicated games such as setting up "camps" with blankets or dressing up. All too often if all the adults are juggling over-full schedules, the long, gentle hours of play will tragically disappear. Although food, talk, books, and bed are central, children cannot mature without play. And as any mom knows, play that is worth the name means untidiness. It takes time to service play!

At this point I'd like to go back to Charlotte Mason and early childhood. She believed that the first years of life were so important as a "quiet growing time" that formal lessons should not be started until the age of six. When lessons did start, these should be very brief, perhaps twenty minutes for learning reading and writing every morning and another fifteen minutes for numbers. Additional time would be spent telling and reading stories to the child, maybe at teatime.

So what did she think younger children should be doing all day? Well, she knew that children needed lots of time to play, explore, run, jump, and climb. She knew they'd want to watch and join grownups at work and ask lots of questions; they should have the opportunity to think. She wanted their imaginations to grow and be used—so they were to have plenty of time for spontaneous play, acting out imaginary situations. This play was fired by stories they had heard or by their eager desire to copy adult life. She knew that children love to draw and paint pictures. She understood how much they love listening to stories too. Children have an urgent desire to communicate. For all of these activities Charlotte thought that homes or homelike places were best.

In the first three years of life every child learns more than at any other period in life. This is true even if he or she were to spend several years in a top university working on a Ph.D. and postdoctoral research later on. For the toddler much more is going on than what we would usually define as "learning." The very being of the child is developing. The joyous sense of well-being and the integration of mind, heart, and spirit are established at the beginning. All future relationships are being started in seed trays, so to speak, in this nursery of life. As any gardener knows, neglect the sprouting seed or young seedling, and you'll have a stunted plant.

These are the first great years of opportunity; they are also the years that can often be enjoyed with the least clutter from the fallen world. It is a time designed by a loving heavenly Father to be spent in an atmosphere of joy within the security of parental care. The early years should be a wonderful time when everything is new for the little person. The sight of his own hand fascinates a three-month-old, while the three-year-old glories in splashing in puddles as if such ecstasy had never before been known. The probing of a lump of dough by a one-year-old finger (that ends in the mouth) is replaced by squatting with concentration as the toddler watches an ant carrying a pine needle.

Thus is *wonder* born. And then the endless questions start, long before this imagination has taken wing. Of course imagination will only mature at four and onwards, but toddlers play endlessly in a world imagined at first in their wonderful heads. A hat, bag, and doll will be basic props for many girls. Boys may gravitate to cars, toy tractors, and creative adventures accompanied by the sound of engine noises. The moral "map" of right and wrong will be well established early on, just after actual babyhood. At first this moral sense will be a pleasant part of the security of being in the tender care of loving parents. The "no, no" response at first comes with a passion to protect the infant from exploring a hot stove or another danger. Well learned, these are lessons for the whole of life.

And so we hold this wonderful infant with wonder! Those eyes seeking and finding ours, the early smile of total friendliness and trust, tell us that we are entrusted with a precious, unique individual. Let us covenant with the Lord, this child's Maker, that we will make this trust our greatest task in life, our vocation. Parenthood is a high calling; do we not look to a Father of "tender mercies," who is "always faithful," "very love of all loves," and wholly righteous?

What exactly *does* this child need?

The child has been produced by a mother and father. This child's well-being is to be nurtured by these very same people. Of course, in this fallen world sometimes a child needs "grafting in." Adoption has a divine precedent. It takes love and trust to graft in a branch that has grown on another tree. The result of this choice is a special kind of belonging together.

The baby needs a mother. As a flower opens in the gentle spring sun and under April showers, so a mother's daily care enables this one particular baby to grow. "My baby," "bone of my bone, flesh of my flesh," both parents say. The mother's special link physically and emotionally almost flows with the milk (at breast is the greatest satisfaction for mother and child), the holding, the gentle touching—and the speech. That little face looking up at ours calls forth speech! Whether we murmur the name of this child or say something else, we've entered together into the great distinguishing feature of humans. Language is unique to those of us creatures who have been "created in the image of God." And language flows as we care for our child, as we enjoy being together as persons. Research keeps emphasizing the importance of all the "talk" we enjoy as we care for our babes. The English national newspaper *The Daily Telegraph*[1] recently reported on Dr. Sally Ward's work. Her seven years of research found that "talking to babies, even when they are too young to reply, can make them brighter."

Parents were instructed to turn off radio or TV noise so the babies (between nine and thirteen months old) could hear the words spoken to them. The parents who spent at least half an hour a day talking about what the baby was interested in had children whose average intelligence tested at a "remarkable" year and three months ahead of the other group of babies left to their own devices.

"Dr. Ward said that there had been huge changes in society that led to the decline in parents talking with their babies. These included the use of video tapes and the need for mothers to go out to work."

Obviously there is a lot to manage in this home-education opportunity that lasts only thirty-six months! The early stages must establish a baby's own routine. Otherwise chaos will so exhaust the parents that the sweet order that allows peaceful, creative, enjoyable family life will not exist. Also routines *are* the early discipline; the child is a person who, for all of life's duration, is *to fit into a community*—not exist as the center of a personal solar system of relationships revolving around "me." This self-centered attitude is increasing in our society. People are more and more concerned primarily about what they want and need, about their rights, and about gratifying their desires. The very dangerous and terrible results in society are evident in every daily newspaper, in statistics, and in unethical business practices designed for personal gain alone.

These early years can give children the correct way of thinking and living. This foundation is started and carried on as the routine comes first—their passing whims or wants do not "call the tune." The first and lifelong orientation we are meant to have is that we are like satellites in orbit around a center that is *not* ourselves. (Later we learn that the center is God.) Of course, the very key to children's future welfare lies in their accepting their own personal place in life. Unlike the orbiting planet that knows its place automatically, children have a choice ahead. They soon should listen and obey cheerfully. Large areas of personal choice and creativity will flower, but children are to remain within the boundaries set for them—a submission.

This idea of having a definite "place" in life is a distinctive of the Christian worldview; its application is best established in the sweet, enjoyable security of those first thirty-six months. Of course, the parents have fifteen or so more years to continue reinforcing and building on the early patterns. But beware of thinking you can change a person's basic orientation after several years of childhood! Habits are always hard to eradicate, especially a self-centered orientation.

A sweet routine and the fact that a child has been born into the functioning community of a family does *not* mean that you don't adjust the feeding and sleep schedule to an infant's changing patterns! Within that schedule of community life, the little child will often need adjusting to, for each child's needs are individual.[2]

A major part of the cost of having a child for many of us is that it means lost sleep at night, resulting in days spent in a mental fog and physical weariness. Some parents experience depression from being depleted. (Hint: Naps for mother are more important than dust-free surfaces or toy-free floors.) Such realities give even more reason to move "slowly with all speed" toward a routine for the baby that serves the family's needs and lifestyle.

I did find the basic Dr. Spock of the sixties very balanced and practical in suggestions about establishing sensible routines from birth through three years of age.[3] He attracted a lot of criticism; he isn't another Charlotte Mason! But for many of us, his advice helped us toward our own sane middle ground—a balance between understanding and listening to the needs of the changing infant and yet respecting our own needs and schedules. It *is* a matter of balance—and no mean feat!

We are bound to get it wrong at times. However, as we take into account a child's individual needs, we also always remember that she is fitting into our family. We can't be governed by what she wants at all times. It is not too strong to say that for parents "all hell breaks loose" if a child finds that *she* is the conductor of this band![4]

A baby is ready to give that great smile, enjoy all the love and fun sounds and talk, and also accept that life is organized by those godlike parents. Mom and Dad decide, so to speak, when the sun rises and sets! Having been loved, enjoyed, and served, a baby full of warm milk may cry when sleep is needed. Don't get into the trap of hovering worriedly. That tiny-looking infant is poised to become a tyrant! If interested, do read my old friend Dr. Spock. He won't explain Christian philosophy or its worldview, but he does know babies and toddlers. Try to find an old secondhand edition (before later revisions in the last twenty or so years made him politically correct). Go back to the old-fashioned family doctor.

So much is achieved through childhood routines that fit into the larger picture of the home's schedule and life. I based mine, as Charlotte Mason would have expected, on the old tried-and-true British nursery. The baby and toddler are cared for at home. Strong bonds are established with the mother, father, other children, and family members. There is a lot of appreciation for this infant, but the baby isn't the center of the stage. A small child will fit into the safe-sounding hum of life being lived kindly, as much as possible without stress. When this family knows something of the love and peace of the Lord, an atmosphere that is entirely wholesome pervades. Forgiveness is a sweet air—and the background sound could be voices raised in snatches of song rather than the endless blast of noise emitting from our present technology. Singing and music go with such a truly blessed home. I am not being romantic;

there can be a pleasant, cheerful calm in the midst of life's activities. Here we make another choice.

The baby and the toddler need a quiet place to sleep. Simple going-to-sleep routines give peace and security to the tiny one. At bedtime nothing should get in the way of that comforting tuck-up, prayer (and maybe a song or two), and a good night with the parent walking out. When children are old enough for stories, I don't think these should be read to them in their beds. Children too easily get wise to the parent's desire to respond educationally to their bright ideas and conversation, and they beg for more stories.

To be ready for the delicious comfort of one's own cozy bed when tired, the child should, obviously, *be tired*. I don't mean exhaustion, but the pleasant weariness of a child who has had in her day plenty of space and time to play; lots of satisfying rhymes, songs, and stories; and best of all, several hours of fresh-air play. And this last is so often the hardest bit for adults to achieve these days for their children. The whole list is crucial for a child's balanced development.

In a good nursery, whether in a humble cottage or great house, babies used to start life with wholesome doses of fresh air. They were put outside to sleep for their naps—warmly tucked into their prams.[5] Alternatively, children slept with windows wide open to the fresh air wafting in. While still very young, tucked up cozily in his pram, most afternoons the baby would "go for a walk" for at least an hour or two. The British are so constituted that only the most extreme weather could put a stop to this essential activity of the day. The young mother gets a good walk herself—essential to ensure that depression doesn't close her in with the house. The parks where I lived in London became loved and a daily vacation in the fresh air for me. I could watch the seasons change, see the clouds and sky, smell the good, damp earth, and glory in the spring flowers.

Soon, of course, the baby is propped up and watches all this with delight. As Mama pushes the pram along, she can see the baby who faces her (the old prams are high—keeping baby away from dust and dogs). The mother will talk and sing nursery rhymes from time to time. Soon the baby can point out interesting things she sees. "Dog," says the mother. By ten months or more the baby will also start to say, "Gog," or whatever.

The out-of-doors is so full of health and interest. It stimulates in an entirely wholesome way. I believe that much hyperactivity and concentration difficulties of later childhood are defused entirely by such a "nursey" childhood. The child's amazing need for vigorous activity can be satisfied in the wonderful out-of-doors without producing frantic overexcitment. In fact the child who spends his or her afternoons outdoors from earliest infancy will be very glad for tea (nursery supper served up after the walk or outside play), followed by storybooks on the couch, and then the welcome warm bath with toys to play with. No more exciting or noisy time here; this is the soothing, quiet time of day. The child goes straight from bath to bed, full of fresh air, with limbs weary from whatever activity he or she is up to developmentally.

This routine is good for marriages; it gives the adults some peaceful, child-free time together. And you'll appreciate an early bedtime yourself to be ready for the next morning. By age two many children are ready to accept a routine that in the earliest morning lets them "read" some favorite books in bed or play with their cars or whatever until it is time to get up. In our family this was one of the first lessons learned that earned much praise! (And by about three years, the issue was tackled by some strong scolding too. Thinking about other people's need to sleep is an excellent start to learning consideration.)

Obviously, afternoon play outside will not always be possible. However, the "Charlotte Mason with Sue Macaulay Way" aims for this tried and true formula. There are also many variations to consider. Three mothers meet in a park that has a grassed-over mound and logs where toddlers can roll and run safely away from swings and frantic older children. Each mother brings a small toddler ride-on toy, some cars or dolls, and some soft, old blankets to sit on. They bring a bottle of water for children's thirst (*not* sweet drinks, says

C. M. Let the children enjoy quenching their thirst with plain water or cold milk), a few apples to slice, a few raisins, or even little peanut butter sandwiches on whole wheat bread. The mothers bring refreshment for themselves (coffee in a thermos?), babies in prams, and older children walking. All sorts of creative ideas can be tried.

Our family's aim and practice was that by three a child could walk at least three miles at one time. Of course this distance would be in spurts—with little rests while the three-year-old was pushed along with baby, legs dangling off the end of the pram, but a *total* of three miles in one afternoon. (And then later four miles at four, five at five, and so on. Ours could usually enjoy a family day hike many times longer than that at three—say, six miles.)

Taking walks outside is a good place to see Charlotte Mason's "education as an atmosphere, discipline, and life" practiced. The atmosphere is the fresh, lovely world God has created. If you live in a hot climate, walking times may be in the sweet dawn or cool evening. Of course, the British "way" has to be adapted if you are somewhere else!

Walking is companionable. It is a "time to talk together along the way." The Lord often used this activity for teaching through conversation. And like the good mother, He'd point out illustrations from objects seen along the path—trees, plants, animals, seasons, light and dark, heat and coolness, persevering to the end of the way. Biblical imagery is related to the visual, the things actually seen and experienced in life.

The atmosphere of this large "classroom" also involves the other senses—balance, touch, smell, hearing. Children are eager to use all of these. They splash in water, pick up stones, wave sticks, balance along walls, run after squirrels. They are ready to be wondering and curious. Soon they ask a myriad of questions or comment on everything. We enjoyed singing, counting steps, and encouraging nursery rhymes.[6] Ranald and I resort to telling stories or playing games when little feet lag. In our family walking along together was one of the earliest disciplines.

Early on our family lived in the great sprawling city of London. My husband was a student, with little money. There was no car for outings. The children (first one, two, and finally three in that chapter of our life) would all have their daily walks "to the swings" about one and a half miles each way through a park or on neighborhood sidewalks.

One precious day a week, in addition to Sunday, Daddy was home with us. That was our together day. We'd pack up rucksacks with a day's food, diapers (cloth nappies), spare garments, etc., and then wait for a bus that would take us about an hour out of London. We'd alight in different places and, map in hand, spend glorious days in woods, by rivers, and on footpaths going through meadows.

Soon we had lots of tactics to entice small people to walk for reasonable distances! First, walking was always a discipline—in the sense that the rule is to keep going, even when you don't feel like it. Occasionally it meant a spanking for an older child. But this gives the wrong impression. Walks and days out were our best times (walks and reading aloud as a family). We'd so often find that the tense and maybe-tired adults had time to expand, soak up beauty, and walk off tensions. We'd also be able to talk together off and on as adults or with older children. The various arrangements that naturally occurred meant sometimes it was husband-wife, sometimes a special time for two sisters, or an older child with one parent.

Another tactic we did use was "hiking medicine." As this was the only, and I mean *only*, time we produced sweets (candy) for our children, this was powerful medicine! "At the top of the hill we'll have some hiking medicine (or a picnic, or sit in the shade and read a story while we have a drink)." Also to entice children along, we played endless games of hiding. The child had to "run past that tree" and then hide near the path. Great squeals of joy erupted as Dad's whistle came excitingly near. Then Dad rushed ahead—yes, quite *far* ahead—and disappeared. Much trotting down the path. Excitement. And the joy of reunion.

Such a childhood "atmosphere, discipline, and life" does give a person a more persevering character. On walks there are discomforts to put up with, obstacles to overcome, reasonable tiredness to push through. Rain and fog can be beautifully soft and sweet;[7] sun shows nature's colors. Eyes, ears, and nose respond to the real world. Then there is the contrast of delicious rest after the slog. This sort of a childhood builds *inner resources* that last a lifetime.[8]

Of course, as soon as the baby is walking around, she will benefit from a safe, enclosed outdoors "garden." The best arrangement would allow the toddler to run in and out of a door into the yard. Ride-on toys, logs to climb, balls, toy cars, dolls in strollers, a sandbox, a pan of water on a low table with lots of plastic cups and spoons—all these can be brought out and left for the child to find and use.

Adults also use this yard for work or relaxation. One of my favorite active "sports" is laundry (if I have a washing machine). It is so rewarding to hang up lines of sweet-smelling clothes in fresh air. Toddlers love to hand up items and pegs to help. Some children like to have their own little line at their height and put out small items such as socks.[9] Gardening is therapy and healthful; it creates beauty. Remember, it was the first occupation offered to people as positive, creative, satisfying work in the good, old days before the Fall.

Children are very sensitive to smells. They will enjoy the smell of freshly cut grass, the scent of rain after a dry day, or crunchy leaves underfoot in the autumn. Even babies will pick dandelions and shower parents with golden bounty.

Fortunate indeed is the child who has an outdoor space. Flat lawn is lovely and welcoming, as is shade in hot climates. Of course we have to live with our own limitations, but sometimes we can make choices. A child who spends (Charlotte Mason's recommended) four to six hours outdoors each day will be much easier to care for if there is such a yard. Many children today are so deprived of this natural heritage that they are like poor hens in cages. Of course they claw, squawk, and grumble! Not only that, in places as far apart as Minnesota and sunny Australia, many children of six have had so little exercise that they have the ideal physical condition for the sort of cardiac problems to develop that used to be the privilege of the middle aged.

Play outdoors is enjoyable alone or with playmates. By the time a baby is toddling around, she will be very interested in other children. First, children find it interesting just being near each other. But by two and certainly by three, some play times should include socializing. It is useful to "borrow" another child who plays well alongside yours. When we lived in London, we had a little neighbor girl almost on permanent loan—not all hours, but she tended to be company during whole afternoons of outdoor play in the yard. "Girls and boys, run out to play" means that children will be in a village-like group! Our children's playmates also played endlessly in our home too. Dressing up and imaginary games all benefit from including friends.

Why have I gone on in such detail about the out-of-doors aspect of a child's early years? Because it is *basic* in the Charlotte Mason philosophy and has been the practice of so many generations of healthy people everywhere. Also, for many, these ideas now seem strange, perhaps an impossible dream. It takes planning and time to provide such a day.

We live in an age where everyone is trying to sell something. People will try to sell you expensive gadgets for your little ones, expensive clothes, and tell you to make "educational" purchases. Videos at one? Computers at two? Classrooms at three? And the answer is, "No, the child *needs* the old-fashioned basics." Parents, home, land. Love, boundaries, routines. Family friends, community. Seasons, earth, sky. Activity, sleep. All stirred with warmth, fun, and lots and lots and *lots* of enjoyment. The main ingredient of this "stew" will be talking together, communication—and then reading books together. Add paper and crayons, old cardboard boxes, play dough (at nearly three), and bath toys. A ride-on toy will be worth its weight in plastic or wood. Little girls love dolls, prams, blankets, and pillows for home corners, old-fashioned as these naturally are, and boys value their cars, airplanes, tractors, sticks, and balls! Interests overlap because individuals are unique, but the general principle holds.

Secondhand is as good as new, and small children don't care about status symbols (not at this untainted age—enjoy it!). And if they've thrived with joy on such a rich diet of activities when small, maybe they'll *never* be cheated by manipulation in our get-rich and have-the-right-label culture. They won't need drugs to calm them down at school age or therapy to "find their identity" years later.[10] The fresh air, sun, and security of early childhood give them sturdy roots like an oak. As they grow up, they are likely to find a rhythm and routine of life for themselves that will be a sweet maturing of the order, discipline, and richness nurtured in nursery days.

Of course, for many families, giving the child the benefit of a full-time mother may seem too expensive. But look again. What, oh, what have we done in accepting this most bitter deprivation and poverty—a child robbed of its *mother?* Can we possibly afford the unbalanced children that we will have if these foundational years are lost?

Yes, it takes a person's full capacity to serve little children. Think! There is also food to get in and prepare, cleaning to be done, laundry to keep going. There are other ongoing commitments—hospitality, other family members, church, and whatever. All this is far more than one person can do. It takes mother and father. There are *no* formulas for saying who does how much and when, for we all lead very different lives. We respond to our own realities when we say, "How can we, how should we 'do it'?" Mothers appreciate and need help in this vocation. Fathers do different things at different stages. They can provide care so the mother gets out, or take the children to the park Sunday afternoon so the exhausted young mum gets a good long nap. (My husband, Ranald, always did this.) And how great is the stress if this team-work doesn't exist.

Everyone benefits from being part of a community that shares each other's burdens. Be friends, act as a group together. It is a sad fact of life in this fallen world that both small and huge things go wrong. Jobs are lost, medical needs loom menacingly—in all sorts of situations we need our neighbors. Friendship is a most precious part of life. Christians should be real neighbors in their area, not just to members of their church. We can offer to baby-sit for a weary father whose wife is in the hospital. We introduce ourselves to an elderly person and offer to shop for him or her. We invite different ones over for a cup of tea or a family meal—this is all part of a living home.

But as I finish this chapter, I'd like to go back to those who need to juggle an outside job with time at home every day. There can be good plans and adaptations; nobody has a picture-perfect life. All sorts of arrangements can provide for children well. A community organization or church can step in if there is an urgent need.

Homes are a good model for substitute child care. Several years ago I read of an urban borough that provided day nursery care in a creative way. They bought ordinary family homes in city areas. Because this was an English project, the houses were small terraced homes.[11] The children could walk to the house, as it would be in their neighborhood. The house interior was not different from most homes. All the usual rooms were there—kitchen, dining/living room, upstairs bathroom, and bedrooms. The rooms were furnished for family use. There was a little strip of garden at the back.

I read how little children would come in with their mums. If they had time, the parents could stop for a cup of tea and develop a friendly relationship with the adult caregivers. A normal home routine was followed. A little four-year-old might be found standing on a chair at the counter chopping carrots for lunch. Another had gone to draw a picture at the table. One child was curled up on the couch having a look at a book in the living room or maybe had asked for a story. There would be the usual basics for play—a box of dress-up clothes, blocks, and toys.

Children would play in the yard and walk or tricycle to the local shop with someone to help bring in groceries. They ate family-style around the table, with a toddler in a high chair. After lunch, those needing a nap were comfortingly tucked up in the bedroom. Children were very much at home here, and so were their parents. They went to the park nearby, played, and generally enjoyed an "at-home" life, free of too much organized activity, but rich in relationships.

It was found that the mothers benefited as well as the children as they learned how to better care for their children in a home setting. More and more young parents have been deprived of such models, so the day care educated parents and befriended them too. I believe that providing such homelike care could be Christian work of great value. Any church that has lone parents or others struggling to go to work and yet care for home life should consider this model.

Sometimes we find (or can provide) well-run nursery schools to care for children who need it. By three years of age children enjoy friends and are normally secure enough to adapt to a more organized day. The ratio of adults to children should be very high.

Some well-run nursery schools have one caregiver designated as a "key worker" for every three or four children. She is the one to help them in their toilet training, washing, and so on. At mealtimes her little family group sits at one table, and she eats a freshly cooked meal with them. They learn to speak one at a time, conversing nicely. A cheerfully relaxed and yet quiet atmosphere pervades the room. After lunch she'll sit down with her arm around one or two, another on her lap, and read a story or two. She fosters a relationship with each child and is the one who will work with the parent on boundaries in behavior and other matters. She needs to have a genuine love of children, enjoy life, and maintain a relaxed yet orderly atmosphere. She will be committed to seeing her group through from three years to the age when they leave nursery care.

All good nursery schools should have access to a garden. The children should be able to play on grass and under trees. There should be a hard-surfaced area for wheeled tricycles and toys. There is a generous sandbox. The PNEU philosophy would insist that children have proper clothes and shoes or boots to play outside in damp, cold, snow, or drizzle and good sun hats for summer. Outside play should be fun. The outdoor area should be well away from the sound of busy road traffic—in a peaceful environment. Tired or unwell children have access to the indoor rooms when they need to go in.

The nursery school should be relaxed, homelike, warm, peaceful, and yet cheerful. Parents should be encouraged to keep their child's "nursery day" as short as possible. A half day is ideal. If a child is in care for more than five hours a day, the provision must be planned more as a daytime "orphanage" than as a nursery class.

Charlotte Mason lived a long time ago. Most of our lives and communities are different now. But some things never change! That is why I'll conclude this chapter with a quote from Dr. Isabelle Fox, who has a long career as a licensed family therapist specializing in developmental psychology. She returned to work when her third child went to school. Her professional insights of the up-to-the-minute child reinforces the old traditions, values, and understanding. I have not yet read her book *Being There*, but I am quoting from an interview in the monthly publication by mothers for mothers, *Welcome Home*.[12] Dr. Fox said:

> The motivation to write *Being There* came from feeling that parents today need to be empowered to "be there" for their young children and from my conviction that the needs of the very young for stability and responsive care should be articulated. Many parents do have a choice to be a home with their children, especially if they prioritize for those first few years.
>
> During the last ten or fifteen years of my thirty-five-year practice, I began to notice that the children referred to me displayed symptoms that were much more difficult to treat. These children were often more aggressive, hyperactive, inattentive, or withdrawn than the children I had worked with earlier. When exploring their histories, I learned that most of these children came from families where both parents

worked, and as infants and toddlers they had constantly changed care givers. . . .

It is because children are and can be a source of enormous pleasure, wonder, laughter and love that I wish to encourage mothers and fathers to participate fully in the parenting process. These commitments to one's developing child are as important as any career for the limited time we are privileged to be the parents of our young children.[13]

We need to give each other all the encouragement we can in the job of homemaking and bringing up children. Whether we work part time or not, whatever our circumstances, homes really are the heart and hearth of our lives. Babies, little and big children, young adults—everyone will benefit from an "alive-and-well" home. Creating home life is a good way to spend time; it is satisfying. Remember, Jesus said, "I prepare a place for you."

13

❧

Homes and Life in Community

We've been looking at our lives at home. The neighborhood, community, friends, schools, and churches have been mentioned, but more needs to be said.

C. S. Lewis's allegory on hell and heaven[1] pictures hell as a dreary city with many boarded-up houses. In this place people's relationships break down, and they move farther and farther away from their neighbors. This idea is biblical; in God's fulfilled plan (the opposite of hell), we are "knit together in love" with fellow believers,[2] "listen to each other and try to serve each other," "give in to other people's ideas and plans,"[3] and "carry each other's burdens,"[4] "share tears and laughter,"[5] and more. As people who are loved by God, we should enjoy a profound sense of worth. We are meant to have deepening relationships with other people who are our "neighbors" and "especially those who are of the family of God."

The hallmark of people who are good models is that they don't stand in judgment over other people;[6] we'll notice that they don't look down on others for choices/lifestyles/opinions different from their own.[7] (This does not mean being confused about what is morally right or wrong.) We are even to act in a loving way to people we find so difficult that we call them enemies (Matthew 5:44). We pray for these people to be helped and blessed. And we try to be friendly in practical ways.

To get the perspective right, we must start with the big picture, the whole of reality. *Where does my life fit in? Then how do we all fit in together as human beings?* It seems natural to start with babies and children's lives, their upbringing and needs, the home's atmosphere, discipline (routines/moral framework), and life. We all have different kinds of lives, situations, and choices. Although many of the "beads on the string" of our days are the same, the hows and whys vary.

First let us look at our lives and homes in relationship to the bigger picture of society. We are most certainly not created to live in the increasing isolation C. S. Lewis so chillingly described. One of the worst fates a human being endures is being put in solitary confinement, especially when he is cut off from the rhythm of natural daylight and regular mealtimes and bedtimes. There are other situations in this fallen world that inflict similar suffering. Deafness can cut off a person from communication. So can certain kinds of brain damage that leave a person with full understanding but unable to communicate. We respond by sometimes heroic efforts to bridge the gap—to educate or devise means for the person to escape isolation.

God has created us to be in relationship. We are not made to live alone. Sadly, the effect of current ideas and lifestyle trends is toward loneliness and isolation. Consider the difference between two scenes: In one you are sauntering down a sidewalk on your street and stop to greet a neighbor working in his garden. A few yards further, you compliment a little girl who is learning to roller-skate. Next you decide that Alice, recently widowed, would love to be invited in for supper with the family. On the way to her house you stop to ring the neighbor's doorbell. Peter comes to the door. "We're going away next weekend, and I've just planted some seeds. Could you water them?" He is more than glad to and responds, "I'm going to be out over lunch tomorrow. Could you put our dog out in the yard for an hour or two?"

Fiction? No, an actual neighborhood street in the year of our Lord 1998. This scenario is about people who make choices concerning how they live as neighbors.

Contrasting with this scene is the sort of isolated life that is becoming all too "normal" today. A harassed person rushes out of a house with two children. The children are enclosed in a metal vehicle on wheels, and restraining straps are tied down. Windows are closed—not even bird song penetrates, let alone the possibility of getting to know the people who live nearby. If they see neighbors as they drive out, the children don't know the people's names. They are too often afraid of talking to the elderly man or lonely widow anyway—aren't they "strangers"? These children are driven to a hangar-like building without windows. They enter to spend seven hours sealed inside.[8]

It is not far-fetched to imagine another scenario. A weary businessman or woman drives along a congested road for an hour or more after an eleven-hour day on the eleventh floor of a sealed-in office building. For several hours he or she may have stared into a lighted screen and pushed keys. The day was filled with tension but not even one conversation with a cheerful friend. This person parks underground and takes an elevator to the eleventh floor, enters an apartment, and dons shorts and T-shirt after a shower and drink. He or she switches on the news and jogs on the spot while watching it. The phone rings but is answered by a machine. The current "steady" relationship has broken up.[9]

A lot of people's leisure hours are spent locked up away from fresh air, all those "dangerous people," and thus also neighborhood chats. Shopping is typically done in huge warehouse-sized places where no one asks your name or how you are getting on while your wife is in the hospital. Not even the weather is discussed. For a lot of the time we act like cogs in a machine rather than like people in relationship with each other and our environment.

What have we lost? The cost is most dreadful. Lives so lived are far, far removed from the sweet satisfaction of being part of a community. It is not human life at all as it has been known in the past. There is a lot of stress and much isolation. Some people only hear conversation at home when they turn on the television.

Living on a residential street or in an apartment building where neighborhood actually functions is not just a "lucky" break. The people who live there have made choices and planned their use of time so as to be *people who live in community*. Any society is made up of young families, older people with nearly adult children still at home, the elderly. There are couples (some married, some not) and single people. Some live in apartments and others in houses. These people together are the community, the neighborhood.

The people who live on our street try to make it a neighborhood of meaningful relationships. We have achieved our goal partly through special occasions as well as taking time to pause in our daily lives to "be there" for each other. For instance, in the largest yard one summer afternoon a year there is a neighborhood potluck lunch. Name tags are donned as people spend a few hours together. Friendships are strengthened, new acquaintances made.

At Christmas a smaller group, including children, sing carols at each residence. One of the families opens their home for the spiced mulled wine (the traditional Christmas drink), fruit drinks, cheese and mince pies that everybody helps provide. The singers mingle with those who stayed home to listen. Recently two of the boys have started an occasional street newspaper. Someone asks for a Scrabble partner; another tells of good exam results. Our postman is retiring. How can we thank him? (He and his wife were invited to the Christmas party, and they were given a gift from everyone, along with a framed picture of small drawings done by each child on the street.)

Why should we let community die? It destroys our humanity. One of the good results of developing relationships with neighbors is that it may enable us to make friends with people of different persuasions. I remember a Christian homemaker in California telling me that her best neighbor is a Muslim mother and her family next door. Both sets of parents care about their families and moral behavior. It is good to have friendships like this. These two families not only enjoy a friendship, but they also help each other in practical ways.

Of course, in the neighborhood one belongs to a church,

another to a mosque or synagogue, while many would say they believe nothing in particular. Christians who understand their faith are persuaded that its truth explains reality. Obviously these varied backgrounds result in different moral and lifestyle choices. For example, we who are Christians believe that the taking of human life is wrong, including abortion. And we believe that a live-together partnership between a man and a woman should only occur within the marriage commitment. Yet holding different convictions from others "in this world" should not stop us from being neighbors. When Jesus said to love our neighbors, these *are* the neighbors He was talking about! In fact we should welcome the opportunity to develop our own understanding through friendships that cross cultural barriers.

So when we do go to our own church or group, we appreciate a special bond; it is good to be with others who believe the same things. If historic Christianity *is* truth, then church actually is the place where we are in harmony with what life is about, what fits into reality's design.[10] Not only is it "nice" to be part of such a group, but it is commanded of us. The order is, first, our responsibility to obey God[11] and to live in His love,[12] and also fulfill family responsibilities. Next we are "to do good to all people especially to those who belong to the family of believers,"[13] and also not to ever give up on being a caring neighbor. "Let us not become weary in doing good, for at the proper time we will reap a harvest if we do not give up" (Gal. 6:9). This is the "salt[14] and light"[15] the Bible speaks of—for an apartment building, a housing project for the elderly, houses along a street, schools, businesses, city or rural areas, and our nation. As Christians we should also see that our lives are concerned with the global community's welfare.

Once more we pull the camera away from the large screen to focus on our individual days of twenty-four hours. Each of us lives a rather feeble little life. Soon the years go by; some of us have shorter lives, others longer. Then we die.

As we've been seeing, the New Testament deals with reality as it is everyday. Jesus expressed our "salt" and "light" in terms of something as small as one cup of cold water given to another person in His name. Every "little" life counts; each day, each hour has its place. In God's sight, there is no "little" life; each person is significant. Together we should add up to a powerful whole—a body where each part is important. One person here and another there, each doing well enough in his own little "patch of life," will add up to permeate society as a whole, as salt flavors a lump of dough. The influence can be for good or evil, for truth or lies. Some things are done by individuals; others we act on as a group.[16]

Some are called to and find themselves in all sorts of situations. Some are the householders making homes, creating warm centers of life that can reach out with hospitality and help. Others are more like Paul, a hard-working person free of domestic constraints.[17] Some such persons live in a dangerous or pioneer situation that would be hard for a family, for instance some areas of our inner cities. Such people are also free to travel around serving widespread areas and bring them the Good News. Others go into war-torn places to give medical help. I've met women and men who've sacrificed their own safety to serve as medics in terrible conditions. Probably we all can give many examples from among our friends. The variety makes it possible for Christians together to be a near- and far-ranging "team of light-givers, salt-producers."

It is a fundamental fact that each personal life counts. We also live and work as members of groups. Although we just have one short life to live, that doesn't make it easy— "nothing in this life is simple." As we are flawed ourselves and live in a flawed reality, things go wrong. We were never perfect or well-rounded in the first place—all of us have needs. That is when we help each other. It is a terrible thing when we are isolated from a working-together community.

Mutual help and support are basic to each one of us. One member of my family was a young mother living in the high Himalayas with no store, no electricity, no telephone. Her husband was away for a few days, and her cooking fire went out. Food was a problem. Her friends and neighbors, the poorest of the poor, came to her rescue that time (not always). One brought a plate of cooked rice, another a cooked potato.

At around the same time her sister lived in a room without a stove in an American inner city. She needed to bake a cake and walked down the street knocking at some doors. She asked a neighbor if she could borrow her kitchen and oven for the afternoon. "Sure, honey," said the woman, very pleased to be asked. While the cake baked, they looked over photo albums to get to know each other. When women in a suburban Christian church heard how the cake had been baked, they reacted with shocked surprise: "Why, we'd be terrified to even drive along *that* street!"

Who will be a neighbor? If we lead such safe, sterile lives, who will help us when we lose our job or become ill? We all are part of the human family. In all traditions people have helped each other in practical ways. The ancient Old Testament culture codified this attitude in its laws. God makes it clear that He looks out very especially for the orphan, the widow, the poor, and the stranger too. He cares about people having a fair deal. He watches as we become His caring hands, His listening sympathy, His practical help.

The community aspect of life needs to be part of a child's everyday experience. How children are brought up affects how they'll live later on. Strange as it might seem, play time is a vital part of a child's preparation for being fully involved in the local community as an adult.

First of all, play is an expression of a child's thoughts and plans; it is a personal response to life. From the earliest stages, a baby wants to share this vital part of life. While enjoying something, even a baby will look up to flash a happy smile at a parent and maybe say "goo" or whatever. Using language to communicate to other people is an integral part of play. Good quality play provides much of life's enjoyment and experience for every child.

The earlier chapters have described how every child needs order and leisure for growth—physical, mental, and emotional. Sadly, for many children today, pushed about hither and yon, overstimulated with entertainment or organized educational effort at all times, leisure is exactly what they do not have. For such children, their young lives are already filled with stress and tension, with no opportunity to discover what "makes them or the world tick" as they amble along with childish interest and play.

As we consider society and the individuals that make it up, we must look at play carefully and provide for it. Play is as natural to the child as life itself and is not taught or organized by adults. A child who is not playing alone and together with friends a lot is deprived.

Play! Early play almost equals discovery. Items are reached for, batted around, held, put into the mouth and tasted. The exploring baby loves to get around. The rooms lived in need to be baby-safe. I used to remove all breakable items from low cupboards. An eight-month-old loves to go through a kitchen cupboard! Pot lids are pulled out, sieves tried on as hats, or measuring spoons put in and out of a bowl.

In the bedroom clothes drawers are unpacked. Underwear will be draped over the baby's person in festive decoration. However, even at this age there are boundaries set by authority—Mom and Dad. These "baby lambs" have "fences around the meadow where they play" (from *For the Children's Sake*). This is the beginning of a child's realization that while play is something he or she thinks up and is free to do, it cannot be *whatever* the child wants. This enjoyable freedom has boundaries. The baby learns the *no* word. *And no must actually always be NO.*

"No, you cannot touch the stove or play here." I would say, "No, no," in a strong, firm voice while actually removing the baby. Take the child away and distract him with something else. (Go to the cupboard. Rattle measuring spoons or plastic containers.) At some point the infant will return to the stove to try again. I might emphasize the boundary by adding to the firm "No" a smack on the hand. Children must not win; you always remove them in your arms and distract them. Until they are three, they need this assistance. Some adults expect a little one to crawl or toddle away! That is not realistic.

In these early stages when a baby is mobile, the family home has enough built-in necessary "no-go" areas to teach the principle and start the habit of obedience. One removes any extra irritations *to make such boundaries really clear and leave a few so that they are noticed.* Stoves, electric plugs, windows, and such will teach the concept well enough. You baby-proof as much as possible otherwise. To begin with, danger decides "the law." Stairs should be blocked until you are confident that they no longer constitute a hazard. Go over the living areas with an eagle eye to safety. Then the baby and little child will not have to be checked in normal joys of exploration, climbing, and pulling. They can be free to play.

Older children who can use small beads, building blocks, scissors, and what not will need to play in separate areas. This arrangement also protects the older children from needless irritation from the baby or toddler. For instance, I once arranged for our three-year-old to have a little "den" with table and chair in the playpen, which she climbed into "to be safe from being bothered by the boys." (A little "gang" of three baby boys only eighteen months old played together daily in our yard and apartment!) Frequently an older school-age child building intricate lands with blocks or Lego was allowed into the parental bedroom to keep her precious constructions safe from marauding toddlers in the family room area.

This brings me to an important point. *Play needs to be protected by the mother/father in charge of the child's day. We act as all-important allies.* We provide the materials. We save grocery boxes for trains, cities, boats, and stores. There should be storage for the dress-up clothes for boys and girls. In it we put interesting cloaks, materials, shoes, bags, hats, dresses, vests—all sorts of items. (Garage sales are useful here.) We provide picnics for garden exploration parties, extra drinks for the dehydrated, bandages for the wounded, along with bedding. We allow our living rooms to be turned into camps on cold, wet days.

We provide (and become) the audience for plays and puppet shows. When our children are wonderfully engrossed in some game, we alter our own ideas about what should be happening that afternoon. Their play is high on the agenda of priorities.

We know how to turn a blind eye when not needed or wanted, and yet we are the immediately available support team when something needs fixing or helping along. Occasionally we tactfully suggest another avenue when a first idea doesn't work out. ("Look, you could have the cars go on roads we can make in the gravel.")

To encourage play as the adult-in-charge is one of the greatest art forms of all. Part of this art is tactfully bringing an enjoyable session to its end. ("You only have fifteen minutes—then we are going to clean up, and Joey will be going home. Do you want a last drink?") This preparation is important, for by now the child is no longer a baby and needs to be respected.

This fact brings me back to an earlier subject—*routines*. If children had free time all day, play would not be so delicious. Even the baby has balance in the day, which he or she learns through peaceful routine. Learning to fit into a structure is all-important. Life has a structure to which we adjust; we do not just follow our impulses such as what "I want" or "I feel like . . ." Rather it should be, "What is it time for?" Later on this idea naturally evolves into the concept "What should I be doing?" or "What ought I to do now?" (Note: In this way we learn about duty and responsibility.)

At each stage there is time for the "musts"—bedtime or nap time, sitting up at the table to eat with the family, going out to the park, getting ready for bed. Later on there are chores (starting at eighteen months or so even the toddler can join in putting away toys). And in *any* properly ordered family there will be story-reading time. This is so appealing to the child, as it heralds a quiet, unwinding time after activity. In fact, should the play time go wrong (end in frustration and tears or a fight), the perfect medicine is often a story together (or a walk outside, food, or a "play bath").

Essex Cholmondeley, Charlotte Mason's biographer who followed on in the work of the PNEU, wrote a booklet with the title *Parents Are Peacemakers*. Making peace is our adult responsibility. We notice if a child is too tired to cope, or we intervene when a new birthday toy is snatched away. We are on each child's "side" and "carry" each through difficulties. In creating the true *Charlotte Mason childhood*, parents make no habitual recourse to television's "virtual reality" to handle difficult, fussy moments. Such random use would deprive the growing child of the opportunity to develop a treasure house of inner riches to cope with the normal ups and downs of life. The child deserves to learn how to get through such times without artificial props. They should be learning in real life how to get through tiredness or "fallow times" (boring patches) until new ideas start growing.[18]

Some children naturally drift toward being alone. They will draw endless pictures, telling stories or singing to themselves all the while. Or they might spend hours making elaborate constructions, road systems for cars, and so on. But these activities are very different from the isolation of a child sitting in front of a computer screen. The hands-on play based on reality gives children skills and creativity. They are creating a world, not pushing a key to make it appear. Should a friend or other sympathetic person appear, a natural joining in is possible; conversations will occur; "community" will grow.

All children should be encouraged to enjoy time alone without entertainment. It helps to have a tidied-up, inviting place to play. No child is attracted to a mess where the Lego pieces are stirred in with crayons or an old hat is under a roller skate. In fact, I found that the key to having a child settle happily to play was to put out inviting groupings of items—a neat table with a clean piece of paper and crayons and pencils laid out, all the cars together in a box on the floor, a basket filled with blocks, the dress-up clothes easily reached, a small plastic tea set on a low shelf, a box upside down with a simple outline drawn in thick felt tip pen that turns the box into a stove with a small (real) pan and wooden spoon on it, a doll's bed made up.

I learned about how to arrange a room or garden for play as a young mother over thirty years ago when I took my three-year-old to a play group. I saw a drab old church hall turned into a place where happy, creative play occurred two or three mornings a week. I'd already been practicing ways to encourage play to a certain extent, but the room gave me new ideas.

With this method you don't say, "Now we'll build blocks" ("paint a picture or play house"). In the room are several centers arranged for various activities, and the children have the opportunity to gravitate to whatever attracts them. One child may always play house. Another paints pictures endlessly. A boy wanders around and finally settles down to play with cars. Because this method allows for actual interests, the children usually find something that they like to do and remain absorbed for long periods. They develop the habit of concentration, focus, and an attentive spirit.

The same ideas work at home. But people often make the mistake of providing such play only for children under seven years old or so. A dress-up box can easily get constant use until children reach the age of fourteen. "Just playing" turns into structured plays. Art supplies can be available for an entire lifetime! A lump of play dough on the kitchen table will attract fingers from age three to thirty! The books on display should be changed from time to time. Library books can be propped up invitingly. Early picture books become illustrated books on subjects various family members are interested in. Then of course the permanent bookshelves are full of old friends. Good lighting and comfortable seating attract readers.

Very soon the little child appreciates having other little ones playing nearby. It is sometimes amazing how in community or extended family life even babies form friendships. I've had children with established playmates from the unbelievable age of six months! When two cousins shared a house, the one-year-old would hide in the curtains. The six-month-old, who crawled very early, would zoom around finding the other child. High glee would ensue! Toddler boys who played together daily in my home also taught me that such children seem to get up to more mischief than one toddler! So I would ensure that boundaries were enforced. My own son would get a spanking; the other boys were told "no more playing now" and sent back to their own apartments and mothers. They soon learned to respect the few sensible limits.

When we lived in London, we encouraged one or two neighbor children who made excellent playmates to come and play at our house. A hard fact is that some children "click" and some don't. Some children are on the same wave length; others just aren't. For instance, little girls playing endless games of home and child care may not gravitate to the cars and toy tractors in the same way their brothers do. Mind you, our girls were active explorers too, and they climbed and swung on ropes with the best of them! Girls and boys were often firm friends who enjoyed imaginative and active play. It has more to do with personality than gender.

The little boys in our community of families certainly were on each other's wave length! Noisy rushing-around games included a huge variety of imaginary exploits. To my chagrin, these often included quite a lot of fighting imaginary enemies, involving many complicated maneuvers. We finally gave in and allowed unrealistic looking guns, as sticks were used anyway in this play, and it seemed churlish to pretend our son had pacifist leanings at four! (This from a child who had no television.) It seems that the masculine person has an instinct of battle built-in, just as female children I've known have a strong homemaking and baby-care instinct. We provided all sorts of toys for all. I once saw the boys playing with the doll our son had been given. They were charging in and out through all the doors of our apartment with the doll under one boy's arm. As they ran, they were all crying, "Save the baby! Save the baby!" It was the only time I saw any of them with a doll in their game.

In any case, in play together with sisters and brothers and then with friends and neighbors, we learn to act as the *communal beings* God has made us to be: We learn to forgive, tolerate, and listen to each other. Sometimes we have ideas, and the others follow. Other times we have ideas, and the others refuse to follow. We get our feelings hurt, make up, and go on. We learn to do what someone else has planned sometimes.

In fact, in playing together with real friends, the child learns how to live life itself. Therefore, we leave this kind of play out at the peril of an individual's welfare as well as society's good.

Ranald and I made an important decision about the friends we had in to play with our children. We had enough work to bring up our own children; we couldn't solve the neighbors' problems. If an invited-in child was what we called frenetic, we did not try to make him a part of our family's life. For us to include a child regularly, he or she had to settle down and become absorbed in wholesome play. They had to "click" and be a real friend to at least one of our children.

We sometimes had in problem children to help their parents or develop a personal contact with the family. But in such cases, we undertook to stay on the scene with these children. Perhaps we'd take them all out to the park and then bring them home for a story over supper. In other words, we could not expect that cheerful, absorbed (and messy) hum of children getting on with their play alone.

Also, we decided that when children came to play, *we* were the ones to decree when the play time was over. "You'll be going home when we have supper." Or if a child came knocking when the family was busy with study, work, reading, or a meal, there was no stress. "No, we're not playing now. You may not come in." Then, "We'll be ready to play at . . ."

Also, should a wonderful camp be spread over the family living room, it was understood by all that the room had to be tidied before supper, as other family members also use that room for their leisure. In other words, we did not grant pure freedom. The parents control who comes and where and how play happens. All is within boundaries. Yet this type of play contrasts with the organized play in nursery classes, kindergartens, etc.

Having generous play time is more important than extra lessons in violin, Latin, or a team sport. These might each be important for a child's education and life. However, *plenty of daily time free for play is a primary need for all children.* Sadly, for many children such time is shrinking and shrinking. For quite a few there is no time left for play in solitude or with chosen friends at home. What kind of a world will these children make when they are adults? Will they have the self-confidence of knowing themselves well enough to enjoy their leisure time with many rich interests that grew out of childhood play? Will they know how to accept and get along with other people in long-term relationships?

Before ending, I'll address one frequent complaint (whine, fuss, grumble) most parents hear time and again: "I have nothing to do." As I am a busy mother and grandmother who has brought up six children, I have just the answer. This is not a method—it is the truth. If a child of over four or five has finished his or her duties (room cleaned up, schoolwork done, jobs finished), then I usually say, "Oh, that's good. I have too much to do today. Nobody has swept down the stairs yet, put away the dishes, put the books back into the bookcase, etc. I have *lots* you can do. Thank you."

It's amazing, but I've found that 95 percent of these complainers, though all have very different personalities, will suddenly remember a most attractive "thing" it seems they've actually been *waiting* to do!

There are days when every child is out of sorts and really doesn't want to play. I prescribe a good long walk together if possible or a special job (washing the front porch or raking leaves *together*). Some children enjoy a special shared cooking session or just a long cuddle on your lap.

It helps if there are different kinds of days in the week's routine—a day off as a family and Sunday with its particular rhythm. It's fun to surprise a child with an unexpected activity or outing sometimes. Also put out only a selection of toys or books at a time. When a toy hasn't been out for a few weeks, it looks fresh again. The child returns to playing with new interest and is perhaps inspired with new ideas.

A child who enjoys constructive, imaginative play in solitude and with friends is prepared for life in a foundational way. Individuality takes shape, and relationships teach about living in community. In their play children often act out helping each other, such as having one be sick or injured, rescuing sheep in a flood, and many other situations they've witnessed or heard about. They practice their adult lives.

At all times a home that is a living part of a community will teach its children the age-old art of being a good neighbor in many ways. Children are thrilled to be helping others. They can feel important and satisfied when they are strong enough at four years old to carry in the groceries for an infirm neighbor. When a child younger than themselves is being cared for while its mother is in the hospital, the older children will feel perfectly splendid when making a room safe for the toddler or in using a book to distract the little one. Often they will run and get a favorite toy. Altruism and sharing should come from the heart and give a glow of satisfaction to the giver. Kindness and generosity flow from a contented child whose imagination is stirred by another person's need.

When I was very, very little in America, the Depression[19] was recent enough that many tramps still came through the neighborhood looking for a hot meal. How I loved helping my mother set a special tray of good food for the hungry man on the back porch. She never, ever turned anyone away! I grew up hearing that indeed we might be serving an angel "unawares."[20] Or if the person smelled and seemed repugnant, I'd be told that maybe his mother had wept over him. That made me realize he was a precious person, and there was hope that he'd be able to change. In other words, my imagination was educated for caring.

Later on when I lived in a tiny Swiss alpine village not too long after World War II, there was real poverty in many chalets. At Christmas we not only prepared to celebrate as a family at home, but my mother would ask around so as to identify a family or old person suffering great need. She'd pack a dinner such as we rarely had—roast meat and all the trimmings. Suitable new warm clothes and special treats would be carried in bags. We'd hike together as an entire family through the snow. Up, up, higher and higher to a family looked after by a care-worn mother. There we might find a child on a bed with a tubercular hip and no comforts to be seen. Another year we ministered to an old crone who peered and muttered at us in disbelief as we entered a scene of extreme need. As we walked home in the moonlight over snow, thoughts were born in me that gave me a lifelong hunger to assuage at least a little grief.

Later, as a young couple in London, Ranald and I attended a large church with people well fed both physically and spiritually. We chatted with a man there after services. He had attended church in that place for over twenty years. His wartime boyhood had scarred him; he was reserved. We wanted to share our Christmas dinner with someone who was alone, and we invited him. Although the shops had been closed when we invited him, he brought me a gift of sweet-smelling lotion, a treat I could not afford. We discovered he had bought this gift and others, "Just in case I was invited out." Later we heard that ours was the first home ever to invite him in for a shared meal.

Oh, busy Christian church! Oh, fellow human beings! We need to take time for each other. This is right. Share this way of life with every child. It is the way to live now and into the future.

14

∾

A Look at the Everyday
All Around Us—All Year Long

The last chapter described a friendly yet nonintrusive community functioning on a little street of houses linked by sidewalks. While familiar to some, this scene may well have left many of us discouraged. I can almost hear a wail, "But I don't live anywhere like that at all! I've never even *seen* neighbors talking over back fences, let alone children knowing people enough to exchange friendly remarks as they roller-skate." And the person might glumly add, "In reality, dear Susan, around me most of the time nobody is at home. People dash in and out without enough time to even listen to their own family, let alone to a neighbor in trouble. You paint a romantic picture."

Friendly neighborhood support *is* disappearing fast. People's lives are so full that they cannot give extra time to others, or they don't even want to. On top of this, the prevalent attitude is that the more information and educational activities that are crammed into children's lives, the more "advanced" youngsters will be. Children are rushed about and have full schedules too. We have got it all wrong. With all the stress and the too-much, we snuff out life. *Motivation is quenched before it blossoms with questions and ideas.*

Our days need to be simplified so that the "string of comforting beads on our routine" do not disappear. We need to take in a lot less of the information and entertainment that pours in from TV, videos, CD-ROMs, and the Internet. Mind you, each of these technologies can be good, depending on *whether it's our servant or our master.* Never before in history have people had to be so discriminating in the effort to add only people-sized portions of information to their lives! A little bit that we assimilate is better than huge avalanches of information or ideas that we cannot digest. We can all do without the trivial—and the degrading.

The same goes for activities. People try to sell us the idea that we should try to do everything. That pressure from the outside turns into an inner sense of destructive false guilt. For instance, people reading books with instructions (like this one!) may immediately feel loaded down by all the suggestions. They might exclaim, "Drat, I really am hopeless! I can't do everything here. My life is not good enough." Or "I really am a worse parent or person than I thought. Look at all I can't fit in!" Instead they could say, for instance, "Oh, I can't go for a walk every day with my family, but maybe we could take two shorter walks and one long Sunday walk a week."

This is terrible! It is just like getting a cookbook and feeling depressed because we don't like every recipe. That is why I used the beads-on-the-string image; we as persons require a basic routine for life. But there are many variations—some simply because of natural differences in ourselves or our environment, others the result of the abnormal world that intrudes into our bodies, minds, and emotions, creating challenges and pain.

The Christian worldview takes all this in. The Shepherd is unfailingly there for us when nobody else is. That is the golden cord that helps to keep us from flying apart and heals too—individuals, married couples, families decimated by death or desertion, our fellowships, churches, and mission groups. *For we alone and together are the needy, the weak, the poor, the unseeing and confused. None of us can claim that we are not in need of God's forgiveness, mercy, and care.*[1]

A beautiful prayer echoes down through the centuries from very early Christian believers. People have had to persevere through the difficulties in life in all generations.

We beseech Thee, Lord and Master, to be our help and suc-
cour. Save those who are in tribulation; have mercy on the
lonely; lift the fallen; show Thyself unto the needy; heal the
ungodly; convert the wanderers of Thy people; feed the hungry; raise up the weak; comfort the faint-hearted. Let all the
peoples know that Thou art God alone, and Jesus Christ is
Thy Son, and that we are Thy people and the sheep of Thy
pasture; for the sake of Christ Jesus. Amen.[2]

ST. CLEMENT OF ROME

There is a story I like, about a frightened little boy who was told
to go upstairs to bed. He was scared of the dark. I guess the adults
were comfortably involved in conversation or books, because he
was told to go up alone. He wailed, and this poor little chap was
told that he should buck up: "Jesus is with you." A pause came,
then a fearful response: "Yes, but Jesus doesn't have skin!"

Jesus knew how he felt. "Blessed are those who have not seen
and yet have believed" (John 20:29). He didn't think it was easy
even to believe in someone unseen, let alone be comforted in the
dark at five years old. So He gave us each other. *We* are the ones
who hug. *We* are the ones who can bring nutritious, hot meals into
a home struck by disaster. *We* are the ones who can sit by someone
facing death, hold that person's hand, or answer questions. We are
meant to be there.

This is probably the most compelling reason for keeping our
calendars and daily plans simple. Caring and friendship takes
time. These are exactly the ingredients we lose in all the rush.

People typically say that they wouldn't have time to write to
their parents every week. (Staying in touch must be part of the com-
mandment: "Honor your father and your mother.")[3] People have
no time for even occasional letters (and visits if possible) to brothers and sisters. Grandparents are so busy with rounds of golf and
healthy swimming (good activities) that they can't have grandchildren visit during a vacation time. Others say there is no time even
for a daily family meal, let alone for reading a book together, hav-

ing conversations, taking walks, or picnics with games. *"No time."*
So this being true, what are the chances that we find ourselves on
a street with anybody at home long enough to nod to, let alone find
time to help each other?

Most of us have to acknowledge we are part of the problem. We
are perhaps isolated because everyone around us is caught up in
nonstop "mechanized" programs. There are no pauses where life
and living happens, no leisure where relationships grow.

Sadly, convinced Christians often operate under a misconception that really compounds the problem. They may have been
brainwashed to think that we are only to offer a good turn to a
neighbor or become a friend so as to have an opportunity to ped-
dle our beliefs.

Of course we know we have life's secret. The message of the
open doorway to life, escape from eternal death and despair, needs
telling. However, *we are fellow human beings first.* Sometimes our
neighbors ask a question or want to know more about our beliefs,
and sometimes they don't. Family and friends who do not share
our worldview probably over time know well what our convictions
are. We pray for them, but we are not to keep ramming these beliefs
down their throats! We pray on and keep alert for openings that
come from them, but day in and day out we go on being faithful
sons, daughters, parents, brothers, sisters, friends, and neighbors.

Other people have a lot to teach us. We enjoy times together. We
give and take. I believe it is a prostitution of our Christian belief to
see helping our neighbor only as a means to the end of "telling
them the Good News." Of course, if we know this Good News and
experience abundant life, we'd love to share it. There is no doubt
that this "telling" will be a priority. However, we cannot determine
when someone is ready to hear. People sometimes ponder over the
ideas and perhaps yearn for faith. Later they may be "prepared
ground" for planting seed.[4] But love is to shine on regardless in
life's relationships.

My grandfather was very angry and disappointed when his
only child, my father, became a Christian. He was dismayed when

Dad battled many odds to go to college and prepare for the ministry, believing this was God's will for his life. Both grandparents stood against Dad's beliefs, life plans, and subsequent pastoral ministry. My dad prayed on faithfully, even though there were no openings to talk to them about Christ. While other working-class men suffering as a result of the Depression were changed through my dad's ministry, my grandfather (and grandmother) were obdurate.

The young couple who were my parents continued in faithful relationship to both sets of parents, the supportive Christian ones and the difficult ones, week in, week out. Dad wrote a weekly letter to his own parents, and my mother wrote to hers. Sacrificially they'd visit at Christmas and other holidays. They tried to be satisfactory children. Then fifteen years after my dad's conversion and new life perspective, a telephone call came. My grandfather had had a massive heart attack and lay sick "unto death" in a Philadelphia hospital. Into the night my parents drove, and then they walked into a darkened hospital room. It was wartime, and in fear of air attack, lights were not allowed. (For some reason there were not adequate black-out curtains.) Dad walked over to the shadowy bed. From it came a voice, "Boy, tell me about your Jesus."

My dear grandfather, whom I can remember loving as a toddler, lay there. His life had been so hard—from a childhood spent as a laborer sorting Pennsylvania coal (which was so scarring he never talked to his son about it) to an unsatisfying marriage. He had an intelligent mind, with no opportunities to fulfill its potential. My grandfather, my neighbor. Love so often comes first, along with a responsive quietness that will be ready to tell about the Source of that love, that truth, the sure and beautiful life when the time is right. We pray that the loved one, the friend, the neighbor will find the pearl of great price.

Words alone, we are told, are "clanging cymbals" and offensive noise, a stench.[5] We dare not, we must not prostitute love. We are not God; we do not see another person's heart or life. We should never sell our friendship and love as a means to an end. The problem for all of us is that our time on earth is so limited. We'd love to be better friends, do more together, be able to help out more. I found it encouraging to be told once, "A little bit of help is a lot of help." Love is powerful and deep. And to be called "love," it has to be pure with no strings attached. My grandfather came to an understanding of Christian belief in the right season in his life.

A friend, a faithful prayer warrior, has had a disappointing life humanly speaking. She was an unmarried Christian worker, and due to a condition she had while she was still young, she became blind. She has a little apartment home and garden, and spends time praying. She both enjoys the companionship of God[6] and also battles away in prayer for many of us everywhere. Twice each week she sets out to a local residential home for needy babies. She brings her loving arms and heart to hold infants suffering from drug addictions that afflicted them while yet unborn. She spends hours rocking them lovingly. The angels must smile in relief that she and others are there for such little ones. These babies will have such short and painful lives. It is Jesus' wish that they should be comforted, talked to, sung over.

God's love. Our love. Real caring. This is needed, and every single good act is important to God. But He knows our frame; we are not to kill ourselves trying to do more than we can. Being friends to one lonely mother is important. Inviting in one isolated foreign student for regular family meals counts. This is how it is done. We together are meant to be permeating society, each being a light: "You in your small corner, and I in mine."[7]

Some of you reading this will be adults who were once the children who played throughout our home. Some among you are now bringing up children, going out to work, or are elders and deacons in churches. Some teach Sunday school, while others still search for life's meaning and truth. You have neighbors in places all around the globe. I hear of parents of a handicapped baby comforted here, children cared for when there is need there. I hear of counsel given to unhappy pregnant women and of a lonely elderly person befriended. A few of you have gone out to distant lands with truth plus love and help for all kinds of poverty. Another flies a mighty aircraft designed to defend and protect citizens against evil powers. Many more tend home fires faithfully, being the sweet strength in everyday life. Some teach school, and others volunteer in needy public schools and youth projects.

What am I meant to do today? What are you meant to do?

Because of the growing failure of communities to function, many find themselves living alienated from any neighborliness.[8] This is as true for many single people with busy work lives as for the increasingly isolated mothers at home full time and the elderly. Such people face streets and backyards empty of supportive relationships. For many, fear stalks just behind loneliness. Because of this reality, we need to devise local strategies.

Solutions can be innovative. I knew of a church in a Canadian city whose members decided that they would all find living accommodations (apartments and houses) in one neighborhood. The criterion was to live within walking distance of each other. Choosing areas with sidewalks makes this possible. The development of residential areas without sidewalks was a giant leap backward for contemporary people. Planners were accommodating the car rather than human beings.

Citizens can work together for the good of their town or city. They can put pressure on civic officials to make changes, bringing back sidewalks, bicycle paths, and parks. We must not be passive in these matters.

I know of people who chose to live near each other in an inner-city area to be "salt" and "light" there. This place had been a lost cause in everyone's minds, including the residents. Christian families and single people started a church after they moved in and became active neighbors. A housing association was formed (as I have mentioned before). People were relieved to have a righteous landlord with reasonable rents and decent dwellings. When I visited one of the streets not long ago, my eye delighted to see that in a vacant lot, instead of broken glass, there were little garden plots, vegetables in neat rows, flowers here and there—all defying the boarded-up windows, the guns, the drunken misery.

In more economically favored neighborhoods other kinds of stark poverty can exist. One of the most neglected children I've ever seen was growing up in a home of immense wealth. The children had professional nannies covering their care in eight-hour shifts. One of the children became a friend to one of mine. How she loved days playing in our apartment and garden! She loved the stories read aloud too and meals all together around the table. When she grew up, she returned once to visit. The sophisticated-looking woman froze to the floor when she walked into the room. She hungrily gazed at every detail and said, "This is where we read stories around the fire. Do you still read?" She was hungry for God's love too.

"Faith, hope and love. But the greatest of these is love" (1 Cor. 13:13).

Many of us are "just" living ordinary, everyday lives. This is great! Life, good and right life, should exist in every corner. Your street and mine will do well.

First of all, having moved in somewhere, we ourselves need to be part of a web of life shared with others. We should take that into consideration when we move. "Where are the churches where I can be part of a community of believers?" is an important question for Christians to ask. For us sound biblical teaching is the very bread of life, as it brings the reality of God and His truth to life for us. Here is our allegiance.

The next question is closely related: Does the church offer a viable fellowship—where friendships can grow, prayer be shared, help given and received? It is not always possible to live within a short drive, let alone at the ideal walking or bicycling distance of our church fellowship. Distance is an issue. Surely Christians should meet with others living nearby if at all possible. How can we operate as a community if we aren't close enough to be friends?

Then what about schools—if we have children? Are the neighborhood's schools the right ones for us? Some will be rightly choosing where to live for their family's sake. (Just as we choose nourishing foods and books that build up and don't deconstruct goodness for us.)

Others know that they are to move into "their corner" for others. Some go to work and live in refugee camps for that reason, others to places with all sorts of great needs—their hometown's inner-city streets or somewhere distant.

Another choice for some is to be near the family. One of my cousins and her husband turned down an attractive job on the East Coast (USA) for a city up in the north. My aging, widowed aunt would otherwise have had no family near her. I know of many missionaries who knew that their place was to come home to be near ailing parents, and still others who stayed on the mission field. *All these different moves represent right choices before God.*

Once we move in somewhere, we must make it a home. We should also start finding a community to fit into. When one of my daughters was pregnant with a first child, she and her husband moved to a new city. On a Monday morning, her first day there, she walked into a reliable church and went to the office. "Is there a women's Bible study meeting today?" There was. She went, and over coffee and open Bibles she suddenly had a roomful of women of all ages who responded warmly to her need for friends. These women stepped in; they gave her useful local information. Immediately she was invited into homes, and then and there friendships started forming. Soon she and her husband were part of a circle of people.

This is just the kind of all-around support people need. A couple of years later when the young couple rented a tiny home near the university, some of these friends were within walking (and stroller-pushing) distance. By this time a few mothers would care for each other's children so they could take turns having free mornings. Husbands helped each other fix cars and do other tasks. This is a practical supportive community.

It is important for groups to pray together regularly. The informal intimacy of women praying together regularly offers a freedom to share personal burdens that would be difficult to bring up in more public mixed gatherings. We mothers will share the "small" but actually heavy concerns of a child not sleeping or a teenager one is worried sick about. Along with prayer comes neighborly support. The group I just wrote about in an American city would help each other move, paint rooms, and lend equipment as well as pray. Such groups provide a substitute neighborhood for people living in scattered areas without functional communities.

Another sort of link is a local church house group that meets weekly. These often include people of all ages, married and unmarried. This is special too; deep friendships can be forged; mutual understanding can grow. A cross section of people is more representative of a "body."

One caution—as well as being in small support groups, we should each develop relationships with those living near us or working with us as much as possible. Our real neighbors need time, and we must leave time for them. It is a question of realistic planning and balance again.

Communities have always had their "all-together" rhythms as well as individual ones. Just as every day has its satisfying routine, so does the week, the month, and the year. We see an excellent example of this in Old Testament society.

According to the Scriptures, God created the seventh day to be free from labor. Having one day to rest each week is actually so important that it is part of the Ten Commandments, right along with laws such as not murdering or stealing![9] If we buy a machine and totally ignore the maker's instructions, of course it will break down. That is what happens to people and societies that break God's laws and life patterns.

The sweet sanity and wholesome effect of one day off every seven is now hard to find. Parking spaces near supermarkets are as difficult to find on Sunday as on weekdays; people commute hither and yon under stress. And it is usual to see stressed children in the backs of cars.

Our culture as a whole has been slowly giving up the health-giving routine of the shared day of rest. Interestingly, when communism wanted to break down former patterns of thought and values, they designed weeks so that there was no day off on Sunday (so worship stopped too). Take this away, and you destroy a lot.

We should choose to respect this creation ordinance. The Sabbath is a gift that is a benefit to us. In Hebrew homes, before the Sabbath many practical preparations were made for this different day. It was (and is) from sundown to sundown and started with the most special family meal of the week. Candlesticks were (and are) polished. The food is the best possible; homemade bread smells good. There is eager anticipation as this break from the tiring round of work draws near. Ordinary relationships and life are celebrated and enjoyed; God is worshiped and remembered. The week is complete.

We were once in a church that had many young families. Often one or both of the parents worked outside the home; the weekend was a key part of the week for all, married or single. We believed it was important to gather for worship and Sunday school, but that it was also important for people to have a simple-enough Sunday schedule so that they could rest and enjoy at-home relationships too. Thus we decided to have only a morning service. During the rest of the day there was time for walks, naps, all sorts of leisurely occupations as individuals chose.

Practical decisions must be made to keep Sunday special. Surely it cannot be right to shop for food or anything else on a Sunday! Are there not six other days? Planning ahead makes the day free of unnecessary work; choices must be made.

Some of us do have to work on Sunday. Of course there are church workers, and for them it can be an exhausting day. Then there are those who work in residential communities for the elderly or for those with other special needs. There are hospitals and ambulances, and we need policemen on duty Sunday too. In such jobs we must find our "one day in seven of rest" on a weekday. Hopefully, when we have a family, it should be on a day when we can relax together. This rhythm is good for individuals, families, and communities.

Many of us nowadays can schedule in other breaks. Some people always have two full days off a week (the weekend). This is especially important in the sort of home situation where one person (often the father) leaves early and only returns by supper time. The weekend gives an extra day for the more relaxed morning start, special projects such as painting a room, gardening together, or doing something necessary. Relationships grow while family or friends enjoy special days out hiking together, visiting an art museum, or doing some other activity that would be refreshing. It is wonderful to have a day like this—and worth careful thought. We must be careful though to include relaxation, doing a bit less, and leisure.

Sometimes it is possible for a married couple to get away alone for a weekend. Such short breaks help counteract stress that can build up in our relationships. We can relax together and talk over matters. Sharing something we both enjoy is a breath of life, and so is laughter. And of course when you are building up a marriage, extra time to enjoy each other physically is good.

Another idea some people can incorporate at regular intervals is setting aside half or whole days for another kind of break in the regular pattern. Some individuals and communities take days for fasting and prayer. This does not need to mean that *necessary* sustenance is neglected. It does mean that the usual "beads on the string" of life are replaced temporarily for extra time and quiet attention to be given to prayer and feeding on God's Word in our hearts with thanksgiving.

A prayer day can be relaxed, a time to look back to give thanks, time to look forward trusting God, time to be able to understand how we feel or identify what is on our minds and then to bring it to God.[10] At other times we have been so worried by something that it has affected our sleep and/or appetite. While it is important to return to our regular routine soon, it is sometimes good to give attention to our unrest. Jesus would spend starry nights in prayer; we can do the same when we toss and turn with sleep far away. Sometimes it is a relief to get up, make a hot drink, and turn to God. I can't think what my nonbelieving friends do with their concerns!

Christians are told that in marriage they are usually to consider each other's sexual needs. But in times of need for special prayer, even this can be put aside "by mutual consent." This is fasting too.[11]

A day set aside for prayer without usual mealtimes or routine tasks is biblical. In L'Abri we've always had such days. Those who cook or help in kitchens appreciate the opportunity to lay down tools and have a whole day to read and pray in quiet. Our custom is to have soup, bread, fruit, and yogurt left in the kitchen for people to help themselves to as the need arises. Each washes the plate used before leaving. It can be a day for extra rest too. Amy Carmichael told her family in Dohnavur that if, on such a day, they fell asleep while praying in the heat of the afternoon, that was good. She quoted, "He giveth his beloved sleep." A nature walk is also appropriate or simply being still before the Lord.

In a busily active life, occasional days are also well spent if there is just a general change of pace. Then perhaps we can read the book that is life-giving to our minds, paint the picture we wanted to, or pick up a hobby. We come back strengthened for the daily routines. It is dangerous to get too lopsided. Prayer includes reading the Bible thoughtfully—the listening part of our conversation, which should not be neglected.

Of course many people are able to take vacations. These can be an excellent way to have a longer change of scene and pace. Those who feel cooped up inside can enjoy skies, coastlines, or forests. Others working outdoors may prefer to visit a lovely city and go to an art museum or concerts.

When we have children, we have to be realistic. It can be counterproductive to plan vacation breaks that aren't really enjoyable due to children's ages or one's financial constraints. Once again we must work within the frame of what is possible.

And this brings me full circle back to the truth that it is the balance of our everyday lives that is vital. We cannot rescue a life that is a sinking ship in one heroic vacation! Our lives should be healthy enough for us individually and together everyday. This is what counts long term.

The Christian year is marked with the great celebrations of Christian hope. We express these in our church life, at home, and in our communities. Easter is at the heart of the Christian year. Then comes Christmas when we remember the birth of our Savior, "God with us."[12] Both holidays have traditionally been considered so important that preparation is made for them weeks ahead. This has nothing to do with commercial pressure to spend more than we can afford or to suffer extra stress doing just that.[13]

Of course, Christian converts from pagan cultures wanted to change their previous festivals. Now they had the good news of forgiveness, love, and life! God who was made man came to dwell among us—the mystery of a young Israelite woman in an impoverished shelter, wrapping her newborn infant in simple bands of cloth and laying Him in an animal's feed box. Those of us who have been pregnant remember the first felt movements of a baby, the birth later, and the first gaze into a little face. This is a miracle in itself. But we enter this shelter with awe as a fellow mother bends over an ordinary-looking baby boy. She looks up, and our glances meet. In the depths of her eyes you see she'll never to her dying day forget the tiniest detail of this birth. Her little one is God. He existed before creation. He was one of three Persons who created everything, including human beings. All of us were made in the image[14] of the one eternal God.[15]

This young mother, like and yet unlike us, knows the dependent cry that is soothed as usual through her milk and loving arms. But uniquely this little child will be the Savior given to all the world,[16] a light for those who live in darkness, a light of revelation, a light that is life.[17] In caring for Him, Mary gives all of us hope. All mothers desire the best for their children; this mother has a once-only calling to bring The Hope of the World to birth and to bring Him up for the good of all.[18] Her Son's life will bring her joy; His suffering will bring her anguish. She will ponder many wonders; a sword will rip through her heart to the center of her being.[19]

We find her again at the cross. Others who are followers, some who will be apostles, have abandoned the Savior at His darkest moment. His mother is there, along with other women. She perse-veres to the end.[20] All history is to call her blessed[21] and remember her life, although the focus is and always will be on her Son. He brings the light. She bore Him into the ordinary everyday of actual history and cared for Him there. This is not just a story. If the bibli-cal narrative is truth, this happened as truly as your birth or mine. Christians have naturally desired to celebrate the birth of their sweet, dear Lord Jesus.

The early church chose Easter as the best moment in the year for new believers and their families to be baptized and to join the inner circle of believers. The converts came from a variety of back-grounds, many being scarred emotionally from past hard lives. Prosperous merchants (both men and women), scruffy odd-job men, slave women who had been used sexually since before puberty, solid Jewish families who already knew about the God of the Scriptures, previously cruel masters needing to learn compas-sion and humility, people with no sense of self-worth who needed building up, women beautifully dressed but imprisoned as chattel of a Roman husband, contrasting with a runaway slave or two—*what* a crowd! Nothing like this had been seen before.

Early church converts represent the varied throng of humanity that chooses to follow Christ: He promised full forgiveness and assurance of eternal life to each and every one. Typically, they started listening to the Gospel and then believed that it was true. They then accepted the lordship of Christ by a personal choice. They could pray right away, but they still had a lot to learn too. They listened carefully to teaching in the Christian fellowship and asked for baptism, thus burning the bridges behind them. This decision was courageous, and it must have felt especially strange to those who usually expected others (such as a slave owner or hus-band) to choose for them!

Newcomers were startled to have their world turned upside down. From then on, they learned, all the long-held traditions about who was more and less important in society had to be for-gotten. Gone. Here there was to be no rift or superiority in any way:

Jew or Greek, Roman, Asian, or African. (The Mediterranean Rim has always been cosmopolitan.) Here were to be no distinctions between rich or poor, slave or free, educated elite or illiterate "scum." Converts must have been startled and offended too when they found out that the lowly were to be respected as much as a Roman centurion in all his fine adornment, as much as a learned rabbi. In this assembly such a one had to listen respectfully to a slave or to a person who shoveled manure. For many the greatest shock was that women were equal with men. Prejudices and habits of lifetimes and entire cultures had to be broken. And this was only the beginning. People would not have drifted into such society, for it asked for a great deal of change. They came because they were sure that Christian claims were true (Gal. 3:26-29).

Anyway, the preparation and anticipation for Easter was enormous. By the time the annual festival came, the baptismal candidates had been instructed carefully. They would have shown that they were trying to follow God's ways[22] in their everyday, ordinary lives as they were waiting to be baptized. Those who had been thieves had given up stealing and had a decent job.[23] Men had stopped visiting female or male prostitutes;[24] some of them had married. They and others were learning how to have homes of order and love, where each person, whatever age or gender, was respected.[25] A few older women helped instruct others in this practical, everyday aspect of learning to live a Christian life.

The whole church waited for the special annual rejoicing of Easter. Poorer families would have saved up so that a special meal could be enjoyed on the big day. Cleanliness really does go with godliness: Houses and forecourt would be swept in readiness for the special celebration.

But they were taught that the visible cleanup was not enough. When we celebrate something very wonderful, we prepare our inner selves too. Of course, in that congregation, some were just stopping the most blatant sins. They struggled to stop cheating with their weights in the market or to stop abusing their wives and so on. Others seemed picture perfect on the outside, but their Lord had told them not to look merely on the outside. God looks on the heart.[26]

There is always internal house-cleaning for people to do. And they were going to take their first Communion after their baptism, which always needs careful inner preparation.[27] Thus it became the custom that the days leading up to Easter were for special personal reflection. "Is my inner self reflecting Christ's life?" They and we also must ask ourselves, "When His light shines into my heart and everyday life, what does it show up that needs changing?"[28]

This type of questioning and subsequent insight clear the way for goodness to be chosen and grow in our everyday lives, with God's help. This is the best preparation for celebrating our response to God's love to us in Jesus! Of course, we listen, read, understand,[29] and pray to have God's help every single day of the year. But busy routines can easily result in habitual complacency. We can get stuck along the way and stop making progress. It is good to set aside a special *thoughtful season* regularly to "take stock" and respond.

Christians came to call this special preparation time Lent.[30] This season emphasizes taking Christ's Word right into our everyday lives and choosing to obey even the hard requirements.

Of course, not all of us who are now Christians are in traditions that still use the beautiful old liturgies for Lent. But we should pause to consider the idea behind the practice. Such a response to Christ's life, death, resurrection, and offer of salvation to each of us personally is more appropriate than getting lost in wrapping paper or chocolate. We are in danger of losing even the concept of a truly Christian celebration. The price for God, for Jesus, was high. Dare we be trivial or materialistic in our memorial times? It is better not to sing hymns of thanks and praise than to do so glibly.

Old wisdom decreed that there should be extra simplicity of life in the weeks before these two momentous times of remembrance for Christians. Such wisdom is practical. Chosen simplicity for a season can mean more time for reflection, prayer, and reading together or alone. Simplicity provides a contrast with the celebration feast! For, yes, we are creatures of body as well as spirit, and it is good to celebrate our Christian belief at home and in our communities with special meals and glad happiness, just as Jewish believers before us had their great festivals.

Sadly, *any* plan we make to help ourselves spiritually can easily become another ossified and meaningless ritual. Worse, it can become a "good deed" that we *do* to earn God's approval, which entirely misses the point of grace and salvation freely received. Maybe we need to make plans flexible to avoid such difficulties.

Of course, the joy of Jesus is with us everyday. But celebrating the most important events with feasts, fun, fellowship, and loving thoughtfulness has always has been part of home and community life. And for Christians, Jesus is the source of all life, hope, and comfort.

As centuries passed, many Christians also set aside a time for expectant preparation for Christmas: Advent. This word comes from the Latin *adventus*, which means "coming." Christians prepared to celebrate the first coming of Christ along with looking forward to His coming again as Judge and King. Hymns such as this twelfth- to thirteenth-century one are sung at Advent services:

> *O come, O come, Emmanuel, and*
> *ransom captive Israel,*
> *That mourns in lonely exile here, until*
> *the Son of God appear. . . .*
> *O come, Thou Key of David, come and*
> *open wide our heavenly home. . . .*

In the 1662 *Book of Common Prayer* the Reformers included both Lent and Advent preparation services, prayers, and readings. The "main" prayer (Collect) for the first Sunday and week of Advent was written by Thomas Cranmer, scholar and reformer (1549). It expresses preparation for Christmas and also for Christ's second coming.

Almighty God, give us grace that we may cast away the works of darkness, and put upon us the armour of light, now in the time of this mortal life, in which thy Son Jesus Christ came to visit us in great humility; that in the last day when he shall come again in his glorious majesty to judge both the quick[31] and the dead, we may rise to the life immortal, through him who liveth and reigneth with thee and the Holy Ghost, now and ever. Amen.

In homes and churches Advent has come to have special traditions such as lighting candles on a wreath on the four Sundays before Christmas. On the first Sunday, one candle is lit; on the second Sunday, two are lit; on the third Sunday, three. On the last Sunday all four candles are glowing. This practice helps create a joyous expectancy in the everyday.

In any celebration Christians are meant to look out for the lonely. Celebrating Jesus' life does not necessarily mean a traditional family day. I've known people who use festive days to help run hospitality centers for the homeless. A family in Canada took over a guest house every year to provide an open home over the Christmas holiday for overseas students of many nationalities and religions. It is very lonely for such people in many of our cultures over these days. Shops close, and they wander past houses with brightly lit windows to return to a solitary lunch of precooked noodles.

The phrase "no room in the inn" should echo in our hearts, for Jesus' sake. Of course, we cannot do everything. We may have babies and young children or elderly folk to think about. Our hands may be full already. We should never feel guilty when we are just within our limit; in such a case we cannot ourselves do anything extra for needy others at Christmas or Easter. But perhaps we could donate the money we would have used for a movie or to eat out to a local center providing a Christmas meal for elderly people who would otherwise sit alone. When we are celebrating Christ's love and life, we should demonstrate His love in practical ways.

For the homemaker, there are lots of ideas for celebrations. We adapt our plans to suit our time, energy, and finances and create meaningful occasions that can be enjoyed by our group of folk.

Birthdays come once a year for every child. Although we love and cherish each child every day, birthdays are opportunities to show this love visibly and enjoyably. Different families have different traditions. These traditions are important. As with Christmas, love is not proved through expensive gifts. However, being made to feel special really is crucial to a child's development. In the West birthdays are often happy opportunities to invite in friends for a suitable social time together.

I find it sad that more and more parents seem to fear that a simple homemade party will be scorned. The reverse is usually true, in my experience. Number of guests invited should be realistic; plans should be made that suit the group. All sorts of other ideas can be fun too. Sometimes it is best to enjoy birthdays just as a special family time. In other years, the child invites home a friend overnight, or the child and friend are taken out to a treat. There is no one way that is "right." Many families have their own customs that suit their own homes.

Different countries have national celebration days too. Americans have Thanksgiving in November and the Fourth of July. England has Harvest Thanksgiving, celebrated in village churches after the harvest is over locally. This special service is attended by those who rarely go to church. The children and women decorate the church with harvest produce and flowers. Food gifts are brought to donate to the needy in the community. Sometimes a village meal is served in the village hall.

In America Thanksgiving Day is a day to thank God for His gifts. This day is traditionally celebrated with a family reunion with a huge meal, typically including roast turkey and pumpkin pies, and nowadays many finish off watching a football game! The celebration commemorates the original Pilgrim fathers who planned a three-day feast to thank the Lord for all His provision and care after the first harvest.

In Switzerland there is the magical *First of August*. Fires are lit on the highest point in villages and mountain peaks commemorating the fact that the light of democracy has shone out here since their Constitution was written in the 1200s. My childish American heart used to beat harder with gladness as we celebrated freedom from tyranny nearly 800 years ago! We'd carry our paper lanterns lit by a burning candle in happy procession up the hill behind the village band. The bonfire would blaze, and the village choir would sing. The pastor would make a speech, and so would the local community representative. Meanwhile children would set off fireworks that whizzed with un-Swiss abandon between people's legs. It was and is always a happy and proud night shared by villages and towns.

All countries have a national identity. These celebrations should usually be entered into and enjoyed. They help bind a people together in a shared aspect of life.

For my Dutch friends, St. Nicholas Day is December's fun moment.[32] Then children receive gifts and chocolate. (And it leaves Christmas to be celebrated with proper Dutch respect.)

Going back to our own homes anywhere, it is good to think about what *our* year's rhythm is—our community and family celebrations, our nation's special days. Some celebrations, such as Halloween, may promote ungodly practices. These practices are discarded or altered totally when people become Christians. They develop locally appropriate celebrations and traditions to replace unclean ones. Fun can and should be as pure as possible.

All cultures feast at special occasions; weddings are a good example. The celebration of a new marriage or birth is a joyous and hopeful time for the whole community.

In a different and yet similar way, death brings us together. Traditions differ, but we have a lot to learn from the more rooted communities of the past. Back then death, like birth, usually occurred right at home. The person was carefully washed by a neighbor and possibly a loved one. In some places it was the tradition for neighbors to come into the home and show support by sitting up with the coffin through the night. This practice exhibited concern and provided company in a hard time ("in the skin," as the little boy said). Many a tired relative who had missed sleep felt freer to drop off to sleep, knowing someone else was "on duty." Or if a person couldn't sleep at all, such a custom meant companionship and a drink together.

Many cultures share the neighborly custom of bringing cooked food to the bereaved family for several days. I've known neighbors in different countries who have offered beds for relatives or care for children. Some sort of reunion of family and friends occurs after a funeral, usually a meal shared along with memories. Someone may say, "Oh, if only (the name of the one who died) could be here; how they'd enjoy it!"

Perhaps that paragraph is as good a place as any to end this book. Like life, this book could go on and on! *For homes are about all of life, from our first weak cry to that last time our eyes close. What happens in between is our life's story.*

Some of us have easier times in life, some harder. We can all look forward to the sure gladness of the life ahead that starts a new chapter when we breathe our last down here. The days in between matter; the weeks matter. Loving God comes first. His light and life slowly can transform our everyday, ordinary round of human life. With His pure goodness comes increased contentment in every part of life. His love and forgiveness can heal our hurts substantially over time; we gradually enjoy our fellow human beings more as we should.

Because of His joy and peace, we are ready to live our lives faithfully in *our* "everyday," whatever that means for us. The ordinary has been blessed. It is good. Faithfulness "in my small corner" helps to redeem life. Thus we find *"the glory of the usual."* Here is true greatness.

O God, who knowest us to be set in the midst of so many and great dangers, that by reason of the frailty of our nature we cannot always stand upright: Grant to us such strength and protection, as may support us in all dangers, and carry us through all temptations; through Jesus Christ our Lord. Amen.[33]

Appendix

Charlotte Maria Shaw Mason

Charlotte M. S. Mason was born in 1842 and died in January 1923 in Ambleside in the Lake District. In 1860 she became a student at the first training college for teachers in England, the Home and Colonial Training College in London. She gained a first-class certificate in 1863.

After several years of teaching, she began to lecture in a teachers' training college. When parents heard of her ideas, they invited her to talk to groups around the country. By 1887 the Parents' National Educational Union (PNEU) was formed to advance her philosophy of education.

A key to the wide influence of the PNEU was that it developed multiple-use programs—for governesses, home-school mothers, and the PNEU schools of such excellent repute. This was no hidden experiment. The PNEU flourished, as did the children. The "graduates" have influenced British culture for a century.

The children's study programs were carefully crafted, and their narrations were examined twice a year, providing a disciplined "gold standard." Usually for young children, the examiners were university academics who knew their subjects at the highest level.

PNEU schools became known for their happy, natural atmosphere and a rich curriculum. Secondary schools welcomed the children from these schools, as the students were well-prepared, with excellent habits of attention and good attitudes.

In 1892 the first students came to Charlotte Mason in Ambleside to be trained as teachers. The next years were ones of constant growth. Charlotte Mason was writing books that many parents and teachers found inspirational. By the time of her death, she had the respect of a whole generation. Elsie Kitching, her coworker and friend wrote, "Charlotte Mason lived to be eighty-one. She did not keep letters or diaries. 'I do not wish my life to be written; it is the work that matters; it will live.' Her work was to her a great adventure. . . ."[1]

Clifford Allbutt, a Cambridge academic, wrote a month after her death in 1923: "Charlotte Mason reanimated and reformed a large part of education in Great Britain. . . ." He describes how after visiting her in Ambleside, he understood how her influence had come about: "One became vividly aware in her of a lucid view of affairs, and an intellectual grasp of principles, animated by the inward warmth and sympathy of hope. . . ."[2]

The *Times Educational Supplement* published the following personal tribute four days after her death on January 20, 1923:

Charlotte Mason was that rare combination, an original thinker and philosopher and at the same time a wonderful organizer and businesswoman. She was wise and witty, keenly interested in the things of the world, birds and flowers, books and people, but with an inner vision for the beyond, and the graciousness of manner and selfless consideration for others which marked the *grande dame* of a passing age. She treated the smallest child with courtesy. She was gracious to the youngest member of her household just as she was to the great of the land who were among her disciples. . . .

Her teaching has spread to almost every corner of the globe; the pupils of her correspondence school are to be found in home schoolrooms, in private and council schools, and many generations of happy children filled with the joy of living and learning will rise up and call her blessed.[3]

Charlotte Mason's influence and the PNEU's unique educational philosophy seemed to have waned as this century came to its close. However, the ideas are timeless and are as true and alive today as they were when she first wrote, spoke, and worked.

There has been a revival of interest in Charlotte Mason's ideas, a movement that is spreading internationally. A new generation of parents and teachers are once again walking up the hill to Scale How to sit at the feet of this wise woman and to learn how to live life "for the children's sake" (motto of the House of Education, Ambleside).

Francis and Edith Schaeffer

The Schaeffers, my parents, were the founders of L'Abri Fellowship. Francis A. Schaeffer was born January 12, 1912, in Philadelphia, Pennsylvania. He died on May 5, 1984. Edith R. Schaeffer was born November 3, 1914, in Wenchow, Chekiang Province, China, of missionary parents. Their combined life story and that of L'Abri Fellowship until 1981 can be read in:

• *The Tapestry* by Edith Schaeffer, Word Books (now out of print, worth borrowing). An unusual and intriguing book with a good story and vital ideas.

• *L'Abri* by Edith Schaeffer. A story about the early days of L'Abri. Updated edition published by Crossway Books, 1992.

The ideas relating historical, biblical Christianity to the reality of thought, culture, and our own lives can be found in the following books by Francis A. Schaeffer. These are all published as separate volumes or in *The Complete Works of Francis A. Schaeffer* by Crossway Books:

• *The God Who Is There*
• *He Is There and He Is Not Silent*
• *Escape from Reason*

• *How Should We Then Live?* by Francis A. Schaeffer. A historical overview of Western culture giving us a perspective on changes in thought, society, and personal choices. Published by Crossway Books, 1983. A companion video series is available from Gospel Films, USA.

• *Whatever Happened to the Human Race?* by Francis A. Schaeffer and Dr. C. Everett Koop. An analysis of human life, its value, and the problem of ethical choices such as abortion, infanticide, and euthanasia—issues we all face at this time. Exposes how human life has been cheapened, as laws based on God's standards have been replaced by laws based on man's standards. Published by Crossway Books, 1983. A companion video series is available from Gospel Films, USA.

Edith Schaeffer's books have become classics. People continually tell me that her writings have had a major influence in their lives. Several books of hers that especially apply to aspects of this book will expand and complement chapters here. The works listed deal with practical matters, the difficulties in everyday life, our choices, and related ideas:

• *Hidden Art of Homemaking*. About creativity in our everyday lives wherever we are. Published by Tyndale, United Kingdom, 1998.

• *What Is a Family?* Published by Baker Books.

• *Affliction*. Published by Paternoster, United Kingdom, 1996, and Baker Books in the USA, 1996.

• *Common Sense Christian Living*. Answers many commonly asked questions. Published by Baker Books, 1997.

• *The Life of Prayer*. Published by Crossway Books, 1992.

• *MeiFuh*. Published by Houghton Mifflin. Delightful stories of Edith Schaeffer's childhood in China at the beginning of the century, with special line drawings that accurately portray the scenes. This outstanding book will appeal to all ages and may be read aloud to children from five years old or so. Appropriate for families and schools.

Ranald and Susan Macaulay

Susan Schaeffer Macaulay—born to Francis and Edith Schaeffer, May 1941 in Pennsylvania.

My father was a Presbyterian minister in Grove City and Chester, Pennsylvania, and then in St. Louis, Missouri. In 1947 a group of churches sent him to make a postwar survey of Protestant Christians across Europe. He returned to the United States with a deep desire to help and encourage the new friends he had made on his trip. In 1948 my family moved to Europe for a four-year assignment of encouraging believers in rebuilding their faith and their lives. They initiated children's work for the uprooted generation of youngsters, believing that biblical truth was necessary for wholeness. Later this work came to include discussions with students.

My parents settled in Switzerland, as it was a central location in Europe. I grew up there, going to French-speaking schools. When I had rheumatic fever at thirteen years of age, I was given a home study course, Calvert School, which I loved.

L'Abri began in 1955 in our home. I enjoyed all the conversations, friendships, and helping with the work when I was well. At seventeen I spent a year at the University of Lausanne studying French literature before leaving for England in September 1959. I'd decided to train as an occupational therapist in a college in Headington, Oxford (not the university). My vision of that career ended not long after I met Ranald, a student from Cambridge. By Easter we knew that our lives were to be combined in marriage and that we'd work together.

Ranald Macaulay was born in South Africa in 1936 to parents of Scottish descent. He grew up there, but his family life was disrupted when his father served in World War II. A year after Ranald's early education was completed, he was accepted at Cambridge University. He arrived at the university in 1956 with no understanding of what life was ultimately about.

The first Sunday a friend took him to an evening church service, and he returned to his rented room. There he knelt and prayed to the Lord God, accepting His promises and choosing to follow Him. Not long afterward, Ranald and this same friend invited my parents to tea in Cambridge. When Ranald met them, they suddenly had his full attention. My dad was answering real questions! An understanding of the truth of Christianity began then for Ranald.

In December 1959, the winter after his graduation, he finally was able to visit the Schaeffers in their Swiss chalet. I had come back home from Oxford too. L'Abri in those days was like a small family get-together. At Easter 1960 we were engaged to be married! By that time Ranald had gone to stay at L'Abri in Huemoz, one of the first three people who came to study there. (Before that people had come as guests. The pattern of studying half a day and working half a day started then.) Ranald also became a L'Abri worker that spring.

In April 1961 we were married. We worked there in Switzerland until the summer of 1964 when L'Abri asked us to begin a nonresidential work in London. In 1971 we were asked to leave that work in someone else's hands and start up a residential branch of L'Abri Fellowship south of London in the rolling Hampshire countryside. Apart from four years back in Switzerland at L'Abri from 1984-88 and a year's sabbatical, we worked on in the lovely Manor House in Hampshire that had been given to L'Abri. We had four children born to us between 1962 and 1972, and two more, ages three and seven, joined our family in 1986 when their own parents died. (We had been named as their guardians.)

In 1997 our years in this bustling L'Abri branch drew to a close. Younger people have taken responsibility for the ongoing life there. We still are part of L'Abri Fellowship, and our days continue to hold much work. But as always, work only grows out of the fundamental fabric of home life with its regular pattern of meals together, chores, leisure, visitors, and so on.

We still have a teenager living at home and going to school every day and another a bit older starting college next fall. Our home is therefore not yet an empty nest! Grandchildren visit from time to time, and it is a particular joy to find that they love books and are read to, take walks and love nature, know about pictures and enjoy art, and are generally brought up according to Charlotte Mason's abundant-life principles.

Ranald and I have always loved God's beautiful out-of-doors, and usually our free time spent relaxing together takes the form of a good tramp or bicycle ride across meadows or hills. We don't have a car, as in this town everything is within walking and cycling distance. We enjoy simplifying our lives in such ways, as we both appreciate quiet time at home for reading, cooking, and conversations around meals or the fire. Ranald plays the piano, gardens, and sometimes paints.

We have not always made light work of our marriage: He has red hair, and I was my father's daughter! That is, we are two passionate people with what might be called eccentric personalities. It has been interesting and a challenge to forge our lives together. Both of us have always been deeply committed to making a home for our family and wanted to be fully involved in bringing up our children—our life's greatest task and its deepest joy. We both are devoted to Christ and have put our lives at His disposal in our own stumbling way.

We feel very, very blessed and enjoy each day of this chapter of our lives as we are allowed to be together in our first *little* home, just one-family big. Our message together is that although there may be dark and confusing days (even depression's gloom), through weariness and glad, happy times, in ups and in downs— God is so good. He has proved every promise reliable, even when the answer was hidden for a time.

The two cords that were our own selves in the marriage could not have held together alone, but the golden cord is there and has held true—strong and dependable. That cord is the Lord, giver of abundant life. "Taste and see that the Lord is good."

• *Being Human—The Nature of Spiritual Experience* by Ranald Macaulay and Jerram Barrs. A key book that answers the questions: Who are we as persons? How do the spiritual and physical sides of our lives fit together? Published by InterVarsity Press. E-mail: mail@ivpress.com.

• *How to Be Your Own Selfish Pig* by Susan Schaeffer Macaulay. Answers to questions people often ask about the truth, life, the Bible, and God—a springboard into the sorts of answers people get at L'Abri. A help with dinner table conversations with high school and college students! Published by Chariot Books, 1982. Due to be reprinted in 2000 by Chariot Victor Publishing.

L'Abri Fellowship

L'Abri Fellowship continues on. As before, it welcomes people from any country to stay from a few days up to three months. In the L'Abri day, everyone shares in the practical side of life together for half a day (cleaning, helping cook, gardening, etc.), and the other half of the day is free for individual study guided by one of the workers on a one-to-one tutorial basis.

All of the areas of "at-home life" function in L'Abri—meals together regularly with conversation, a day "off" for leisure, times for reading books, discussing ideas, and bringing up children (in most of the L'Abri places).

The work continues month by month as a testimony to answered prayer: It has no organizational income or resources. We believe that this is a particular calling for some Christian work, demonstrating that *the Lord hears us in whatever area we appropriately ask for His help*. (Most people are working for a salary in life; this is normative.)

Single and married people from different backgrounds and countries work together in L'Abri. All have their own home base, be it a studio apartment or larger wing of a house. L'Abri is not a commune, and the individuals working together make different personal choices. There is no director over the whole Fellowship or a local branch; we pray that God will direct us as we trust in Him and work together, both men and women.

L'Abri Branches

England: The Manor House, Greatham, Liss. Hants. GU33 6HF England. Tel: (INT)+ 01420 538436 Fax: 01420 538432. E-mail: labri_uk@compuserve.com.

Switzerland: Chalet Bellevue, 1884 Huemoz, Switzerland. Tel: (INT)+ 41 24 495 2139. Fax: 00 41 24 495 7647. E-mail: 101502.171@ compuserve.com.

Holland: Kromme Nieuwe Gracht 90, 3512 HM Utrecht, Holland. Tel: (INT)+ 31 302 316933. Fax: 00 31 30 236 8545 (personal fax). E-mail: labri@labri.nl. Eck-en-Wiel: 00 31 344 691914 (phone & fax).

Sweden: Bidevindsvagen 4, S-260 42 Molle, Sweden. Tel: (INT)+ 46 42 347632. Fax: 00 46 42 347832.

Korea: 50-2 Hooamdong, Yongsangu, Seoul 140-190, South Korea. Tel: (INT)+ 82 2 773 5309. Fax: 00 82 2 318 2595. E-mail: labri@unitel.co.kr.

United States

Southborough: 49 Lynbrook Road, Southborough, MA 01772. Tel: 508 481 6490. Fax: 508 460 5021. E-mail: 76312.3146@ compuserve.com.

Rochester: 1465 Twelfth Avenue N.E., Rochester, MN 55906. Tel: 507 282 3292. Fax: 507 282 2334. E-mail: 75551.1702@compu serve.com.

L'Abri Fellowship Resource Centers

For information, materials, occasional conferences.

Australia: Frank Stootman, 10 River Road, Elderslie, (Camden), NSW 2570, Australia. Tel: (INT)+ 61 246 580227. Fax: 00 61 246 580051. E-mail: f.stootman@uws.edu.au.

India: Vishal and Ruth Mangalwadi, Ivy Cottage, Landour, Mussoorie, UP 248 179, India. E-mail: library@wdstock.globe mail.com.

Germany: Petra and Andreas Hartmann, Haydnweg 3, 38471 Ruhen, Germany. Tel/Fax: (INT)+ 00 49 5367 981955.

Cassette Tapes

L'Abri also has many recorded L'Abri lectures and teaching sessions on cassette tapes. These can be purchased or, in Europe, borrowed as well.

For Cassettes in the USA and Canada:

Sound Word Associates, P.O. Box 2035, Mall Station, Michigan City, IN 46360. Tel: 219 879-7753 for their catalog.

For Cassettes in Australia and New Zealand:

L'Abri Cassettes, 10 River Road, Elderslie. NSW 2570, Australia. Tel: (INT)+ 61 46 580227.

For Cassettes in the United Kingdom and Europe:

L'Abri Cassettes, The Manor House, Greatham, Liss. Hants. GU33 6HF England. Tel: (INT)+ 01420 538436. Fax: 01420 538432.

Amy Carmichael and the Dohnavur Fellowship

Amy Carmichael was born in 1867 in Northern Ireland. She worked in India for fifty-five years, mostly in Dohnavur. She died in 1951.

Here is a woman whose life, achievements, and books stand out as a lighted city shines in the midst of a dark landmass as one flies over it. Her books have given a new dimension of life to many. She possessed a poetic vision and art of expression on one hand, and yet rock-hard realism and everyday practical common sense on the other. Underneath all these qualities was the breath of life and the sweet, refreshing coolness of living water. That water was Christ.

As a young woman, she left all that is usual in life, and many felt she was burying herself alive in a hot, unknown corner of the world. To her, each little scrap of a child was immensely precious, worth her Savior's dear life, and so serving each one seemed a happy privilege.

In all the loving, serving, homemaking, through courageous steps of faith, she grew as a person. She was open to life and people, and although her belief in the Lord and His Word was like a steel infrastructure for her soul, she was tender. She took an interest in Indian culture too and thus gained her adopted people's acceptance and a high esteem for her life and work.

Around her gathered young Indian and English women who committed themselves to a life of homemaking, child-rearing, teaching, hospital work, and later village evangelism. They all served Christ together. Later men joined the fellowship, and boys were given a safe home too.

"Amma," as Amy Carmichael was known by her family, lived and taught an abundant life centered around prayer and trust in God. Her books combine all of this. They are unusual and surely will live on.

• *Gold Cord*. Published by Christian Literature Crusade. This is the story of the Dohnavur Fellowship and contains many spiritual and practical insights.

• *Kohila—The Shaping of an Indian Nurse*. Published by SPCK, London, 1947. This book describes the spiritual formation of one of the Dohnavur women who came to Amy as a little girl.

Margaret Wilkinson's personal account of her life at Dohnavur is also helpful. She joined the Fellowship toward the end of Amma's life and helped lead the mission in a time of great change.

• *At B.B.C. Corner I Remember Amy Carmichael* by Margaret Wilkinson. Privately published and distributed through the Dohnavur Fellowship (address below).

• *Amma: The Life and Words of Amy Carmichael* by Elizabeth R. Skoglund. A personal friend and coworker of Amma's at Dohnavur has said that this book truly reflects Amma as a person and her teachings and wisdom. Published by Baker Books. (Available in bookshops.)

Information about these books and about the Fellowship can be

obtained from the London office: The Dohnavur Fellowship, 15
Elm Drive, Harrow, Middlesex HA2 7BS. In the United States contact: Mrs. J. Sessions, 3737 West Lake Drive, Augusta, Georgia
30907-9407.

Child Light and Charlotte Mason Schools International (CMSI)

When my husband, Ranald, and I discovered Charlotte Mason's
books on children at home and in school, we felt we'd found what
we'd been searching for. She had put together elements central to
the Christian worldview in relationship to children's lives and education. After others began to express their interest, Ranald encouraged me to write a book explaining this educational philosophy. Its
title is *For the Children's Sake*, published in 1984 by Crossway Books,
Wheaton, Illinois.

Soon letters started coming from many corners of the world. It
seemed that many parents and educators discovered Charlotte
Mason with relief. It was just what many of them were looking for.
Children's lives started benefiting; they enjoyed learning this way.
We ourselves could not respond to the interest or even the letters.
This is why Child Light was started—as a charitable educational
trust. The parents, educators, and we ourselves felt that these life-
giving ideas could endure into another century. Children are persons and are much the same today as they have always been. Many
have testified that their attitude to children, the atmosphere in
homes and schools, and the new breadth of life enjoyed have been
good results.

Along with the welcome renewal of interest in the writings and
work of Charlotte Mason, some publications have emerged that are
unhelpful and inaccurate in their interpretation of her ideas.
Anything using Charlotte Mason's name does not necessarily properly represent her attitudes and work.

Child Light aims to inform, encourage, and inspire people

serving children in all sorts of ways. Occasional newsletters, seminars, and conferences offer information and provide a forum for the sharing of ideas and practical wisdom. We also answer letters and put people in touch with each other.

Child Light, P. O. Box 59, Petersfield, Hants GU32 3YL, England. Fax: 011 41 1223 35 85 65. E-mail: ecatcl@aol.com.

Or in the USA:

Charlotte Mason Institute of Classroom Teachers, c/o Mr. Bobby Scott, Principal, Perimeter Christian School, 9500 Medlock Bridge Road, Duluth, GA 30097. Fax: 770 582 6685.

For well over a decade individual classroom teachers and entire schools have been practicing Charlotte Mason's ideas. The schools are usually small and privately run, but Mason's principles have been found to work well too when adapted for public education. In the United States followers of Charlotte Mason have formed a professional association and meet twice a year for conferences.

Out of these developments has grown a need for a consultant, and one of the school principals will now take on this task full time. The expertise that has been carefully forged with help from a British Charlotte-Mason-trained teacher will be available to all teachers and schools, including home-school groups.

Provision of teacher training and curriculum are two main aims of the association, and the accomplishment of these goals is at last on the way. Contact Mary Ellen Marschke, CMSI, P. O. Box 4035, Atlanta, GA 30302. E-mail: maryellen@camtechnologies.net.

Books published by or about Charlotte Mason:

• Six-volume reference set of books on Education, Home, School, Character, and Philosophy reprinted as The Original Home Schooling Series by Tyndale House Publishers. (Now out of print.)

• *The Story of Charlotte Mason* by Essex Cholmondeley. Published by the Charlotte Mason Foundation, for the Charlotte Mason College Assn., 1960, Aldine Press, Letchworth, Hertfordshire, for the PNEU, London. Out of print. A biography of Charlotte Mason and also an excellent explanation of her ideas.

• *For the Children's Sake* by Susan Schaeffer Macaulay. Published by Crossway Books, 1984. The most accessible and accurate introduction to Charlotte Mason and her ideas. Before publication the manuscript was scrutinized by Joan Molyneux, who was at that time the head of the PNEU and was trained by the Charlotte Mason College.

• *I Buy a School* by Marion Berry. Published by Avon Books, London, 1996. ISBN 1 860332838. This is a delightful description of an era of education when Charlotte Mason's ideas were being practiced in the Parents' National Education Union Schools across England and the world. Through the eyes of a former headmistress, we can see many applications of Charlotte Mason's ideas in real life. (Available through Child Light)

It can be lonely for an at-home, all-day mother with young children if everyone leaves the neighborhood to go out to work. Although there is no substitute for an actual network of friends, the monthly publication *Welcome Home*, by mothers for mothers, goes a long way in encouraging us all. I look forward to its arrival and also like to give it as a gift to mothers: Mothers at Home, P. O. Box 2192, 8310A Old Courthouse Road, Vienna, VA 22182. Web site: www.mah.org. E-mail: wh@mah.org. or Tel: 800-783-4666 for a free information packet.

Also available from Mothers at Home is an insightful and challenging book entitled *What's a Smart Woman Like You Doing at Home?* by Linda Burton, Janet Dittmer, and Cheri Loveless. Published by Mothers at Home.

In England there is the national support group for full-time mothers: Full-Time Mothers, P. O. Box 186, London SW3 5RF, England. The organization publishes a useful newsletter and has ideas for active involvement in presenting to society and the media the important issues of a mother's care for her child, child development, and nurture in the home. They welcome letters from interested people.

If you have a child or children under six years of age at home and would like help with educational activities/conversation/time together each day, you might set aside an hour or more for that purpose. Calvert School has one-year kindergarten courses you might like to use. It is fun for parent and child to do the course together, and the child is given opportunity to blossom. The course can also assist a child who is being introduced into a new home or who has special medical problems that restrict activities. As well as being fun to do, such time together helps build a positive relationship. The Calvert package comes complete with all you'll need. In addition to the kindergarten materials, the school provides an excellent education for grades one to eight. I used Calvert School myself as an older child and enjoyed the expertise and care put into the courses. Since then I've taught all the grades to various children. The cost of a course is money well spent: Calvert School, 105 Tuscany Road, Baltimore, MD 21210. Tel: 888 487 4652. Fax: 410 366 0674. Web site: www.calvertschool.org.

Bookshelf

It is said that one picture can be worth a thousand words. However, a good story can plunge us into a completely different situation from our own and vividly show us another way of life.

Today some people wanting to make homes complain that they have few memories to draw on. Perhaps they've never experienced the warmth of a family home where little children are loved and respected and yet are guided firmly within a moral framework. Others have only seen marriages where husband or wife use each other or where everyone is working so hard there is no enjoyable everyday life left.

Here are a few books that might be a help. They are fiction, and through them we can walk into other homes and taste different atmospheres. Relaxing with a story not only encourages us but also gives us a break. There are many more books of course; this is merely a start.

• *Understood Betsy* by Dorothy Canfield Fisher. Originally published by Henry Holt & Company in 1917 (many editions). This is a lovely story for children about a little girl who goes to live with relatives in Vermont. She is cared for by an aunt who makes a great success of homemaking and brings a wilting child to robust abundant life. The book also makes a good comment on schooling that serves a child rather than forcing a child into a mold. Adults benefit from reading this.

The following books by Elizabeth Goudge form a trilogy:
• *The Bird in the Tree*
• *The Herb of Grace*
• *The Heart of the Family*

One family's story, they are to be read in the order given here. As Goudge was a popular author in the United States and Canada (she died in the early 1980s), you may be able to locate copies in libraries. Some of her books have been put back into print, but unfortunately the ones I've seen are abridged. This author has the unusual gift of portraying the everyday life of married and unmarried people with warmth, realism, and depth. The books are endlessly encouraging on many levels. This trilogy concerns a marriage where love was lost and then chosen again.

Two of Goudge's books focus on single person's lives (as she herself was). These books include people with difficulties such as emotional and mental suffering. But the stories are alive with warm human joy and friendships, and help comes with new insights. It is interesting also to read them with the question: What exactly does love mean?
• *The Dean's Watch*
• *The Scent of Water*

If a mother feels tempted to walk out on a child and "unsatisfactory" husband, the Goudge trilogy is one thing to read. Another is:
• *A Solitary Blue* by Cynthia Voigt

This is a poignant story about what happens to a little boy whose mother walks away, leaving him with an aloof, academic father. The boy's empty life and home become suffused with life again. Instructive. So are two other Voigt books, although they are an eccentric portrayal of a home! Published in paperback by Fawcett Juniper, New York, the two books must be read as one story:

- *Homecoming*
- *Dicey's Song*

Another family/home-life book, written for older children and early teens but giving insight to adults too, is a series on one family by Madeleine L'Engle. The series was first published by Farrar, Straus, and Giroux, Inc. in 1960.

- *Meet the Austins.* In this story a family with four children suddenly is joined by a recently orphaned child.
- *The Moon by Night*
- *A Ring of Endless Light.*

Note: You may want to know that the authors listed here have varying worldviews.

NOTES

CHAPTER 1
Who Needs a Home?

1. You can visit her home in Chawton, Hampshire, England, near the market town of Alton. Jane Austen loved her home life. She enjoyed cooking, serving meals, and writing letters to her scattered loved ones. She found pleasure in taking long walks through the surrounding countryside.

2. Deidre Le Faye, ed., *Jane Austen's Letters* (Oxford, England: Oxford University Press, 1995).

3. Sods are pieces of turf cut from peat and used for fuel.

4. Poem chosen by Sir Arthur Quiller-Couch for *The Oxford Book of English Verse* (Oxford, England: Oxford University Press, 1939).

5. In 1984 the book *For the Children's Sake*, which I wrote about Charlotte Mason's ideas for the education of children, was published by Crossway Books.

6. Brief accounts of the various people and organizations that are referred to in this book can be found in the Appendix.

CHAPTER 2
Home—the Best Growing Ground for Children

1. Charlotte Mason, *Home Education*, from chapter 1 (London: Kegan Paul, Trench, Trubner & Co. Ltd., 1935).

2. Charlotte Mason, *The Saviour of the World*, vol. 2, book 2 (London: Kegan Paul, Trench, Trubner, 1908), p. 80.

3. Essex Cholmondeley, *The Story of Charlotte Mason* (Letchworth, Herts, U.K.: Aldine Press for PNEU, Charlotte Mason Foundation), p. 188.

4. Ibid., p. 185.

5. Isaiah 50:7 (transposed and partial).

6. In the United Kingdom A-levels are the exams at the end of preparatory school before the student enters the university.

7. Susan Schaeffer Macaulay, *How to Be Your Own Selfish Pig* (Colorado Springs: Chariot Victor Publishing, 1982).

8. Francis Schaeffer, *The God Who Is There*, in *The Complete Works of Francis Schaeffer*, Section IV (Wheaton, Ill.: Crossway Books, 1982), p. 145.

9. Ibid., p. 146.

10. All Biblical exegesis must be carried out within the context of the entire Word—both Testaments. We lack integrity if we take phrases or short passages out of chapters or books or change the system of thought being expressed by the whole. Proper reading of the text does not solve all honest differences of opinion, but these differences are of detail, not of substance.

11. The lecture *"De Descriptione Temporum"* may be found in C. S. Lewis, *They Asked for a Paper* (London: Geoffrey Bles, 1962), p. 9, 20.

12. Jesus always taught the enormity of hindering a child's well-being. (Luke 18:16; also Mark 9:36-37, 42.) Charlotte Mason often used the phrase "hinder not the child" to refer to any sort of hindering in their lives.

13. Hampshire is a county in southern England.

14. The Downs are a long ridge of chalk hills running along the south of England.

15. A market town in Hampshire.

16. In 1948 my parents moved to Switzerland where I spent the rest of my growing-up years.

17. Ambleside Geography Books by Charlotte Mason.

18. At that time the "board schools" (public education) had huge classes, typically of over fifty or sixty children. The teacher relied on older pupils to "student-teach" smaller groups under supervision. These were the monitors and monitresses.

19. Calvert School, Baltimore, Maryland, USA. Address in Appendix.

20. Charlotte Mason, *Essay Towards a Philosophy of Education* (London: Kegan Paul, Trench, Trubner, 1925).

21. Ibid. For example, Charlotte Mason contrasts children as she found them with the existing view that children had no innate powers of judgment, intellect, imagination, moral insight, and no generous impulses.

22. A large number of parents helped by Charlotte Mason were influential, and so her influence spread.

23. John 10:10 in Essex Cholmondeley, *The Story of Charlotte Mason* (Letchworth, Herts, England: Aldine Press for the PNEU, Charlotte Mason Foundation, for the Charlotte Mason College Assn., 1960), p. 190.

24. Ibid., p. 191.

CHAPTER 3
"Free as a Bird, Dutiful and Humble as the Angels"

1. Benjamin Spock, M.D., and Michael B. Rothenberg, M.D., *Dr. Spock's Baby and Child Care* (New York: Pocket Books, 1945), p. 423.

2. Essex Cholmondeley, *The Story of Charlotte Mason* (Letchworth, Herts, England: Aldine Press for the PNEU, Charlotte Mason Foundation, for the Charlotte Mason College Assn., 1960), p. 190.

3. A French expression for a life lived with joy.

4. Why are angels humble? Because serving God is the aim of their lives, not personal success. With a self-centered person that self-interest and a sense of being better or worse than others creeps in. With God as the center, we are not comparing ourselves to others, and *He is always bigger and wiser!* Proper humility gives proper self-confidence too.

5. Benedict, Prologue in *St. Benedict's Rule: A New Translation for Today*, trans. Patrick Barry, OSB (York, England: Ampleforth Abbey Press, 1997).

CHAPTER 4
This Is Where I Put My Feet Up and Thank God

1. Aldous Huxley presents a striking illustration of a society based on the "man as machine" view in the novel *Brave New World*.
2. Ellis Peters, *Ellis Peters's Shropshire* (Gloucestershire, U.K.: Sutton Publishing, 1992), pp. 8-9.
3. An Aga is a solid fuel stove for cooking, warmth, and heating hot water. In damp weather the room with the Aga is the warm heart of the home.
4. Peters, *Shropshire*, p. 165.
5. Quoted in my childhood's beloved book (a collection of poetry), *This Singing World*, comp. Louis Untermeyer (San Diego: Harcourt, Brace & Co., 1951).
6. *Homecoming GI*, original oil painting for *Saturday Evening Post* cover, May 26, 1945. Collection of Mrs. Ben Hibbs.
7. Single women whose lives are good examples of homemaking and who also gave their lives to the works mentioned in this book are Charlotte Mason, Ellis Peters, Amy Carmichael, and Elizabeth Goudge. There would also be a long list of men: C. S. Lewis is only one example.
8. This verse refers to friendship. Marriage is to be a more permanent and intimate relationship. Of course, the taking of a vow of marriage has to be done with a big dose of common sense and wisdom. There are many human beings anyone would *not* be wise to marry!

CHAPTER 5
The Home's Weight-Bearing Beams

1. Deuteronomy 22:8.
2. See his *Childhood and Society*, first published in the U.K. by Imago Publishing Company in 1951.
3. Some single persons tend to think that a home will come along with a marriage—always "tomorrow." They may even feel guilty about using time and resources for normal everyday life and its routines.
4. It is quite normal to be upset and unhappy upon discovering a pregnancy. Regardless of the reaction, a person has a responsibility, in pregnancy or at any other time, to care for and protect that child's life.
5. The passage 1 Peter 3:4, as translated in the NIV, encourages wives to have the "unfading beauty of a gentle and quiet spirit." This spirit is not just a quality for women only. Note verse 7, which says that husbands are to be in the same way considerate. Most biblical references to meekness are to men and women, and Jesus is our example.

CHAPTER 6
Taking Time and Care to Create the Home's Atmosphere

1. "If a man has recently married, he must not be sent to war or have any other duty laid on him. For one year he is to be free to stay at home and bring happiness to the wife he has married" (Deut. 24:5).

2. The PNEU was established in 1892 as a national society for parents and teachers to promulgate Charlotte Mason's educational philosophy and practices. This goal was carried out through a journal called *The Parents' Review* and through local branches established in many different parts of the United Kingdom that also developed into schools. "Someday," wrote Miss Mason to a friend, "we hope to see each branch a sort of center for the spiritual (including intellectual) profit of all classes in the neighborhood."

3. As quoted by Essex Cholmondeley, *The Story of Charlotte Mason* (Letchworth, Herts, England: Aldine Press for the PNEU, Charlotte Mason Foundation, for the Charlotte Mason College Assn., 1960).

4. The definition given to the word *sensibility* in the *Collins Concise English Dictionary* highlights emotional feelings. And this dictionary tells us that emotion is "any strong feeling such as (joy), sorrow or fear." In this context I'd add shame.

5. Form and freedom—stability and security on one hand, and yet exploration and experimentation on the other.

6. Galatians 5:16 tells us to "live by the Spirit," and verse 22 says that His fruits are love, joy, peace, etc. Verse 25 adds that since we "live by the Spirit," we *should keep in step with the Spirit.* This directive is interesting. It is not talking about a vague feeling. We've been told to lift one foot and then the other; do our part; get on with it.

7. Sometimes we have to respond to the spouse's choices that actually are "like death" (habitual adultery), or we face the threat of injury if she or he is dangerous. We may have to leave if the spouse makes no effort to change.

8. "Abide in me, and I in you. As the branch cannot bear fruit of itself, except it abide in the vine; no more can ye, except ye abide in me" (John 15:4 KJV).

9. Taken from a "Sunday Meditation" leaflet by Charlotte Mason and quoted in Cholmondeley, *Story of Charlotte Mason*, p. 189.

10. *For the Children's Sake* (Wheaton, Ill.: Crossway Books, 1984).

11. *Meditate* is used here as in the *Collins Concise English Dictionary*—to think about something deeply (in this case the Scriptures). From the Latin *meditari*—to reflect upon.

12. Cholmondeley, *Story of Charlotte Mason*, p. 185.

13. Italics mine.

14. A basic recipe is: 1 cup flour, 1 cup salt, enough water to make dough. This home-made clay will dry hard and can be painted.

   Or try: 1 cup salt, 1 1/2 cups flour, 1/2 cup water, 2 tablespoons cooking oil. This play dough will keep in a covered jar in the refrigerator.

15. Elsie Kitching, "Children up to School Age and Beyond," Parents' National Education Union, p. 8.

CHAPTER 7
"The Glory of the Usual" or Jack of All Trades

1. Patrick Barry, O.S.B., *Saint Benedict's Rule—A New Translation for Today* (York, England: Ampleforth Abbey Press, 1997), p. 44. Barry was the former abbot of Ampleforth.

2. Ibid., chapter 37.

3. In this discussion, I am not touching on Jesus' work of salvation.

4. Charlotte Mason, *Home Education* (London: Kegan Paul, Trench, Trubner, 1920).

5. Ibid., pp. 17-18.

6. Michelle Magorian, *Goodnight, Mr. Tom* (London: Puffin Books, 1983).

7. Amy Carmichael was born in 1867, went to India in 1895, and died in 1957. In 1899 the first child "ran away" to Amma (Amy's Indian name. It means "mother" in Tamil), who provided a home for her and for many others in Dohnavur.

8. Amy Carmichael, *Gold Cord* (Ft. Washington, Penn.: Christian Literature Crusade, 1992), p. 75.

9. Ibid., p. 76.

10. Ibid., p. 142.

11. Read about this and about Charlotte Mason's ideas in Susan Schaeffer Macaulay, *For the Children's Sake* (Wheaton, Ill.: Crossway, 1984).

12. Margaret Wilkinson, *At B.B.C. Corner I Remember Amy Carmichael* (Self-published, 1996). Available from Dohnavur Fellowship, 15 Elm Drive, North Harrow, Middlesex, HA2 7BS, England.

13. The original six-volume series of Charlotte Mason's books for parents and schools was published by Kegan Paul, Trench, & Trubner in London in 1920.

14. Wilkinson, *At B. B. C. Corner*, p. 41.

15. The motto of the Charlotte Mason College at Ambleside.

16. Amy Carmichael, *Kohila: The Shaping of an Indian Nurse* (London: Society for the Propagation of Christian Knowledge, 1947).

17. Amy Carmichael, *Lotus Buds* (London: Morgan and Scott, Ltd., 1910).

18. Wilkinson, *At B. B. C. Corner*, p. 63.

19. At the time Amma was writing, Tara was three years old and Evu two and a half.

20. Carmichael, *Lotus Buds*, p. 37.

21. Wilkinson, *At B. B. C. Corner*.

22. Carmichael, *Lotus Buds*.

23. Wilkinson, *At B. B. C. Corner*, p. 64.

24. Carmichael, *Lotus Buds*, p. 227.

25. Ibid., p. 228.

CHAPTER 8
The Infrastructure of Routine

1. Charlotte Mason's careful schedule or pattern for life in the House of Education in Ambleside would be unexpectedly changed sometimes when a beautiful day dawned. (The Lake District is the rainiest area in England.) A bell would ring, and everything would be canceled so that many parties could hike up high, skate on the lake, or enjoy the woods and meadows, depending on the season.

2. Richard Winter, *The Roots of Sorrow* (Basingstoke, England: Marshall, Morgan and Scott, 1985), p. 62. Chapter 3 —"There are other forms of postpartum depression. . . . One, like the other forms of depression, is associated with such factors as the loss of mother before the age of 11, an unsupportive husband, poor housing and few friends."

3. Luke 22:26-27.

4. We don't so much have "roles," as responsibilities and situations that we live in and respond to.

5. "Like as a Father pitieth his children, so the Lord pitieth them that fear him. For he knoweth our frame" (Psalm 103:13-14 KJV). In other words, our makeup has a built-in limit; we cannot transcend it.

6. In Mediterranean societies the midday break was longer so as to allow a wonderful siesta. Children came home from school at lunchtime and stayed home.

7. This is the recipe for the real Swiss *Birchemusli*: 2 tablespoons oats covered with water until mushy, 1 tablespoon fresh lemon juice, 1 tablespoon sweetened condensed milk. Grate raw apple into this mixture (including skin and core), add raisins, flaked almonds, other diced fruit, yogurt, as desired. (This is one portion.)

8. Oxbridge—the word commonly used to designate Oxford and Cambridge.

9. This describes the Macaulay family room between 1971 and 1996.

10. Sometimes the best childhood kitchen in the world cannot save us from later depression or anxiety. Just as we all get sick sooner or later, so we all suffer mentally. This is a *fallen* world—no longer balanced and satisfying in itself. It is good to seek and receive understanding help when we need it, and this can include professional help.

11. Studies have demonstrated that stable, friendly adults who are content in their work and home life tend to come from homes where as children they worked together with the adults regularly. The team effort may be helping with meals, working in the garden, or assisting in the family store, etc. The main thing is that people work as part of the team, not alone. Interestingly, this cooperation was more important than the level of income, location (whether in the inner city or suburbs), success of the parents' marriage, or educational opportunities.

12. Jack Dominion, *Human Relationships* (Middlegreen, Slough: St. Paul Publications, 1989). Full quote:

"It is essential we treat each other as persons of love and not things. The object of personal relationships is to donate ourselves and receive the other. The object of things is to use them." These words appeared just previously: "Through Jesus we have learned that God is a trinity of persons—the Father, the Son and the Spirit who relate to each other, in and through love. At the center of the Godhead are persons in a relationship of love with each other. This God created the world out of love and relates to each one of us in a relationship of love. Furthermore, our relationships with one another, aiming to realize love, mirror the life of God."

13. C. S. Lewis, *The Lion, the Witch and the Wardrobe* (London: William Collins & Sons, 1974), pp. 69-72.

14. Amy Carmichael, *Gold Cord* (Ft. Washington, Penn.: Christian Literature Crusade, 1992), pp. 323-324.

CHAPTER 9
Of Beds, Balance, and Books

1. Robert Louis Stevenson, "The Land of Counterpane," in *Complete Poems: A Child's Garden of Verses* (New York: Scribner's Sons, 1914), p. 14. The last verse of this poem goes:

    I was the Giant great and still / That sits upon the pillow hill,
    And sees before him, dale and plain, / The pleasant land of Counterpane.

2. "Wynken, Blynken and Nod" was my favorite. Eugene Field, *With Trumpet and Drum* (New York: Scribner's Sons, 1899), p. 46-48.

    Wynken, Blynken and Nod one night / Sailed off in a wooden shoe—
    Sailed on a river of crystal light, / into a sea of dew.

3. The familiar schedule for being in bed with lights out is roughly up to age five— 6:00 to 6:30 P.M., up to seven or so—7:00 P.M., eight years—7:30 P.M., nine years—7:45 to 8:00 P.M., ten years—8:15 to 8:30 P.M. This schedule depends somewhat on the child, and in summer bedtimes are later than in winter.

4. Search secondhand bookstores, garage sales, etc. Many libraries discard their best older books—see ideas in *Books Children Love* by Elizabeth Wilson, published by Crossway, and *Honey for a Child's Heart* by Gladys Hunt, published by Zondervan.

5. I'd firmly outlaw Winnie-the-Pooh and any C. S. Lewis Narnia tales on video. These videos are disrespectful to the authors as they are not their work. It is impossible for the child using these products to have the joy and richness of contact with the great, creative minds behind the original series and the work they produced—the entire books. Also avoid abridged versions of books. In contrast, a good Shakespeare play on video is excellent. I recommend those by the BBC.

6. *Stones of Fire* and *Nests Above the Abyss* by Isobel Kuhn are available from the Overseas Missionary Fellowship, 1-888-663-2665. E-mail: omfus@omf.org. In U.K.: omf@omf.org.uk.

7. See Edith R. Schaeffer, *Mei Fuh, Memories from China* (Boston: Houghton Mifflin, 1998).

8. Cristina Roy, *Sunshine Country* (Crockett, Ky.: Rod and Staff Publishers, Inc., 1967).

9. Marion Berry, *I Buy a School* (London: Avon Books, 1996). Distributed by Thomas Lister, Ltd., U.K. Tel: 01695 575 112.

10. Ibid.

11. As the mother of a family in the distracting community of L'Abri, I chose to be at home for the children from afternoon on, including evenings, almost always. Otherwise our apartment would have been a set of rooms, not a home.

12. Ranald and I are now living in a little row house (terrace) set right on the sidewalk. Thus we are in a more ordinary situation at this point in our lives.

13. Ideally, the habit of choosing to use our time well starts in childhood and endures whatever our circumstances. Those who marry may have great loneliness due to incompatibility or the spouse's absence. A majority of married people will become single again due to death (or separation).

CHAPTER 10
Contentment, Thanks, and Enjoyment

1. The Reformation "was, in its heart, a mighty movement towards God. It came of a long-felt, though dimly understood, hunger and thirst for a better and larger spiritual life, for a real and present peace with God, a free and full approach to God, a clear hearing of His voice in the open oracle of His Word." From H. G. Moule, D.D., *The Story of the Prayer Book*, English Church Manual #13 (London: Longmans, Green & Co., 1908).

2. In about 1380 the Bible was translated into English for the first time by John Wycliffe.

3. Moule, *Story of the Prayer Book.*

4. Amy Bjork Harris and Thomas A. Harris, M.D., founders of the Institute for Transactional Analysis in Sacramento, California, wrote something that grabbed my attention in their book *Staying OK* (London: Pan Books Ltd., 1986), pp. 270-271. A couple were asking about leaving their one-year-old daughter Elizabeth while they both went out to work. They asked, "Will she be OK?" The answer: "Probably not. A day in the life of a working woman with small children is a mixture of fantasy, frustration and frenzy. It probably also contains a sizable portion of failure." The authors then give the following advice:

   It is our belief that the minimum requirement is that one parent should be at home, or constantly available to the child until the child has made a decision about whether or not he is a good reader. A child makes such a decision about the time of first or second grade, sometimes later, sometimes earlier. . . . Reading is the primary tool of the child's independence. When a child reads well, and knows it, he or she can, with confidence, read instructions on the refrigerator, shop from a list. . . .

5. L'Abri Fellowship was founded by Francis and Edith Schaeffer in Switzerland in 1955 when they opened their home as a spiritual and intellectual "shelter," a place where people could be helped both to know and to live the truth of biblical Christianity. See appendix.

6. Christian believers will include in their life routine various activities that stem from their relationship with God. For instance, most of us pray before meals and when tucking a child up in bed. We often talk (pray) to the Lord—He is so much with us that we will naturally mention or refer to Him. Also we read the Bible and Bible stories.

7. Although seat belts are important for safety, some children spend too much time buckled down. We should try to free a child from the tyranny of hours spent in cars.

8. These conditions are complex, and a depressed person may need medical help. If in doubt, ask for help!

9. Ranald and I lived in Huemoz, Switzerland, for the first three and a half years of our marriage.

10. Niles Newton, *The Family Book of Child Care* (New York: Harper & Brothers, 1957).

11. Warning! Early days are not usually comfortable for nursing mothers. The nipples are not accustomed to hard use and, like feet going on a first long trek, protest until hardened up. La Leche League (1400 N. Meacham Rd., Schaumburg, IL 60173. Tel: 847-519-7730) advises mothers, gives support, and answers questions.

CHAPTER 11
Choose Wisely and Leave Time for the Daily Rhythms

1. Because we live in a world in which the basic pattern of life has been fragmented and damaged, sometimes our wholeness is fundamentally affected. None of us has a perfect body, mind, or situation anyway: This is life as it is "in the fallen world."

2. We do have a problem—we've already failed. But all is not lost. Jesus bought a way back for us. He offers a new chapter for anybody. Secondly, none of us is strong or good enough to be perfect in obeying God. That is why we've been promised help. "Get up, brush yourself off, and keep on" is the word to us all, just as it is for a child who falls off a bike or who disobeys and gets hurt.

3. In the King James Version Genesis 3:16 states, "I will greatly multiply thy sorrow *and* thy conception. . . ." The Fall altered all areas of life, including conception and childbirth. Just as we seek to alleviate the Fall's result in, say, penicillin for strep throats, so we use ideas to make the spacing of children appropriate for a couple, we are thankful for pain control in childbirth, and so on.

4. Although the example of a lone parent is used in this section, two-parent families also need to consider these realities and the various choices or strategies in their lives.

5. There will always be people who disagree with any plan we make! In the end, having listened to advice, we go ahead with whatever seems best.

6. Luke 2:36-38. Anna is at the end of the Old Testament period of waiting for the Messiah. Her way of life is part of that chapter.

7. Luke 2:25-32.

8. 1 Corinthians 7:25-28.

9. 1 Corinthians 7:2-4.

10. Although I'm addressing women's strengths—their awareness of other people and their needs—obviously men are expected to be trustworthy and faithful in the same ways.

11. Because prayer is efficient in bringing help into human need, prayer will obviously be part of our response. But, when taken into confidence, we ask for *permission* to tell husband, wife, elder, or other praying friends. But confidentiality is not broken if child abuse or similar matters are at issue.

12. "Things"—here used as physical extras that can be purchased: cars, new furniture, vacations, fancy foodstuffs, some kinds of education and medical care, etc. Much pressure comes from advertising sources that make us covet (desire) things we don't have.

13. The Father of creation speaks of two kinds of children—those who know Him clearly through listening to and following His Word and those who are created by Him and thus are children in that general way. The Psalms make it abundantly clear that God's concern and love go out to *all the poor*. The related references are too numerous to list here. A few at random: Psalms 9:18; 10:14; 12:5; 35:10; 41:1; 109:30-31; 140:11-12; Proverbs 14:21. Do make a study of these passages and more. They can be generally described by Proverbs 14:31: "He who oppresses the poor shows contempt for their Maker, but whoever is kind to the needy honors God."

14. Matthew 6:19; Luke 12:18-21.

15. Matthew 18:5-7.

16. Chapter 10. The quote here is from the *Book of Common Prayer* published in 1662.

17. Note: *Sober* in this context means carefully responsible, sensible.

18. How to serve others is a complex question! One response to human need is to give up a settled lifestyle to serve "like a soldier on a battlefront." Such a person endures special hardship (2 Tim. 2:3). We must seek God's "right" path for each of us.

19. I started doing this only when the youngest child was nine years of age and would enjoy a visit to a farm, grandparent, or camp.

20. No school can provide all the help or teaching a child needs. Careful attention at home is a great advantage and joy. It can mean that an extra skill, such as playing a musical instrument, is learned and enjoyed. Other children are slow to learn to read and/or write and may need daily practice. Many children are not stretched enough at school. We have supplemented their education by reading biblical history narrative stories, history, art, nature study, and so on. In contrast, a child being educated at home for some reason benefits by going out to enjoy other adults' input.

21. A compact house means quick cleaning efficiency—getting more of any sort of room or garden means more to look after. Good storage and limited clutter streamlines this old-fashioned lifestyle.

CHAPTER 12
Early Days, Vital Days

1. October 14, 1998.

2. Established routines make up another area where people tend to go to extremes. Either parents have tended to be too rigorous, with a mechanical routine, or too lax. The first is harmful, as a child's individual needs must be served; the second is harmful because it brings chaos, which is destructive to all.

3. Benjamin Spock, M.D., and Michael B. Rothenberg, M.D., *Dr. Spock's Baby and Child Care* (New York: Simon & Schuster, 1945). Good chapters on babies, toddlers, and children in general. Also comforting reference for when to contact a doctor, what to do for croup or a rash, etc.

4. Another aspect of childhood is the constant exceptions to the usual—colds, fevers, teething. The list is endless!

5. This is a baby carriage. I have friends who tell me that parents still follow the custom in two very cold countries, Finland and Canada, as well as in our more temperate Great Britain.

6. When a child found a hill steep work, we'd sing "The Grand Old Duke of York" while snappily marching, and then "Jack and Jill Go Up the Hill."

7. Charlotte Mason never thought normal rain or snow would be a reason not to go out to play or walk (except when a child was ill). Good waterproof outer wear is easier to get than it used to be. And *every child* should have plastic or rubber boots to pull on. These are essential.

8. Amy Carmichael found that hiking up to the forest vacation bungalows was character-building for her children. Charlotte Mason scheduled walks and lots of time outdoors for her student teachers and all school children.

9. With washing machines, cloth diapers are easy to manage. They save lots of money and are kinder to the environment. Disposable diapers in a landfill take *500 years* to disappear and are a health hazard too. What are we doing to our planet? Sun and fresh air are an inexpensive answer to the family's drying needs, and we should all cut down on the total energy we use. (In wet weather my friends and I use clotheslines in our kitchens. I hardly know anyone with a drier.)

10. Children might occasionally need special medication for behavior caused by a chemical imbalance. But in my fifty-seven years I've never met such a child. It must be rare.

11. These are called row houses in the United States.

12. Vol. 15, No. 4—April 1998. *Welcome Home* is a nonsectarian, nonpartisan publication of the national nonprofit organization Mothers at Home, 8310A Old Courthouse Road, Vienna, VA 22182, USA. (Recommended!) www.mah.org.

13. Dr. Isabelle Fox and Norman M. Lobsenz, *Being There: The Benefits of a Stay-At-Home Parent* (Hauppauge, N.Y.: Barron's Educational Series, Inc., 1996). Available through bookstores or by calling Barron's at 800-645-3476. The book includes a chapter dealing with Stable Substitute Care

CHAPTER 13
Homes and Life in Community

1. C. S. Lewis, *The Great Divorce* (London: Geoffrey Bles, 1946).

2. Colossians 2:2 KJV (The *New International Version* says, "united in love").

3. 1 Corinthians 16:16 deals with submitting (giving in to another person's ideas/plans) to each other in Christian work.

4. Galatians 6:2.

5. Romans 12:15.

6. Matthew 7:1-2.

7. James 2:1-4.

8. Schools, surrounded by a desert of parking lots, have too often been built more with saving energy in mind than with growing children. Just as we've developed factory farming, we've specialized in "factory childhood." Typically the child may be one of a thousand students—too big a group to know and be known in community.

9. Watch the film *Local Hero* for a dramatized story that depicts such a "life." The movie is produced by David Puttnam and written and directed by Bill Forsyth. (P.G. rating.)

10. Although obviously I am a committed Christian, the principles governing wholesome home life are the same, whatever we believe. Even if your beliefs differ from mine, you and your children will certainly benefit from the patterns and ideas given throughout the book. Much of what I say is common wisdom that is simply true of life.

11. Acts 5:29; Hebrews 5:9; James 1:22-25.

12. John 13:35; 1 Thessalonians 4:9-10.

13. Galatians 6:10.

14. Salt seasons and preserves (as in bacon). Salt flavors the whole. An illustration would be a street with four out of fifteen households behaving as neighbors. Their goodness would preserve much that is good and season the whole atmosphere. (See Matt. 5:13.)

15. Light shines into darkness, and then those in darkness are enabled to see. Here Jesus speaks of our good deeds being a light. It is easy to illustrate that.

16. 1 Corinthians 12:12-31.

17. Paul was a single man when we read about him. He might have been married before.

18. Should you choose to use a video or television program, it would be part of the planned schedule only.

19. In the early 1930s.

20. Hebrews 13:2.

CHAPTER 14
A Look at the Everyday
All Around Us—All Year Long

1. See Matthew 5:3-10.

2. Selina Fitzherbert Fox, comp., *A Chain of Prayer Across the Ages* (London: John Murray, 1913), p. 86.

3. Exodus 20:12.

4. "What, after all, is Apollos? And what is Paul? Only servants, through whom you came to believe—as the Lord has assigned to each his task. I planted the seed, Apollos watered it, but God made it grow" (1 Corinthians 3:5-6).

5. 1 Corinthians 13:1-13.

6. John 14:23.

7. There are those in the body who have specially designated roles, according to Ephesians 4:11-13. "It was he [Christ] who gave some to be apostles, some to be prophets, some to be evangelists, and some to be pastors and teachers, to prepare God's people for works of service, so that the body of Christ may be built up until we all reach unity in the faith and in the knowledge of the son of God and become mature. . . ."

8. Constant moving from home areas has meant the breakup of lifelong ties with family and friends. People easily become rootless.

9. Exodus 20:8-11.

10. The Psalms are full of such reflections. They include joy, sorrow, confusion, anger—all are there.

11. 1 Corinthians 7:5-6.

12. Matthew 1:23; Isaiah 7:14.

13. It is a great relief to free up the Christmas preparations and day from present-giving. That choice can mean more time spent together, on hospitality, and in worship as well as freedom from the commercial aspect of the season. Present-giving to loved ones can then be spread over the year. However, I personally would keep the gift tradition for children under eighteen or so. We limited the quantity of gifts our children received, which also made the day peaceful. Too much at once encourages a child's greed. A gift to each other in the family circle on the day, a new board game or toy for the family room, plus a stocking seemed to keep frenetic attitudes at bay! Children are perfectly satisfied with this if they are started young. In this plan gifts from other relations are kept for the subsequent "twelve days of Christmas." One gift each a day (as long as gifts last). This gives each gift the recipient's attention and proper appreciation. It also makes for a Christmas *season*—it's fun!

14. Genesis 1:26.

15. Father, Son, and Holy Spirit equal the ONE LORD GOD, Creator of heaven and earth (Isa. 40:28; John 4:24.)

16. Luke 1:68-79; Luke 3:6.

17. Matthew 4:16; Luke 2:32; John 1:4.

18. Luke 2:19.

19. Luke 2:35.

20. John 19:25-27.

21. Luke 1:42, 48.

22. 1 Thessalonians 4:1-3.

23. 1 Thessalonians 4:11-12.

24. 1 Thessalonians 4:3-5; 1 Corinthians 6:9—7:2.

25. The church leaders were to be examples for the others (1 Tim. 3:2-5, 8-9, 11-13).

26. Matthew 15:8-9, 18-20.

27. 1 Corinthians 11:28.

28. 1 John 1:3–10.

29. The word *understand* is interesting. It literally means "to stand under" an idea, to give it attention, and to put effort into being clear about meaning.

30. Lent is the preparation for Easter. Advent is the preparation for Christmas.

31. *Quick* is an old word for "living."

32. On December 6.

33. Collect for the fourth Sunday after Epiphany, from the *Book of Common Prayer*.

APPENDIX

1. Quoted in Essex Cholmondeley, *The Story of Charlotte Mason* (Letchworth, Herts, England: Aldine Press for the PNEU, Charlotte Mason Foundation, for the Charlotte Mason College Assn., 1960), p. IX.

2. Allbutt was the Regius Professor of Physics at Cambridge University writing in the book *In Memoriam, Charlotte M. Mason*, published by the PNEU in 1923 very shortly after her death.

3. "In Memoriam," *Times Educational Supplement*, January 20, 1923.